EXEGETICAL JOURNEYS

IN BIBLICAL GREEK

90 DAYS
of Guided Reading

BENJAMIN L. MERKLE

Baker Academic
a division of Baker Publishing Group
Grand Rapids, Michigan

Published by Baker Academic
a division of Baker Publishing Group
Grand Rapids, Michigan
www.bakeracademic.com

Printed in the United States of America

Library of Congress Cataloging-in-Publication Data
Names: Merkle, Benjamin L., 1971– author.
Title: Exegetical journeys in biblical Greek : 90 days of guided reading / Benjamin L. Merkle.
Description: Grand Rapids, Michigan : Baker Academic, a division of Baker Publishing Group, [2023] | Includes bibliographical references and index.
Identifiers: LCCN 2023009796 | ISBN 9781540965103 (paperback) | ISBN 9781540966858 (casebound) | ISBN 9781493442942 (ebook) | ISBN 9781493442959 (pdf)
Subjects: LCSH: Greek language, Biblical—Grammar—Problems, exercises, etc. | Greek language, Biblical—Readers. | Bible. New Testament—Language, style.
Classification: LCC PA817 .M45 2023 | DDC 487/.4—dc23/eng/20230412
LC record available at https://lccn.loc.gov/2023009796

Except where indicated, translations from the Greek are provided by the author.

Baker Publishing Group publications use paper produced from sustainable forestry practices and post-consumer waste whenever possible.

23   24   25   26   27   28   29   7   6   5   4   3   2   1

CONTENTS

CONTENTS

ACKNOWLEDGMENTS

I am grateful to all the friends who helped me proofread my manuscripts. In particular, I thank Lauren Lockhart, Faith Haberer, and Alex Carr. Once again, I also acknowledge Bryan Dyer and the entire team at Baker Academic for their continued partnership.

ABBREVIATIONS

General and Bibliographic

AD   [Latin] anno Domini (in the year of our Lord)

BC   before Christ

BDAG   Frederick W. Danker, Walter Bauer, William F. Arndt, and F. Wil-
              bur Gingrich. *A Greek-English Lexicon of the New Testament
              and Other Early Christian Literature*. 3rd ed. Chicago: Univer-
              sity of Chicago Press, 2000.

BDF   Friedrich Blass and Albert Debrunner. *A Greek Grammar of the
              New Testament and Other Early Christian Literature*. Trans-
              lated and edited by Robert W. Funk. Chicago: University of Chi-
              cago Press, 1961.

BECNT   Baker Exegetical Commentary on the New Testament

BHGNT   Baylor Handbook on the Greek New Testament

BTCP   Biblical Theology for Christian Proclamation

cf.   *confer* (Latin for *compare*)

CSB   Christian Standard Bible

CSC   Christian Standard Commentary

e.g.   *exempli gratia*, for example

EGGNT   Exegetical Guide to the Greek New Testament

ESV   English Standard Version

GGBB   Daniel B. Wallace. *Greek Grammar beyond the Basics*. Grand
              Rapids: Zondervan, 1996.

i.e.   *id est* (Latin for *that is*)

KJV   King James Version

L&N   Johannes P. Louw and Eugene A. Nida, eds. *Greek-English Lexi-
              con of the New Testament Based on Semantic Domains*. New
              York: United Bible Societies, 1988.

LW	*Luther's Works* [American edition]. 82 vols. projected. St. Louis: Concordia; Philadelphia: Fortress, 1955–86, 2009–.
LXX	Septuagint (the Greek OT)
NAC	New American Commentary
NASB1995	New American Standard Bible (1995 edition)
NET	New English Translation
NICNT	New International Commentary on the New Testament
NIGTC	New International Greek Testament Commentary
NIV	New International Version (2011 edition)
NJB	New Jerusalem Bible
NKJV	New King James Version
NLT	New Living Translation
NRSVue	New Revised Standard Version, Updated Edition (2021)
NT	New Testament
OT	Old Testament
PNTC	Pillar New Testament Commentary
RSV	Revised Standard Version
v(v).	verse(s)
WBC	Word Biblical Commentary
YLT	Young's Literal Translation
ZECNT	Zondervan Exegetical Commentary on the New Testament

Grammatical

1st	first person	masc.	masculine
2nd	second person	mid.	middle
3rd	third person	neut.	neuter
acc.	accusative	nom.	nominative
act.	active	num.	number
adj.	adjective	opt.	optative
adv.	adverb	pass.	passive
aor.	aorist	perf.	perfect
dat.	dative	pers.	person
fem.	feminine	pl.	plural
fut.	future	pluperf.	pluperfect
gen.	genitive	pres.	present
impf.	imperfect	ptc.	participle
impv.	imperative	sg.	singular
ind.	indicative	subj.	subjunctive
inf.	infinitive	voc.	vocative

Old Testament

Gen.	Genesis	Eccles.	Ecclesiastes
Exod.	Exodus	Song	Song of Songs
Lev.	Leviticus	Isa.	Isaiah
Num.	Numbers	Jer.	Jeremiah
Deut.	Deuteronomy	Lam.	Lamentations
Josh.	Joshua	Ezek.	Ezekiel
Judg.	Judges	Dan.	Daniel
Ruth	Ruth	Hosea	Hosea
1 Sam.	1 Samuel	Joel	Joel
2 Sam.	2 Samuel	Amos	Amos
1 Kings	1 Kings	Obad.	Obadiah
2 Kings	2 Kings	Jon.	Jonah
1 Chron.	1 Chronicles	Mic.	Micah
2 Chron.	2 Chronicles	Nah.	Nahum
Ezra	Ezra	Hab.	Habakkuk
Neh.	Nehemiah	Zeph.	Zephaniah
Esther	Esther	Hag.	Haggai
Job	Job	Zech.	Zechariah
Ps(s).	Psalm(s)	Mal.	Malachi
Prov.	Proverbs		

New Testament

Matt.	Matthew	1 Tim.	1 Timothy
Mark	Mark	2 Tim.	2 Timothy
Luke	Luke	Titus	Titus
John	John	Philem.	Philemon
Acts	Acts	Heb.	Hebrews
Rom.	Romans	James	James
1 Cor.	1 Corinthians	1 Pet.	1 Peter
2 Cor.	2 Corinthians	2 Pet.	2 Peter
Gal.	Galatians	1 John	1 John
Eph.	Ephesians	2 John	2 John
Phil.	Philippians	3 John	3 John
Col.	Colossians	Jude	Jude
1 Thess.	1 Thessalonians	Rev.	Revelation
2 Thess.	2 Thessalonians		

INTRODUCTION

The question that students ask me, perhaps more than any other, is "What should I do now that I am done with Greek?" This is a great question. I'm thankful when students ask it because it communicates their desire to continue their study of the Greek language. In the past, I would usually tell students "Stay in the text. Read a few verses of the Greek New Testament every day." I still believe that such advice is sound and should be heeded.

The problem is that the students' follow-up question is "Which book should I read?" In the past I might have said, "Read the Gospel of Mark or the Gospel of John." Although this is good advice, students may come across material that is difficult for them and become frustrated or discouraged (which is usually why I don't tell them to read the last half of Acts, 2 Corinthians, Hebrews, or 2 Peter). Another potential roadblock is the length of the Gospels. Although the Greek in the Gospels is generally easier than what is found in the Epistles, the sheer length of the Gospels can be daunting.

This book is designed to answer the question regarding what NT book students or former students should read. The correct answer is "all of them, . . . in the *right place* and at the *right time*." This book contains 90 days of guided reading. These readings are divided into three 30-day journeys, and the three journeys are further divided into six routes. Each route consists of five days of reading in the same passage (e.g., Rom. 1:11–17), with some longer passages spanning two routes. These routes and journeys start out easy and become progressively harder. The readings also include every NT author and highlight a variety of literary genres.

Each day's work consists of the following components, which should take 10–15 minutes to complete:

1. **Read** aloud the text in the original language at least five times. *This helps to facilitate learning and confidence in the language.*
2. **Parse** all the verbs in the reading, omitting participles and infinitives. *An answer key is provided at the end of each chapter.*
3. **Identify** the nouns in the reading. *Again, an answer key is provided at the end of each chapter.*
4. **Translate** the Greek text into understandable English. *Vocabulary words that occur fewer than 50 times in the NT are provided for each reading. Words that occur more than 50 times in the NT are listed in the appendix.*
5. **Notice** significant exegetical and syntactical insights. *Short, level-appropriate discussions of each important construction are included for guidance.*
6. A final section, **For the Journey**, offers a paragraph elaborating on the significance of the daily passage and connecting it with a wider theme for devotional reflection.

In a way, this book is a sequel to *Exegetical Gems from Biblical Greek* (Baker Academic, 2019). That book provides a way for students to review the basics of Greek syntax without needing to reread a reference grammar. Each of its 35 chapters presents an exegetical gem that highlights a different element of Greek syntax. *Exegetical Journeys* represents another attempt to prevent linguistic apostasy (the act of leaving behind and forsaking one's language skills). Instead of reviewing previously learned grammar and syntax, it aims to keep students reading the Greek text and growing in their vocabulary knowledge.

I envision this book being used in several ways. First, I intend it to keep students in the text between semesters. In the school where I teach, the time gap between the end of the fall semester (Greek 1) and the beginning of the spring semester (Greek 2) is about six weeks, which is a long time to allow a newly learned language to lie dormant. So between the fall and spring semesters, I assign my students the first 30-day journey. By completing that work, they earn either a designated number of points or even extra credit. The same approach could also be used during the summer break.

This book will also be helpful for students who have completed their classroom study of Greek and will no longer be under a professor's guidance. Instead of wandering aimlessly in their reading, they can follow a prescribed course that is appropriate to their current level.

Finally, this book can be used by those who have fallen out of the habit of regularly reading the Greek NT. Sometimes we just need a little encouragement and someone to point us down the right path. This book provides such encouragement and eases the return to daily Greek study.

To all those using this book, I wish the deep satisfaction and spiritual enrichment that comes from spending time daily in the Greek NT.

Journey 1

EASY

ROUTE 1

John 1:1–9

STEP ONE: **Read** aloud the text at least five times.

Ἐν ἀρχῇ ἦν ὁ λόγος, καὶ ὁ λόγος ἦν πρὸς τὸν θεόν, καὶ θεὸς ἦν ὁ λόγος. οὗτος ἦν ἐν ἀρχῇ πρὸς τὸν θεόν.

STEP TWO: **Parse** the following verb.

	Lexical Form	Tense	Voice	Mood	Pers.	Num.	Translation
ἦν							

STEP THREE: **Identify** the gender, case, and number of the following words.

	Gender	Case	Num.		Gender	Case	Num.
(1) ἀρχῇ				(4) θεός			
(2) ὁ λόγος				(5) οὗτος			
(3) τὸν θεόν							

7

STEP FOUR: **Translate** the text into understandable English.

_____

_____

STEP FIVE: **Notice** significant exegetical and syntactical insights.

- **ἐν ἀρχῇ:** This prepositional phrase contains no article, and yet it is usually translated "in _the_ beginning." A prepositional phrase can be definite even if there is no article. Because the word ἀρχή is naturally definite (there is only one "beginning"), this translation is justified. The preposition ἐν is always followed by the dative case.

- **ἦν:** This form of the verb εἰμί (3rd sg.) occurs over 400 times in the NT, accounting for over 90 percent of the uses of the imperfect tense. It occurs four times in just the first two verses of John 1!

- **πρὸς τὸν θεόν:** The preposition πρός is typically translated "to" or "toward," indicating direction. It can also be translated "with" or "in the presence of," indicating personal relationship, which is the best translation here.[1] The object of πρός is almost always in the accusative case.

- **θεὸς ἦν ὁ λόγος:** This well-known phrase has been the center of much controversy. Because the verb εἰμί is a copulative or equative verb, it takes a predicate nominative as its complement (not an accusative). Since both the subject and the complement are in the nominative case, the subject is usually the pronoun or proper name (if there is one), or the noun with the article. In this passage, because ὁ λόγος has the article (is articular) and θεός lacks the article (is anarthrous), ὁ λόγος is clearly the subject. But the question remains as to why θεός lacks the article. The construction that John uses indicates that the Word (Jesus) shares all the attributes of God (the Father) but is a distinct person. If the article were included with θεός, John would have been affirming that Christ was completely identified with God so that there is no distinction of person. But as it is, Jesus possesses the essence of the Father but is not identified as the Father.

---

1. See BDF 125 (§239.1); BDAG 874.

FOR THE JOURNEY

The opening statement of John's Gospel ("In the beginning was the Word") echoes the opening statement of Gen. 1:1 ("In the beginning God created the heavens and the earth"). Jesus was there in the beginning because he has no origin: his existence is beyond time and history. John 1:1 could be paraphrased as follows: "At the very beginning of creation and time, the Word as the perfect expression of God the Father had already existed, and this Word was in active communion with God, and this Word inherently shared the same nature as God."[2] Jesus was not only in the beginning "with" or "in the presence of God"; he also has all the divine attributes of the Father. He is fully God, though the Word does not exhaustively express all of who God is. He shares the same essence but is a unique person. Thankfully, this unique Person of the Trinity (God's one and only Son) became human and lived among us.

ANSWER KEY

1. *Parse:* ἦν (εἰμί, impf. act. ind. 3rd sg.).
2. *Identify:* (1) ἀρχῇ (fem. dat. sg.), (2) ὁ λόγος (masc. nom. sg.), (3) τὸν θεόν (masc. acc. sg.), (4) θεός (masc. nom. sg.), (5) οὗτος (masc. nom. sg.).
3. *Translate:* "In the beginning was the Word, and the Word was with God, and the Word was God. This one was in the beginning with God."

2. Murray J. Harris, *John*, EGGNT (Nashville: B&H Academic, 2015), 20.

DAY 2: JOHN 1:3

STEP ONE: **Read** aloud the text at least five times.

πάντα δι' αὐτοῦ ἐγένετο, καὶ χωρὶς αὐτοῦ ἐγένετο οὐδὲ ἕν ὃ γέγονεν.

STEP TWO: **Parse** the following verbs.

	Lexical Form	Tense	Voice	Mood	Pers.	Num.	Translation
(1) ἐγένετο							
(2) γέγονεν							

STEP THREE: **Identify** the gender, case, and number of the following words.

	Gender	Case	Num.		Gender	Case	Num.
(1) πάντα				(3) ἕν			
(2) αὐτοῦ				(4) ὃ			

STEP FOUR: **Translate** the text into understandable English.

_____

_____

_____

VOCABULARY

χωρίς, without, apart from

STEP FIVE: **Notice** significant exegetical and syntactical insights.

- **πάντα:** This adjective is functioning as a noun (substantival use). Because it is neuter and plural, the word "things" needs to be added in translation (i.e., "all things").

- **δι':** The lexical form of δι' is διά. The alpha drops when the following word begins with a vowel (e.g., δι' αὐτοῦ). The apostrophe is added to indicate that a letter is missing. When the preposition διά is followed by the genitive case, it means "through" (when it is followed by the accusative case, it means "because of"). Thus Jesus, the "Word," is the agent who caused all things to exist.

• ἐγένετο οὐδὲ ἕν ὃ γέγονεν: The form ἐγένετο occurs six times in John's Prologue (John 1:1–18; vv. 3 [2×], 6, 10, 14, 17). The phrase οὐδὲ ἕν is emphatic and does not simply mean that "nothing" was created without Christ; it means that "not one single thing" was created without him. The relative pronoun ὃ ("that") refers back to the term ἕν ("one thing").

FOR THE JOURNEY

This short but jam-packed verse declares that Jesus, the λόγος, is the agent through whom all the universe was created. John expresses this both positively ("all things were made through him") and negatively ("without him not one thing was made"). The apostle Paul says that all things were created "by him" (ἐν αὐτῷ), "through him" (δι' αὐτοῦ), and also "for him" (εἰς αὐτόν; Col. 1:16). Indeed, "he is before all things, and in him all things hold together" (Col. 1:17). The author of Hebrews describes the Son as the one "through whom also [God] created the universe" (Heb. 1:2). The apostle John, in the final book of the NT, calls Jesus "the faithful and true witness" and "the originator of God's creation" (Rev. 3:14 CSB). Jesus is the Son of God, the Second Person of the Trinity, and the one who created the heavens and the earth. To him be the glory!

ANSWER KEY

1. *Parse:* (1) ἐγένετο (γίνομαι, aor. mid. ind. 3rd sg.), (2) γέγονεν (γίνομαι, perf. act. ind. 3rd sg.).
2. *Identify:* (1) πάντα (neut. nom. pl.), (2) αὐτοῦ (masc. gen. sg.), (3) ἕν (neut. nom. sg.), (4) ὃ (neut. nom. sg.).
3. *Translate:* "All things were made through him, and without him not one thing was made that was made."

DAY 3: JOHN 1:4–5

STEP ONE: **Read** aloud the text at least five times.

ἐν αὐτῷ ζωὴ ἦν, καὶ ἡ ζωὴ ἦν τὸ φῶς τῶν ἀνθρώπων. καὶ τὸ φῶς
ἐν τῇ σκοτίᾳ φαίνει, καὶ ἡ σκοτία αὐτὸ οὐ κατέλαβεν.

STEP TWO: **Parse** the following verbs.

	Lexical Form	Tense	Voice	Mood	Pers.	Num.	Translation
(1) ἦν							
(2) φαίνει							
(3) κατέλαβεν							

STEP THREE: **Identify** the gender, case, and number of the following words.

	Gender	Case	Num.		Gender	Case	Num.
(1) αὐτῷ				(5) τῇ σκοτίᾳ			
(2) ἡ ζωή				(6) ἡ σκοτία			
(3) τὸ φῶς				(7) αὐτό			
(4) τῶν ἀνθρώπων							

STEP FOUR: **Translate** the text into understandable English.

VOCABULARY

σκοτία, ἡ, darkness
φαίνω, I shine
καταλαμβάνω, I overcome; comprehend

12

STEP FIVE: **Notice** significant exegetical and syntactical insights.

- **ἐν αὐτῷ ζωὴ ἦν, καὶ ἡ ζωὴ:** The first time John references ζωή ("life"), no article is used (i.e., it is anarthrous). The second time, however, the article is included (ἡ ζωή). This use of the article points back to the first occurrence of the term (previous reference, also called anaphoric). Consequently, several English versions render the phrase "that life" (CSB, NIV), signaling that the second use of the term points back to the first use.

- **τὸ φῶς τῶν ἀνθρώπων:** Jesus is the light of all human beings in the sense that he "endows everyone with the divine image (Gen. 1:27) as part of their constitution, and through his incarnation brings spiritual enlightenment to all humanity, male and female, Jew and Gentile" (Harris, *John*, 23).

- **ἡ σκοτία αὐτὸ οὐ κατέλαβεν:** The verb καταλαμβάνω can mean (1) to overtake, overcome, overpower, or it can mean (2) to comprehend or understand. The first option is best in the present context since the subject of the verb is "darkness." Darkness is not able to resist the light, which is able to overpower the darkness and continue to shine.

FOR THE JOURNEY

The unseen battle that rages does not consist of two equal forces dueling for the upper hand. John is not presenting a dualistic understanding of the universe, in which light and darkness (good and evil) are equally matched opponents, forever feuding. Instead, he describes the victory of the light over darkness. Jesus himself claimed to be "the light of the world" (8:12; 9:5) and "the life" (11:25; 14:6). Just as God spoke in the Genesis creation account and created light, so also Jesus, the Word of God, shines in the darkness and provides salvation for a renewed creation. John later reminds us that "the light has come into the world, and people loved darkness rather than the light because their deeds were evil" (John 3:19 CSB). The light of Jesus causes the world to hate the light itself and to hate him because the light exposes their deeds. But in this world we can have peace, even amid tribulation, because Jesus has "overcome the world" (John 16:33).

ANSWER KEY

1. *Parse:* (1) ἦν (εἰμί, impf. act. ind. 3rd sg.), (2) φαίνει (φαίνω, pres. act. ind. 3rd sg.), (3) κατέλαβεν (καταλαμβάνω, aor. act. ind. 3rd sg.).

2. *Identify:* (1) αὐτῷ (masc. dat. sg.), (2) ἡ ζωή (fem. nom. sg.), (3) τὸ φῶς (neut. nom. sg.), (4) τῶν ἀνθρώπων (masc. gen. pl.), (5) τῇ σκοτίᾳ (fem. dat. sg.), (6) ἡ σκοτία (fem. nom. sg.), (7) αὐτό (neut. acc. sg.).

3. *Translate:* "In him was life, and the life was the light of all people. And the light shines in the darkness, and the darkness did not overcome it."

14

DAY 4: JOHN 1:6–7

STEP ONE: **Read** aloud the text at least five times.

Ἐγένετο ἄνθρωπος, ἀπεσταλμένος παρὰ θεοῦ, ὄνομα αὐτῷ Ἰωάννης· οὗτος ἦλθεν εἰς μαρτυρίαν ἵνα μαρτυρήσῃ περὶ τοῦ φωτός, ἵνα πάντες πιστεύσωσιν δι᾽ αὐτοῦ.

STEP TWO: **Parse** the following verbs.

	Lexical Form	Tense	Voice	Mood	Pers.	Num.	Translation
(1) ἐγένετο							
(2) ἦλθεν							
(3) μαρτυρήσῃ							
(4) πιστεύσωσιν							

STEP THREE: **Identify** the gender, case, and number of the following words.

	Gender	Case	Num.		Gender	Case	Num.
(1) ἄνθρωπος				(6) μαρτυρίαν			
(2) θεοῦ				(7) τοῦ φωτός			
(3) ὄνομα				(8) πάντες			
(4) αὐτῷ				(9) αὐτοῦ			
(5) οὗτος							

STEP FOUR: **Translate** the text into understandable English.

_____

_____

VOCABULARY

μαρτυρία, ἡ, testimony

STEP FIVE: **Notice** significant exegetical and syntactical insights.

- Ἐγένετο ἄνθρωπος: The verb ἐγένετο here functions as a marker of new information (scene, character). The same form occurs 17 times in John's Gospel and 202 times in the NT.

- ἀπεσταλμένος παρὰ θεοῦ: The participle ἀπεσταλμένος (aor. pass. ptc. masc. nom. sg. of ἀποστέλλω) gives us further information about John: he was sent by God.

- ὄνομα αὐτῷ Ἰωάννης: Literally, this phrase is rendered "a name to him [was] John." The dative case can sometimes be used to convey a possessive meaning (i.e., "his/whose name was John").

- εἰς μαρτυρίαν: The preposition εἰς is always followed by the accusative case. Typically the meaning is "into," but here it functions to describe John's vocation ("as a witness," BDAG 290).

- ἵνα μαρτυρήσῃ . . . ἵνα πάντες πιστεύσωσιν: The word ἵνα triggers the subjunctive mood and typically conveys purpose (or sometimes result). John came as a witness *in order to* testify, and he testifies *in order that* all might believe.

FOR THE JOURNEY

Jesus *is* the light, dispelling the darkness. But John the Baptist comes to testify to and confirm the truth, declaring that Jesus is who he claims to be. John does not come on his own authority but is sent by God on a divine mission to be the forerunner and prepare the way of the Lord. The apostle John emphasizes John the Baptist's role as a valid witness by using two cognates ("he came as a *witness* to bear *witness*"). Later in John's Gospel, the Samaritan woman bears witness about Jesus, and many Samaritans believe (4:39). Jesus's own works bear witness to himself (5:36; 10:25). Additionally, the Father (5:32, 37; 8:18), the OT (5:39–40), and the Holy Spirit along with the apostles (15:26–27) bear witness to Jesus. The apostle John tells us that his very purpose for writing is "so that you may believe that Jesus is the Christ, the Son of God, and that by believing you may have life in his name" (20:31).

ANSWER KEY

1. *Parse:* (1) ἐγένετο (γίνομαι, aor. mid. ind. 3rd sg.), (2) ἦλθεν (ἔρχομαι, aor. act. ind. 3rd sg.), (3) μαρτυρήσῃ (μαρτυρέω, aor. act. subj. 3rd sg.), (4) πιστεύσωσιν (πιστεύω, aor. act. subj. 3rd pl.).

2. *Identify:* (1) ἄνθρωπος (masc. nom. sg.), (2) θεοῦ (masc. gen. sg.), (3) ὄνομα (neut. nom. sg.), (4) αὐτῷ (masc. dat. sg.), (5) οὗτος (masc. nom. sg.), (6) μαρτυρίαν (fem. acc. sg.), (7) τοῦ φωτός (neut. gen. sg.), (8) πάντες (masc. nom. pl.), (9) αὐτοῦ (masc. gen. sg.).

3. *Translate:* "There was a man who was sent from God; his name was John. This one came as a witness to bear witness concerning the light, that all might believe through him."

DAY 5: JOHN 1:8–9

STEP ONE: Read aloud the text at least five times.

οὐκ ἦν ἐκεῖνος τὸ φῶς, ἀλλ' ἵνα μαρτυρήσῃ περὶ τοῦ φωτός. Ἦν τὸ φῶς τὸ ἀληθινόν, ὃ φωτίζει πάντα ἄνθρωπον, ἐρχόμενον εἰς τὸν κόσμον.

STEP TWO: Parse the following verbs.

	Lexical Form	Tense	Voice	Mood	Pers.	Num.	Translation
(1) ἦν							
(2) μαρτυρήσῃ							
(3) φωτίζει							

STEP THREE: Identify the gender, case, and number of the following words.

	Gender	Case	Num.		Gender	Case	Num.
(1) ἐκεῖνος				(5) ὅ			
(2) τὸ φῶς				(6) πάντα			
(3) τοῦ φωτός				(7) ἄνθρωπον			
(4) τὸ ἀληθινόν				(8) τὸν κόσμον			

STEP FOUR: Translate the text into understandable English.

_____

_____

VOCABULARY

ἀληθινός, ή, true, genuine

φωτίζω, I give light

STEP FIVE: **Notice** significant exegetical and syntactical insights.

- **οὐκ ἦν ἐκεῖνος τὸ φῶς:** The far demonstrative pronoun ἐκεῖνος is typically "that [one/man]," but many English versions translate it as "he." It is likely that this pronoun is emphatic (*"That man* was not the light").

- **ἀλλ' ἵνα μαρτυρήσῃ περὶ τοῦ φωτός:** The verb ἦλθεν ("he came") is implied from the context: "but [he came] that he might bear witness concerning the light."

- **Ἦν τὸ φῶς τὸ ἀληθινόν, ὃ φωτίζει πάντα ἄνθρωπον:** Even though the subject of the verbs ἦν and φωτίζει is not explicitly stated, the context clarifies that it is "the Word" (ὁ λόγος, v. 1), or "this one" (οὗτος, v. 2). That is, the Word and not John the Baptist was the true light.

- **ἐρχόμενον εἰς τὸν κόσμον:** The participle ἐρχόμενον (pres. mid. ptc. neut. acc. sg. of ἔρχομαι) functions attributively, modifying τὸ φῶς ("the light was coming") and not πάντα ἄνθρωπον ("every person who comes into the world").

FOR THE JOURNEY

John the Baptist was the forerunner of the Messiah but was not the Messiah. He testified to the light and therefore was not the light himself. Only Jesus is the true light (3:19, 8:12; 9:5), just as he later is called the "true bread from heaven" (6:32) and the "true vine" (15:1). The idea of "true" in John often signifies that which is genuine, especially in relation to what fulfills OT expectations. In the past, God gave Israel manna, but now Jesus is the true bread from heaven. In the past, God gave his people revelations of himself, but now Jesus is the true light who reveals the intention of the Father. In the Gospel of John, the term "world" often identifies what is in opposition to God. D. A. Carson reminds us that "God's love is to be admired not because the world is so big but because the world is so bad."[3] In the incarnation, Jesus provides the revelation of God so that all can see God's love.

3. D. A. Carson, *John*, PNTC (Grand Rapids: Eerdmans, 1990), 123.

ANSWER KEY

1. *Parse:* (1) ἦν (εἰμί, impf. act. ind. 3rd sg.), (2) μαρτυρήσῃ (μαρτυρέω, aor. act. subj. 3rd sg.), (3) φωτίζει (φωτίζω, pres. act. ind. 3rd sg.).

2. *Identify:* (1) ἐκεῖνος (masc. nom. sg.), (2) τὸ φῶς (neut. nom. sg.), (3) τοῦ φωτός (neut. gen. sg.), (4) τὸ ἀληθινόν (neut. nom. sg.), (5) ὅ (neut. nom. sg.), (6) πάντα (masc. acc. sg.), (7) ἄνθρωπον (masc. acc. sg.), (8) τὸν κόσμον (masc. acc. sg.).

3. *Translate:* "That man was not the light, but [he came] that he might bear witness concerning the light. The true light, which gives light to every person, was coming into the world."

ROUTE 2

John 1:10–18

STEP ONE: **Read** aloud the text at least five times.

ἐν τῷ κόσμῳ ἦν, καὶ ὁ κόσμος δι' αὐτοῦ ἐγένετο, καὶ ὁ κόσμος αὐτὸν
οὐκ ἔγνω. εἰς τὰ ἴδια ἦλθεν, καὶ οἱ ἴδιοι αὐτὸν οὐ παρέλαβον.

STEP TWO: **Parse** the following verbs.

	Lexical Form	Tense	Voice	Mood	Pers.	Num.	Translation
(1) ἦν							
(2) ἐγένετο							
(3) ἔγνω							
(4) ἦλθεν							
(5) παρέλαβον							

STEP THREE: **Identify** the gender, case, and number of the following
words.

	Gender	Case	Num.		Gender	Case	Num.
(1) τῷ κόσμῳ				(4) αὐτόν			
(2) ὁ κόσμος				(5) τὰ ἴδια			
(3) αὐτοῦ				(6) οἱ ἴδιοι			

21

STEP FOUR: **Translate** the text into understandable English.

VOCABULARY

παραλαμβάνω, I receive, accept

STEP FIVE: **Notice** significant exegetical and syntactical insights.

- ἐν τῷ κόσμῳ ἦν, καὶ ὁ κόσμος δι' αὐτοῦ ἐγένετο, καὶ ὁ κόσμος αὐτὸν οὐκ ἔγνω: The term κόσμος occurs three times in verse 10. It is often stated or assumed that the same word in the same context must mean the same thing. Such a conclusion, though sometimes true, is not necessarily so. Context must decide: here it is clear that the same term is used differently. Harris explains, "In verse 10a ὁ κόσμος refers to the earth as inhabited by human beings (cf. 16:21). . . . In verse 10b it denotes the whole universe, . . . while in verse 10c it signifies humanity in its opposition to God."[1] Also, the antecedent for the personal pronoun αὐτόν is τὸ φῶς (v. 9). Consequently, we expect a neuter form of the pronoun (αὐτό). This shift suggests that John "is thinking of the Logos in personal terms and of the earthly ministry of Jesus" (Harris, *John*, 30).

- εἰς τὰ ἴδια ἦλθεν, καὶ οἱ ἴδιοι αὐτὸν οὐ παρέλαβον: Notice that there are two different genders of ἴδιος: neuter (τὰ ἴδια) and masculine (οἱ ἴδιοι). The neuter form refers to the world as that which the Word possessed. The masculine form, however, refers to his own people. "The first clause shows the intimacy between the Creator and his world, the second clause shows the intimacy between the man and his race."[2]

---

1. Murray J. Harris, *John*, EGGNT (Nashville: B&H Academic, 2015), 30.
2. Edward W. Klink III, *John*, ZECNT (Grand Rapids: Zondervan, 2016), 103.

FOR THE JOURNEY

These verses demonstrate the intention of God to save a people in spite of their continued rebellion. The very world that Jesus created refused to know and embrace him. This was not only true of Israel's rejection of Jesus, but it was also true of Israel's rejection of God in the OT. In Isaiah, God calls out, "All day long I have held out my hands to an obstinate people, who walk in ways not good, pursuing their own imaginations" (Isa. 65:2 NIV). Through their history, God sent the people prophets, "But they did not listen to me or pay attention. They were stiff-necked and did more evil than their ancestors" (Jer. 7:26 NIV). It was to this world that God sent Jesus, the light of the world, to illuminate the love of God and call a people out of darkness into his marvelous light.

ANSWER KEY

1. *Parse:* (1) ἦν (εἰμί, impf. act. ind. 3rd sg.), (2) ἐγένετο (γίνομαι, aor. mid. ind. 3rd sg.), (3) ἔγνω (γινώσκω, aor. act. ind. 3rd sg.), (4) ἦλθεν (ἔρχομαι, aor. act. ind. 3rd sg.), (5) παρέλαβον (παραλαμβάνω, aor. act. ind. 3rd pl.).

2. *Identify:* (1) τῷ κόσμῳ (masc. dat. sg.), (2) ὁ κόσμος (masc. nom. sg.), (3) αὐτοῦ (masc. gen. sg.), (4) αὐτόν (masc. acc. sg.), (5) τὰ ἴδια (neut. acc. pl.), (6) οἱ ἴδιοι (masc. nom. pl.).

3. *Translate:* "He was in the world, and the world was made through him, and the world did not know him. He came into his own, and his own did not receive him."

DAY 7: JOHN 1:12-13

STEP ONE: **Read** aloud the text at least five times.

ὅσοι δὲ ἔλαβον αὐτόν, ἔδωκεν αὐτοῖς ἐξουσίαν τέκνα θεοῦ γενέσθαι, τοῖς πιστεύουσιν εἰς τὸ ὄνομα αὐτοῦ οἳ οὐκ ἐξ αἱμάτων οὐδὲ ἐκ θελήματος σαρκὸς οὐδὲ ἐκ θελήματος ἀνδρὸς ἀλλ' ἐκ θεοῦ ἐγεννήθησαν.

STEP TWO: **Parse** the following verbs.

	Lexical Form	Tense	Voice	Mood	Pers.	Num.	Translation
(1) ἔλαβον							
(2) ἔδωκεν							
(3) ἐγεννήθησαν							

STEP THREE: **Identify** the gender, case, and number of the following words.

	Gender	Case	Num.		Gender	Case	Num.
(1) ὅσοι				(7) τὸ ὄνομα			
(2) αὐτόν				(8) οἵ			
(3) αὐτοῖς				(9) αἱμάτων			
(4) ἐξουσίαν				(10) θελήματος			
(5) τέκνα				(11) σαρκός			
(6) θεοῦ				(12) ἀνδρός			

STEP FOUR: **Translate** the text into understandable English.

_____

_____

STEP FIVE: **Notice** significant exegetical and syntactical insights.

- **δέ:** This conjunction is postpositive, meaning that it never comes first in a sentence or clause. In English, however, it is best to translate it first. This verse, then, qualifies verse 11 ("but") because not everyone fails to receive the Word, who has entered the world he made.

- **αὐτοῖς . . . , τοῖς πιστεύουσιν εἰς τὸ ὄνομα αὐτοῦ:** The dative phrase "to those who believe in his name" (τοῖς πιστεύουσιν) is an expansion of the dative pronoun "to them" (αὐτοῖς). This is known as a dative of apposition.

- **οἵ:** This relative pronoun matches the gender, number, and case of its antecedent, which is the pronoun ὅσοι.

- **οὐκ ἐξ αἱμάτων:** Notice that the word for blood (αἱμάτων) is actually plural (i.e., "bloods"). This probably refers to blood of both parents (bloodlines). The assumption is that the process of procreation involves mixing the blood of the parents.

FOR THE JOURNEY

In John's Gospel, Jesus alone is the "Son of God" (υἱὸς θεοῦ), and believers are called the "children of God" (τέκνα θεοῦ). Jesus's sonship is unique. His sonship is essential to his nature; the sonship of believers is adoptive. The means by which someone comes into God's family is by receiving Jesus and believing in his name. These twin concepts are parallel in verse 12, demonstrating that they are describing the same spiritual reality: forsaking one's own merits and trusting in the Word. Such a transformation does not come through natural means. It is not through our ancestry ("not from blood"), or from our own choice ("nor from the will of the flesh"), or from our own initiative ("nor from the will of man") but from God (ἐκ θεοῦ). We become children of God through his work of re-creation in us: "Behold: new things have come" (ἰδοὺ γέγονεν καινά, 2 Cor. 5:17).

ANSWER KEY

1. *Parse:* (1) ἔλαβον (λαμβάνω, aor. act. ind. 3rd pl.), (2) ἔδωκεν (δίδωμι, aor. act. ind. 3rd sg.), (3) ἐγεννήθησαν (γεννάω, aor. pass. ind. 3rd pl.).

2. *Identify:* (1) ὅσοι (masc. nom. pl.), (2) αὐτόν (masc. acc. sg.), (3) αὐτοῖς (masc. dat. pl.), (4) ἐξουσίαν (fem. acc. sg.), (5) τέκνα (neut. acc. pl.), (6) θεοῦ (masc. gen. sg.), (7) τὸ ὄνομα (neut. acc. sg.), (8) οἵ (masc. nom. pl.), (9) αἱμάτων (neut. gen. pl.), (10) θελήματος (neut. gen. sg.), (11) σαρκός (fem. gen. sg.), (12) ἀνδρός (masc. gen. sg.).

3. *Translate:* "But as many as received him, to them he gave the right to be children of God—to those who believe in his name, who were born not from blood nor from the will of the flesh nor from the will of man, but from God."

DAY 8: JOHN 1:14

STEP ONE: **Read** aloud the text at least five times.

Καὶ ὁ λόγος σὰρξ ἐγένετο καὶ ἐσκήνωσεν ἐν ἡμῖν, καὶ ἐθεασάμεθα τὴν δόξαν αὐτοῦ, δόξαν ὡς μονογενοῦς παρὰ πατρός, πλήρης χάριτος καὶ ἀληθείας.

STEP TWO: **Parse** the following verbs.

	Lexical Form	Tense	Voice	Mood	Pers.	Num.	Translation
(1) ἐγένετο							
(2) ἐσκήνωσεν							
(3) ἐθεασάμεθα							

STEP THREE: **Identify** the gender, case, and number of the following words.

	Gender	Case	Num.		Gender	Case	Num.
(1) ὁ λόγος				(6) μονογενοῦς			
(2) σάρξ				(7) πατρός			
(3) ἡμῖν				(8) πλήρης			
(4) τὴν δόξαν				(9) χάριτος			
(5) αὐτοῦ				(10) ἀληθείας			

STEP FOUR: **Translate** the text into understandable English.

VOCABULARY

σκηνόω, I dwell, live
θεάομαι, I see, behold
μονογενής, unique, one of a kind
πλήρης, filled, full

STEP FIVE: **Notice** significant exegetical and syntactical insights.

- **ὁ λόγος σὰρξ ἐγένετο:** The verb γίνομαι is similar to εἰμί in that it takes a predicate nominative (and not an accusative direct object). Consequently, both ὁ λόγος (the subject) and σάρξ (the predicate nominative) are in the nominative case.

- **μονογενοῦς:** There is significant debate about whether the meaning of μονογενής stems from (1) μόνος + γεννάω = "only begotten" (KJV, NKJV); or (2) μόνος + γενής = "pertaining to being the only one of its kind . . . or class, *unique (in kind)*" (BDAG 658). Most scholars today choose the second option, which is reflected in most modern English versions: "the one and only Son" (CSB, NIV), "the only Son" (ESV, NRSVue).

- **πλήρης χάριτος καὶ ἀληθείας:** The genitive is the most versatile of the cases. Sometimes the genitive case is used following certain verbs (e.g., ἀκούω, ἅπτομαι, ἄρχω, πληρόω) or certain nouns, such as πλήρης.

FOR THE JOURNEY

Jesus was with the Father from the beginning. He himself has no beginning and no end. But Jesus became something he previously was not. He became flesh (σάρξ): that is, he became fully human, with bones and blood and soul. In doing so, he did not cease to be God (θεός). Instead, he added his existence as a fully human person to what he already was, a fully divine person. This divine-man dwelt or tabernacled (from σκηνόω) among us. This term recalls the OT tabernacle (σκηνή), the place where God met with Israel before the temple was built in Jerusalem. Jesus becomes the ultimate manifestation of God's presence among humanity. Similar to the glory that was associated with the presence of God, Jesus displays the glory of God. John reminds us that Jesus is the Word, and the Word is the God-man who came into our world to dispel the darkness.

ANSWER KEY

1. *Parse:* (1) ἐγένετο (γίνομαι, aor. mid. ind. 3rd sg.), (2) ἐσκήνωσεν (σκηνόω, aor. act. ind. 3rd sg.), (3) ἐθεασάμεθα (θεάομαι, aor. mid. ind. 1st pl.).

2. *Identify:* (1) ὁ λόγος (masc. nom. sg.), (2) σάρξ (fem. nom. sg.), (3) ἡμῖν (dat. pl.), (4) τὴν δόξαν (fem. acc. sg.), (5) αὐτοῦ (masc. gen. sg.), (6) μονογενοῦς (masc. gen. sg.), (7) πατρός (masc. gen. sg.), (8) πλήρης (masc. gen. sg.), (9) χάριτος (fem. gen. sg.), (10) ἀληθείας (fem. gen. sg.).

3. *Translate:* "And the Word became flesh and dwelt among us, and we beheld his glory, as the glory of the only Son from the Father, full of grace and truth."

JOURNEY 1 · EASY

DAY 9: JOHN 1:15-16

STEP ONE: **Read** aloud the text at least five times.

Ἰωάννης μαρτυρεῖ περὶ αὐτοῦ καὶ κέκραγεν λέγων, Οὗτος ἦν ὃν
εἶπον, Ὁ ὀπίσω μου ἐρχόμενος ἔμπροσθέν μου γέγονεν, ὅτι πρῶτός
μου ἦν. ὅτι ἐκ τοῦ πληρώματος αὐτοῦ ἡμεῖς πάντες ἐλάβομεν καὶ
χάριν ἀντὶ χάριτος.

STEP TWO: **Parse** the following verbs.

	Lexical Form	Tense	Voice	Mood	Pers.	Num.	Translation
(1) μαρτυρεῖ							
(2) κέκραγεν							
(3) ἦν							
(4) εἶπον							
(5) γέγονεν							
(6) ἐλάβομεν							

STEP THREE: **Identify** the gender, case, and number of the following words.

	Gender	Case	Num.		Gender	Case	Num.
(1) αὐτοῦ				(6) πληρώματος			
(2) οὗτος				(7) ἡμεῖς			
(3) ὅν				(8) πάντες			
(4) μου				(9) χάριν			
(5) πρῶτός				(10) χάριτος			

STEP FOUR: **Translate** the text into understandable English.

VOCABULARY

ὀπίσω, after
ἔμπροσθεν, before, in front of (rank)
πλήρωμα, fullness
ἀντί, for, in place of

STEP FIVE: **Notice** significant exegetical and syntactical insights.

- **μαρτυρεῖ:** The verb μαρτυρέω is a contract verb: its stem ends with a vowel (-ε). Thus, when the third-person singular ending (ει) is added to the stem, a contraction occurs (μαρτυρε + ει → μαρτυρεει = μαρτυρεῖ). The circumflex accent above the iota (ῖ) signals that a contraction has occurred. This verb is also categorized as a historical present, describing a past event (perhaps used to indicate emphasis or a change in location or the introduction of a new person). The present form is translated as a past-tense verb in English ("cried out").

- **λέγων . . . ἐρχόμενος:** These two participles function differently. λέγων (pres. act. ptc. masc. nom. sg. of λέγω) is adverbial and introduces a quote. ἐρχόμενος (pres. mid. ptc. masc. nom. sg. of ἔρχομαι) is substantival and connected to the article ὁ (ὁ . . . ἐρχόμενος = "the one coming"). The words between the article and the participle (ὀπίσω μου) are placed there to show that they are closely connected to the surrounding form ("the one who comes after me"). This type of construction is sometimes called a Greek sandwich.

- **ὅτι πρῶτός μου ἦν:** The superlative πρῶτος ("first") is used in the place of a comparison (πρότερος "earlier," "prior"). Even though Jesus was born after John the Baptist (see Luke 1:24–27), John recognized that Jesus existed before he "became flesh and dwelt among us" (John 1:14). The pronoun μου can be classified as a genitive of comparison ("than me").

- **χάριν ἀντὶ χάριτος:** There are two main interpretations of the preposition ἀντί: (1) accumulation ("upon," "in addition to"); or (2) replacement ("for," "in the place of"). The second option is preferable because "in the place of" or "instead of" is the most common use and fits the context better. Typically, when an author intends "upon," ἐπί is used.

31

FOR THE JOURNEY

What does it mean that we receive "grace in the place of grace"? The idea is that one form of grace is exchanged for another (in this case, a superior) grace. With the coming of Jesus, grace is sent from the Father. The old covenant, even with its laws, rules, and regulations, was a covenant of grace. God was gracious in choosing Israel and making a covenant with them though they were a small and obstinate people. In the new covenant, however, that grace is multiplied. The God of the OT is the same God of the NT. But in the new covenant, God's grace is amplified as the Word humbles himself, takes on the form of a servant, and dies on a criminal's cross.

ANSWER KEY

1. *Parse:* (1) μαρτυρεῖ (μαρτυρέω, pres. act. ind. 3rd sg.), (2) κέκραγεν (κράζω, perf. act. ind. 3rd sg.), (3) ἦν (εἰμί, impf. act. ind. 3rd sg.), (4) εἶπον (λέγω, aor. act. ind. 1st sg.), (5) γέγονεν (γίνομαι, perf. act. ind. 3rd sg.), (6) ἐλάβομεν (λαμβάνω, aor. act. ind. 1st pl.).

2. *Identify:* (1) αὐτοῦ (masc. gen. sg.), (2) οὗτος (masc. nom. sg.), (3) ὅν (masc. acc. sg.), (4) μου (gen. sg.), (5) πρῶτός (masc. nom. sg.), (6) πληρώματος (neut. gen. sg.), (7) ἡμεῖς (masc./fem. nom. pl.), (8) πάντες (masc. nom. pl.), (9) χάριν (fem. acc. sg.), (10) χάριτος (fem. gen. sg.).

3. *Translate:* "John bore witness concerning him and cried out, saying, 'This one was the one whom I said, The one who comes after (in time) is before me (in status), because he was before (in time) me. Because from his fullness we all received grace in the place of grace.'"

DAY 10: JOHN 1:17–18

STEP ONE: **Read** aloud the text at least five times.

ὅτι ὁ νόμος διὰ Μωϋσέως ἐδόθη, ἡ χάρις καὶ ἡ ἀλήθεια διὰ Ἰησοῦ Χριστοῦ ἐγένετο. θεὸν οὐδεὶς ἑώρακεν πώποτε· μονογενὴς θεὸς ὁ ὢν εἰς τὸν κόλπον τοῦ πατρὸς ἐκεῖνος ἐξηγήσατο.

STEP TWO: **Parse** the following verbs.

	Lexical Form	Tense	Voice	Mood	Pers.	Num.	Translation
(1) ἐδόθη							
(2) ἐγένετο							
(3) ἑώρακεν							
(4) ἐξηγήσατο							

STEP THREE: **Identify** the gender, case, and number of the following words.

	Gender	Case	Num.		Gender	Case	Num.
(1) ὁ νόμος				(7) μονογενής			
(2) ἡ χάρις				(8) θεός			
(3) ἡ ἀλήθεια				(9) τὸν κόλπον			
(4) Ἰησοῦ Χριστοῦ				(10) τοῦ πατρός			
(5) θεόν				(11) ἐκεῖνος			
(6) οὐδείς							

STEP FOUR: **Translate** the text into understandable English.

> VOCABULARY
>
> πώποτε, ever, at any time
> μονογενής, unique, one of a kind
> κόλπος, ὁ, chest, side
> ἐξηγέομαι, I reveal, make known, explain

33

STEP FIVE: **Notice** significant exegetical and syntactical insights.

- ἐδόθη . . . ἐγένετο: The difference between these two verbs is significant. The first verb ἐδόθη is a passive form (also known as a "divine passive" since God is the implied subject) with Moses as the intermediary (God gave the law through Moses). In contrast, grace and truth came (ἐγένετο) directly through Jesus, which "implies that grace and truth were Christ's own intrinsic possession, not extraneous virtues that he simply mediated" (Harris, *John*, 37).

- μονογενὴς θεός: Verse 18 contains a textual variant, with some texts reading μονογενὴς υἱός ("the one and only Son" or "only begotten Son"). The reading in our text (μονογενὴς θεός, "the one and only God") is preferable because (1) it has stronger textual support; (2) it best explains the other reading; (3) it is the more difficult reading (cf. John 3:16, 18; 1 John 4:9); and (4) it forms a fitting climax to John's Prologue.

- ὁ ὢν εἰς τὸν κόλπον τοῦ πατρὸς ἐκεῖνος: This entire phrase, which is governed by the initial article ὁ, is in apposition to μονογενὴς θεός. In other words, "the one who is at the Father's side" further explains "the one and only God."

FOR THE JOURNEY

John ends his prologue with a universal truth: "No one has ever seen God" (1:18 NIV). Although Moses saw the Lord's glory (Exod. 33–34), and although he spoke to God "face to face" (Exod. 33:11; Deut. 5:4; 34:10), such contact was veiled and never involved viewing God's essential being. He was seen only in shadows and figures but never in his person. But now, through Jesus the God-man, God has been more fully revealed. "The beloved Son, the incarnate Word (1:14), himself God while being *at the Father's side*, . . . has broken the barrier that made it impossible for human beings to see God, and *has made him known*."[3] Jesus is the great revealer. But how did he reveal the Father? The answer is found in John 14:9, where Jesus claims, "The one who has seen me has seen the Father" (CSB).

3. D. A. Carson, *John*, PNTC (Grand Rapids: Eerdmans, 1990), 134.

ANSWER KEY

1. *Parse:* (1) ἐδόθη (δίδωμι, aor. pass. ind. 3rd sg.), (2) ἐγένετο (γίνομαι, aor. mid. ind. 3rd sg.), (3) ἑώρακεν (ὁράω, perf. act. ind. 3rd sg.), (4) ἐξηγήσατο (ἐξηγέομαι, aor. mid. ind. 3rd sg.).

2. *Identify:* (1) ὁ νόμος (masc. nom. sg.), (2) ἡ χάρις (fem. nom. sg.), (3) ἡ ἀλήθεια (fem. nom. sg.), (4) Ἰησοῦ Χριστοῦ (masc. gen. sg.), (5) θεόν (masc. acc. sg.), (6) οὐδείς (masc. nom. sg.), (7) μονογενής (masc. nom. sg.), (8) θεός (masc. nom. sg.), (9) τὸν κόλπον (masc. acc. sg.), (10) τοῦ πατρός (masc. gen. sg.), (11) ἐκεῖνος (masc. nom. sg.).

3. *Translate:* "Because the law was given through Moses; grace and truth came through Jesus Christ. No one has ever seen God; the only God who is at the Father's side, that one has revealed [him]."

ROUTE 3

Revelation 1:4–9

STEP ONE: **Read** aloud the text at least five times.

Ἰωάννης ταῖς ἑπτὰ ἐκκλησίαις ταῖς ἐν τῇ Ἀσίᾳ· χάρις ὑμῖν καὶ εἰρήνη ἀπὸ ὁ ὢν καὶ ὁ ἦν καὶ ὁ ἐρχόμενος καὶ ἀπὸ τῶν ἑπτὰ πνευμάτων ἃ ἐνώπιον τοῦ θρόνου αὐτοῦ.

STEP TWO: **Parse** the following verb.

	Lexical Form	Tense	Voice	Mood	Pers.	Num.	Translation
ἦν							

STEP THREE: **Identify** the gender, case, and number of the following words.

	Gender	Case	Num.		Gender	Case	Num.
(1) ταῖς ἐκκλησίαις				(5) εἰρήνη			
(2) τῇ Ἀσίᾳ				(6) τῶν πνευμάτων			
(3) χάρις				(7) ἃ			
(4) ὑμῖν				(8) τοῦ θρόνου			

STEP FOUR: **Translate** the text into understandable English.

STEP FIVE: **Notice** significant exegetical and syntactical insights.

- **Ἰωάννης...χάρις...εἰρήνη:** These nouns are all in the nominative case although they do not function as the subjects of any verb. Such nouns are typically categorized as nominative absolutes (the term "absolute" in grammar refers to something that is syntactically independent).

- **ταῖς ἑπτὰ ἐκκλησίαις ταῖς ἐν τῇ Ἀσίᾳ:** This construction follows a common article + noun + article + adjective construction. The phrase ταῖς ἐν τῇ Ἀσίᾳ functions as a giant adjective that modifies "the seven churches" (ταῖς ἑπτὰ ἐκκλησίαις). As such, the article (ταῖς) turns the prepositional phrase ἐν τῇ Ἀσίᾳ into an adjective. Literally, it reads, "the seven in-Asia churches," which is smoothed out to "the seven churches that are in Asia."

- **ἀπὸ ὁ ὢν καὶ ὁ ἦν καὶ ὁ ἐρχόμενος:** This phrase includes two anomalies in Greek grammar, often called solecisms.[1] For example, the preposition ἀπό takes its object in the genitive case. But here (and only here in biblical Greek) ἀπό is followed by objects in the nominative case (ὁ ὢν, ὁ ἦν, ὁ ἐρχόμενος). This grammatical incongruity is most likely the result of the author intentionally wanting "to draw attention to the titular nature of this expression and the OT text from which it comes: Exodus 3:14: ἐγώ εἰμι ὁ ὢν" (LXX).[2] The second anomaly is found in the phrase ὁ ἦν ("the one who was"). It is not unusual for a (substantival) participle to be articular (ὁ ὢν, ὁ ἐρχόμενος). But what is surprising is to have an article attached to an indicative (imperfect) verb. The reason for this usage is probably because there is no imperfect form of a participle.

- **ἀπὸ τῶν ἑπτὰ πνευμάτων:** Notice here that the expected genitive case follows the preposition ἀπό. This use, along with the 31 other

---

1. A solecism is a breach in accepted grammatical rules.
2. David L. Mathewson, *Revelation*, BHGNT (Waco: Baylor University Press, 2016), 4.

uses of ἀπό in Revelation, demonstrates that John is not ignorant of Greek grammar. The seven Spirits represent the Holy Spirit, with the number seven representing the full perfections of God.

FOR THE JOURNEY

John opens his letter with a greeting and doxology to the seven churches located in Asia Minor. These seven churches, though they represent actual local churches at that time, also represent all churches everywhere (as suggested by the number seven). John's message to us, then, is one that conveys the grace and peace of the triune God. Revelation uniquely addresses God with the threefold title as the One who is, the One who was, and the One who is to come (also see 1:8; 4:8). John begins, not in chronological order (who was, is, is to come) but in the present (who is). Not only is God in control of the past and the future; he is also in control of the present. We can therefore take comfort that even in the midst of difficulties or hardships that may come our way, God is the sovereign Lord of the past, the future, and even the present situation.

ANSWER KEY

1. *Parse:* ἦν (εἰμί, impf. act. ind. 3rd sg.).
2. *Identify:* (1) ταῖς ἐκκλησίαις (fem. dat. pl.), (2) τῇ Ἀσίᾳ (fem. dat. sg.), (3) χάρις (fem. nom. sg.), (4) ὑμῖν (dat. pl.), (5) εἰρήνη (fem. nom. sg.), (6) τῶν πνευμάτων (neut. gen. pl.), (7) ἅ (neut. nom. pl.), (8) τοῦ θρόνου (masc. gen. sg.).
3. *Translate:* "John, to the seven churches that [are] in Asia: Grace to you and peace from the one who is and who was and who is coming, and from the seven spirits who are before his throne."

DAY 12: REVELATION 1:5–6

STEP ONE: **Read** aloud the text at least five times.

καὶ ἀπὸ Ἰησοῦ Χριστοῦ, ὁ μάρτυς, ὁ πιστός, ὁ πρωτότοκος τῶν νεκρῶν καὶ ὁ ἄρχων τῶν βασιλέων τῆς γῆς. Τῷ ἀγαπῶντι ἡμᾶς καὶ λύσαντι ἡμᾶς ἐκ τῶν ἁμαρτιῶν ἡμῶν ἐν τῷ αἵματι αὐτοῦ. καὶ ἐποίησεν ἡμᾶς βασιλείαν, ἱερεῖς τῷ θεῷ καὶ πατρὶ αὐτοῦ, αὐτῷ ἡ δόξα καὶ τὸ κράτος εἰς τοὺς αἰῶνας [τῶν αἰώνων]· ἀμήν.

STEP TWO: **Parse** the following verb.

	Lexical Form	Tense	Voice	Mood	Pers.	Num.	Translation
ἐποίησεν							

STEP THREE: **Identify** the gender, case, and number of the following words.

	Gender	Case	Num.		Gender	Case	Num.
(1) ὁ μάρτυς				(8) βασιλείαν			
(2) τῶν νεκρῶν				(9) τῷ θεῷ			
(3) ὁ ἄρχων				(10) πατρί			
(4) τῶν βασιλέων				(11) ἡ δόξα			
(5) τῆς γῆς				(12) τὸ κράτος			
(6) τῶν ἁμαρτιῶν				(13) τοὺς αἰῶνας			
(7) τῷ αἵματι				(14) τῶν αἰώνων			

STEP FOUR: **Translate** the text into understandable English.

VOCABULARY

μάρτυς, ὁ, witness
πρωτότοκος, firstborn
ἄρχων, ὁ, ruler

ἱερεύς, ὁ, priest
κράτος, τό, dominion, power

STEP FIVE: **Notice** significant exegetical and syntactical insights.

- ὁ μάρτυς, ὁ πιστός, ὁ πρωτότοκος, . . . ὁ ἄρχων: These nominative forms are in apposition to Ἰησοῦ Χριστοῦ, even though Ἰησοῦ Χριστοῦ is in the genitive case. The nominative form may indicate the titular use of the terms. The editors of several critical Greek New Testaments have placed a comma between ὁ μάρτυς and ὁ πιστός, thus creating two separate substantives ("the witness" and "the faithful one"). Most English versions, however, rightly take the adjective πιστός attributively, modifying the noun μάρτυς ("the faithful witness"). Consequently, John presents a threefold statement about Christ: "the faithful witness, the firstborn, . . . the ruler" (cf. Rev. 2:13; 3:14).

- Τῷ ἀγαπῶντι ἡμᾶς καὶ λύσαντι ἡμᾶς: The doxology is addressed "to the one who loves us and freed us." Two substantival participles are used here, both of which are linked to the same article (τῷ ἀγαπῶντι . . . καὶ λύσαντι). The first participle (ἀγαπῶντι, pres. act. ptc. masc. dat. sg. of ἀγαπάω) is present tense (imperfective aspect) while the second (λύσαντι, aor. act. ptc. masc. dat. sg. of λύω) is aorist tense (perfective aspect). These different tense-forms highlight "Christ's ongoing, eternal disposition toward people that caused him to act in the specific event of the cross to bring release from sin."[3]

- ἡ δόξα καὶ τὸ κράτος εἰς τοὺς αἰῶνας [τῶν αἰώνων]· ἀμήν: The nominative nouns ἡ δόξα and τὸ κράτος are the subjects of the clause in which the verb is implied (i.e., a verbless clause). The brackets around the form τῶν αἰώνων indicate some uncertainty regarding its authenticity due to its absence from several key manuscripts. It is possible that these words were added to conform to the use of this formula elsewhere in Revelation.

---

3. Buist Fanning, *Revelation*, ZECNT (Grand Rapids: Zondervan Academic, 2020), 82.

FOR THE JOURNEY

John transitions from the trinitarian source of grace and peace to a doxology. Jesus is first identified as the "faithful witness, the firstborn from the dead, and the ruler of the kings of the earth." After John describes who Christ is, he next specifies what he does by using a similar threefold approach. These two triads mirror Jesus's (1) life ("faithful witness" and "who loves us"), (2) resurrection ("firstborn from the dead" and "who freed us from our sins"), and (3) second coming ("ruler of the kings of the earth" and "made us a kingdom, priests to his God and Father"). Although the last of these is already true to some extent, it will only be fully consummated at Christ's return. Christ loves us, freed us, and is making us priests to God. The correct response to this truth is to break out in doxology: "To him [be] glory and dominion forever and ever. Amen."

ANSWER KEY

1. *Parse:* ἐποίησεν (ποιέω, aor. act. ind. 3rd sg.).
2. *Identify:* (1) ὁ μάρτυς (masc. nom. sg.), (2) τῶν νεκρῶν (masc. gen. pl.), (3) ὁ ἄρχων (masc. nom. sg.), (4) τῶν βασιλέων (masc. gen. pl.), (5) τῆς γῆς (fem. gen. sg.), (6) τῶν ἁμαρτιῶν (masc. gen. pl.), (7) τῷ αἵματι (neut. dat. sg.), (8) βασιλείαν (fem. acc. sg.), (9) τῷ θεῷ (masc. dat. sg.), (10) πατρί (masc. dat. sg.), (11) ἡ δόξα (fem. nom. sg.), (12) τὸ κράτος (neut. nom. sg.), (13) τοὺς αἰῶνας (masc. acc. pl.), (14) τῶν αἰώνων (masc. gen. pl.).
3. *Translate:* "and from Jesus Christ, the faithful witness, the firstborn from the dead, and the ruler of the kings of the earth. To the one who loves us and freed us from our sins by his blood and made us a kingdom, priests to his God and Father, to him [be] glory and dominion forever and ever. Amen."

DAY 13: REVELATION 1:7

STEP ONE: **Read** aloud the text at least five times.

Ἰδοὺ ἔρχεται μετὰ τῶν νεφελῶν, καὶ ὄψεται αὐτὸν πᾶς ὀφθαλμὸς καὶ οἵτινες αὐτὸν ἐξεκέντησαν, καὶ κόψονται ἐπ᾽ αὐτὸν πᾶσαι αἱ φυλαὶ τῆς γῆς. ναί, ἀμήν.

STEP TWO: **Parse** the following verbs.

	Lexical Form	Tense	Voice	Mood	Pers.	Num.	Translation
(1) ἔρχεται							
(2) ὄψεται							
(3) ἐξεκέντησαν							
(4) κόψονται							

STEP THREE: **Identify** the gender, case, and number of the following words.

	Gender	Case	Num.		Gender	Case	Num.
(1) τῶν νεφελῶν				(5) οἵτινες			
(2) αὐτόν				(6) πᾶσαι			
(3) πᾶς				(7) αἱ φυλαί			
(4) ὀφθαλμός				(8) τῆς γῆς			

STEP FOUR: **Translate** the text into understandable English.

_____

_____

VOCABULARY

νεφέλη, ἡ, cloud
ἐκκεντέω, I pierce
κόπτω, I mourn
φυλή, ἡ, tribe
ναί, yes, even so

STEP FIVE: **Notice** significant exegetical and syntactical insights.

- Ἰδοὺ, . . . ναί, ἀμήν: The particle ἰδού (technically an aor. mid. impv. of εἶδον) is an emphatic marker, often used "to highlight critical prophet oracles."[4] It occurs 26 times in Revelation. Additionally, the particles ναί (Greek) and ἀμήν (from the Hebrew) together are emphatic, indicating a solemn affirmation. Thus, "these words about Jesus's future coming and rule evoke John's—and our—hearty affirmation and longing for it to be so" (Fanning, *Revelation*, 87).

- ἔρχεται . . . ὄψεται . . . κόψονται: A commonality between all three of these forms is that they are in the middle voice. The verb ἔρχεται (from ἔρχομαι) is also known as a middle-only form since it has no active (or passive) forms. The present tense-form of this verb often has a future reference ("he is coming" = "he will come"). The verbs ὄψεται (from ὁράω) and κόψονται (from κόπτω) are both future forms. In the active voice κόπτω means "to cut (off)," whereas in the middle voice it means to "beat one's breast as an act of mourning" (BDAG 559).

FOR THE JOURNEY

John alludes to both Dan. 7:13 ("I saw in the night visions, and behold, with the clouds of heaven there came one like a son of man, and he came to the Ancient of Days and was presented before him") and Zech. 12:10 ("And I will pour out on the house of David and the inhabitants of Jerusalem a spirit of grace and pleas for mercy, so that, when they look on me, on him whom they have pierced, they shall mourn for him, as one mourns for an only child, and weep bitterly over him, as one weeps over a firstborn"). He presents Jesus as the King of kings and the Lord of lords, who will one day return from heaven to earth to bring judgment and final redemption. Those who refuse to acknowledge and submit to his lordship will be condemned and judged, whereas those who long for his return will enter into eternal life with their King.

---

4. Grant Osborne, *Revelation*, BECNT (Grand Rapids: Baker Academic, 2002), 69.

ANSWER KEY

1. *Parse:* (1) ἔρχεται (ἔρχομαι, pres. mid. ind. 3rd sg.), (2) ὄψεται (ὁράω, fut. mid. ind. 3rd sg.), (3) ἐξεκέντησαν (ἐκκεντέω, aor. act. ind. 3rd pl.), (4) κόψονται (κόπτω, fut. mid. ind. 3rd pl.).

2. *Identify:* (1) τῶν νεφελῶν (fem. gen. pl.), (2) αὐτόν (masc. acc. sg.), (3) πᾶς (masc. nom. sg.), (4) ὀφθαλμός (masc. nom. sg.), (5) οἵτινες (masc. nom. pl.), (6) πᾶσαι (fem. nom. pl.), (7) αἱ φυλαί (fem. nom. pl.), (8) τῆς γῆς (fem. gen. sg.).

3. *Translate:* "Behold, he is coming with the clouds, and every eye will see him, even those who pierced him, and all the tribes of the earth will mourn over him. Yes, amen."

DAY 14: REVELATION 1:8

STEP ONE: **Read** aloud the text at least five times.

Ἐγώ εἰμι τὸ Ἄλφα καὶ τὸ Ὦ, λέγει κύριος ὁ θεός, ὁ ὢν καὶ ὁ ἦν καὶ ὁ ἐρχόμενος, ὁ παντοκράτωρ.

STEP TWO: **Parse** the following verbs.

	Lexical Form	Tense	Voice	Mood	Pers.	Num.	Translation
(1) εἰμι							
(2) λέγει							
(3) ἦν							

STEP THREE: **Identify** the gender, case, and number of the following words.

	Gender	Case	Num.		Gender	Case	Num.
(1) ἐγώ				(4) κύριος			
(2) τὸ Ἄλφα				(5) ὁ θεός			
(3) τὸ Ὦ				(6) ὁ παντοκράτωρ			

STEP FOUR: **Translate** the text into understandable English.

VOCABULARY

παντοκράτωρ, ὁ, Almighty (One)

STEP FIVE: **Notice** significant exegetical and syntactical insights.

- **τὸ Ἄλφα καὶ τὸ Ὦ**: This expression is a merism: two extremes that include everything in between. Thus, when God states that he is the alpha and the omega, he is stating that he is not only the beginning and end but also the one in control of all things at all times. Interestingly, the name of the first letter of the Greek alphabet is spelled out (ἄλφα), whereas the last letter appears only as a single character (Ὤ). This imbalance is probably because the name of the letter Ὤ was not usually written out until about the seventh century. This big (long) *o* (ὦ μέγα) was distinguished from omicron (ὄ μικρόν), the small (short) *o*.

* κύριος ὁ θεός, ὁ ὢν καὶ ὁ ἦν καὶ ὁ ἐρχόμενος, ὁ παντοκράτωρ: A series of nouns are in apposition to κύριος, all matching the gender (masc.), case (nom.), and number (sg.) of that noun: (1) ὁ θεός, (2) ὁ ὢν καὶ ὁ ἦν καὶ ὁ ἐρχόμενος, and (3) ὁ παντοκράτωρ. Of course, the second of these is itself a triad, seen earlier in 1:4.

FOR THE JOURNEY

John concludes his prologue in a way similar to how he began it, with a declaration of God's sovereign control over all history as the one who is, who was, and who is to come. In Rev. 22:13 Jesus claims a similar title for himself, and in 1:17 he declares that he is "the first and the last" (ἐγώ εἰμι ὁ πρῶτος καὶ ὁ ἔσχατος). This, coupled with other statements in Revelation, leads Richard Bauckham to maintain that "Revelation has the most developed trinitarian theology in the New Testament."[5] He continues by stating that these titles "designate God as eternal in relation to the world. He precedes and originates all things, as their Creator, and he will bring all things to their eschatological fulfilment. The titles cannot mean anything else when they are used of Christ in 22:13. . . . [Because these designations state] unambiguously that Jesus Christ belongs to the fullness of the eternal being of God, this surpasses anything in the New Testament."[6] Jesus, the self-existent and eternal ruler of heaven, will soon intervene to accomplish God's perfect will on earth. Until then, we continue to walk with the assurance that "if God is for us, who [or what] can be against us?" (Rom. 8:31).

---

5. Richard Bauckham, *The Theology of the Book of Revelation* (Cambridge: Cambridge University Press, 1993), 164.

6. Bauckham, *Theology*, 55, 57.

ANSWER KEY

1. *Parse:* (1) εἰμι (εἰμί, pres. act. ind. 1st sg.), (2) λέγει (λέγω, pres. act. ind. 3rd sg.), (3) ἦν (εἰμί, impf. act. ind. 3rd sg.).

2. *Identify:* (1) ἐγώ (nom. sg.), (2) τὸ Ἄλφα (neut. nom. sg.), (3) τὸ Ὦ (neut. nom. sg.), (4) κύριος (masc. nom. sg.), (5) ὁ θεός (masc. nom. sg.), (6) ὁ παντοκράτωρ (masc. nom. sg.).

3. *Translate:* "I am the Alpha and the Omega, says the Lord God, the one who is and who was and who is coming, the Almighty."

DAY 15: REVELATION 1:9

STEP ONE: **Read** aloud the text at least five times.

Ἐγὼ Ἰωάννης, ὁ ἀδελφὸς ὑμῶν καὶ συγκοινωνὸς ἐν τῇ θλίψει καὶ βασιλείᾳ καὶ ὑπομονῇ ἐν Ἰησοῦ, ἐγενόμην ἐν τῇ νήσῳ τῇ καλουμένῃ Πάτμῳ διὰ τὸν λόγον τοῦ θεοῦ καὶ τὴν μαρτυρίαν Ἰησοῦ.

STEP TWO: **Parse** the following verb.

	Lexical Form	Tense	Voice	Mood	Pers.	Num.	Translation
ἐγενόμην							

STEP THREE: **Identify** the gender, case, and number of the following words.

	Gender	Case	Num.		Gender	Case	Num.
(1) ὁ ἀδελφός				(6) ὑπομονῇ			
(2) ὑμῶν				(7) τῇ νήσῳ			
(3) συγκοινωνός				(8) τὸν λόγον			
(4) τῇ θλίψει				(9) τοῦ θεοῦ			
(5) βασιλείᾳ				(10) τὴν μαρτυρίαν			

STEP FOUR: **Translate** the text into understandable English.

_____

_____

> VOCABULARY
>
> συγκοινωνός, ὁ, partner
> θλῖψις, ἡ, tribulation
> ὑπομονή, ἡ, endurance
> νῆσος, ἡ, island
> μαρτυρία, ἡ, testimony

STEP FIVE: **Notice** significant exegetical and syntactical insights.

- **Ἐγὼ Ἰωάννης, ὁ ἀδελφὸς ὑμῶν καὶ συγκοινωνὸς:** Similar to the previous verse, here are a series of nominative nouns in apposition (further explaining or clarifying a previous noun). That is, "John" (Ἰωάννης) is in apposition to "I" (ἐγώ). Furthermore, the nouns "brother" (ὁ ἀδελφός) and "partner" (συγκοινωνός) are in apposition to "John."

- **ἐν τῇ νήσῳ τῇ καλουμένῃ Πάτμῳ:** The participle τῇ καλουμένῃ (pres. pass. ptc. fem. dat. sg. of καλέω) functions attributively, modifying τῇ νήσῳ ("the island *called* Patmos").

- **ἐν τῇ θλίψει καὶ βασιλείᾳ καὶ ὑπομονῇ ἐν Ἰησοῦ, ἐγενόμην ἐν τῇ νήσῳ τῇ καλουμένῃ Πάτμῳ διὰ τὸν λόγον τοῦ θεοῦ καὶ τὴν μαρτυρίαν Ἰησοῦ:** Prepositions appear four times in this verse (ἐν three times and διά once) and are used differently each time. The first preposition (ἐν τῇ θλίψει καὶ βασιλείᾳ καὶ ὑπομονῇ) "indicates the thing in which one shares" (following the noun συγκοινωνός).[7] The second preposition (ἐν Ἰησοῦ) relates to the sphere or metaphorical location. The third preposition (ἐν τῇ νήσῳ τῇ καλουμένῃ Πάτμῳ) indicates the location or place where John experienced his vision. The final preposition (διὰ τὸν λόγον τοῦ θεοῦ καὶ τὴν μαρτυρίαν Ἰησοῦ) expresses the cause for which John was sent to the island of Patmos.

FOR THE JOURNEY

John is not only an apostle; he also self-identifies as a prophet by using the stylized phrase "I, John" (ἐγὼ Ἰωάννης). This description may seem too subtle to be seen as a prophetic designation, but when compared with other prophets, we see that John is conforming to a standard convention used in prophetic writings. For example, Daniel often writes "I, Daniel" (Dan. 7:15; 8:15, 27; 9:2; 10:2, 7; 12:5). This makes John's comments in Rev. 1:9 even more surprising when he identifies with his audience in their suffering by referring to himself as their "brother" (ἀδελφός) and "partner" (συγκοινωνός). Familial imagery, like "brother," is commonly used in the NT to describe how believers ought to relate, value, and love each other. The term "partner" emphasizes the mutual

---

7. Mathewson, *Revelation*, 9.

participation and shared experience that believers encounter together. John, the apostle and prophet of God, also identifies with his readers in their trials. But John brackets the difficulties that believers will undergo (i.e., tribulation and endurance) with the hope of God's eternal kingdom. Ultimately, when Christ returns, he will right all wrongs and fully establish his kingdom.

ANSWER KEY

1. *Parse:* ἐγενόμην (γίνομαι, aor. mid. ind. 1st sg.).
2. *Identify:* (1) ὁ ἀδελφός (masc. nom. sg.), (2) ὑμῶν (gen. pl.), (3) συγκοινωνός (masc. nom. sg.), (4) τῇ θλίψει (fem. dat. sg.), (5) βασιλείᾳ (fem. dat. sg.), (6) ὑπομονῇ (fem. dat. sg.), (7) τῇ νήσῳ (fem. dat. sg.), (8) τὸν λόγον (masc. acc. sg.), (9) τοῦ θεοῦ (masc. gen. sg.), (10) τὴν μαρτυρίαν (fem. acc. sg.).
3. *Translate:* "I, John, your brother and partner in the tribulation and the kingdom and endurance in Jesus, was on the island called Patmos because of the word of God and the testimony of Jesus."

ROUTE 4

Revelation 7:9–17

STEP ONE: **Read** aloud the text at least five times.

Μετὰ ταῦτα εἶδον, καὶ ἰδοὺ ὄχλος πολύς . . . ἐκ παντὸς ἔθνους καὶ φυλῶν καὶ λαῶν καὶ γλωσσῶν . . . , καὶ κράζουσιν φωνῇ μεγάλῃ . . . · Ἡ σωτηρία τῷ θεῷ ἡμῶν τῷ καθημένῳ ἐπὶ τῷ θρόνῳ καὶ τῷ ἀρνίῳ.

STEP TWO: **Parse** the following verbs.

	Lexical Form	Tense	Voice	Mood	Pers.	Num.	Translation
(1) εἶδον							
(2) κράζουσιν							

STEP THREE: **Identify** the gender, case, and number of the following words.

	Gender	Case	Num.		Gender	Case	Num.
(1) ταῦτα				(7) φωνῇ			
(2) ὄχλος				(8) ἡ σωτηρία			
(3) ἔθνους				(9) τῷ θεῷ			
(4) φυλῶν				(10) ἡμῶν			
(5) λαῶν				(11) τῷ θρόνῳ			
(6) γλωσσῶν				(12) τῷ ἀρνίῳ			

STEP FOUR: **Translate** the text into understandable English.

> VOCABULARY
>
> φυλή, ἡ, tribe
>
> σωτηρία, ἡ, salvation
>
> ἀρνίον, τό, lamb

STEP FIVE: **Notice** significant exegetical and syntactical insights.

- **Μετὰ ταῦτα εἶδον:** John's vision in Revelation involves him recounting what he "saw." The form εἶδον occurs 45 times, and the phrase μετὰ ταῦτα εἶδον occurs four times (see also 4:1; 15:5; 18:1; cf. μετὰ τοῦτο εἶδον in 7:1 and μετὰ ταῦτα ἤκουσα in 19:1).

- **ὄχλος πολύς . . . κράζουσιν:** The singular noun ὄχλος is the subject of the plural verb κράζουσιν. This common phenomenon is known as a *constructio ad sensum* (a construction according to sense) because, although it is singular, ὄχλος is a collective noun (i.e., by definition, a crowd or multitude is more than one person). Also, κράζουσιν is a historical present that draws attention to the worship of God by the heavenly multitude that follows.

- **ἐκ παντὸς ἔθνους καὶ φυλῶν καὶ λαῶν καὶ γλωσσῶν:** Interestingly, the singular form of παντὸς ἔθνους ("every nation") is followed by the plural forms of φυλῶν ("tribes"), καὶ λαῶν ("peoples"), and γλωσσῶν ("languages"). This fourfold formula occurs four other times (5:9; 11:9; 13:7; 14:6; cf. 10:11), though in an order different from the one here in 7:9.

- **τῷ θεῷ ἡμῶν τῷ καθημένῳ:** The participle τῷ καθημένῳ (pres. mid. ptc. masc. dat. sg. of κάθημαι) functions attributively and modifies τῷ θεῷ ("the God *who sits*")

FOR THE JOURNEY

John is given a vision of an innumerable multitude from every nation, tribe, people, and language. This terminology echoes God's promise to Abraham that he would be the father of "many nations" (πλήθους ἐθνῶν; Gen. 17:4 LXX). But as Fanning reminds us, "The anticipation that . . . end-time people from every nation will worship God and the Lamb is not just a dream for the future. It constitutes a mission that Jesus gave his followers at the beginning and continues throughout the age (Matt 28:19–20; Luke 24:47; John 10:16; Acts 1:8)."[1] We can have certainty that people from every nation will worship the Lamb. But we also have a mission to take the good news to every nation, to fulfill the commission that Jesus gave to the church.

ANSWER KEY

1. *Parse:* (1) εἶδον (βλέπω/ὁράω, aor. act. ind. 1st sg.), (2) κράζουσιν (κράζω, pres. act. ind. 3rd pl.).

2. *Identify:* (1) ταῦτα (neut. acc. pl.), (2) ὄχλος (masc. nom. sg.), (3) ἔθνους (neut. gen. sg.), (4) φυλῶν (fem. gen. pl.), (5) λαῶν (masc. gen. pl.), (6) γλωσσῶν (fem. gen. pl.), (7) φωνῇ (fem. dat. sg.), (8) ἡ σωτηρία (fem. nom. sg.), (9) τῷ θεῷ (masc. dat. sg.), (10) ἡμῶν (gen. pl.), (11) τῷ θρόνῳ (masc. dat. sg.), (12) τῷ ἀρνίῳ (neut. dat. sg.).

3. *Translate:* "After these things I looked, and behold, a great multitude . . . from every nation, and tribes and peoples and languages, . . . and they cry out with a loud voice . . . , 'Salvation [belongs] to our God, who sits on the throne, and to the Lamb.'"

1. Buist Fanning, *Revelation*, ZECNT (Grand Rapids: Zondervan Academic, 2020), 267.

DAY 17: REVELATION 7:11

STEP ONE: **Read** aloud the text at least five times.

καὶ πάντες οἱ ἄγγελοι εἱστήκεισαν κύκλῳ τοῦ θρόνου καὶ τῶν πρεσβυτέρων καὶ τῶν τεσσάρων ζῴων καὶ ἔπεσαν ἐνώπιον τοῦ θρόνου
ἐπὶ τὰ πρόσωπα αὐτῶν καὶ προσεκύνησαν τῷ θεῷ.

STEP TWO: **Parse** the following verbs.

	Lexical Form	Tense	Voice	Mood	Pers.	Num.	Translation
(1) εἱστήκεισαν							
(2) ἔπεσαν							
(3) προσεκύνησαν							

STEP THREE: **Identify** the gender, case, and number of the following words.

	Gender	Case	Num.		Gender	Case	Num.
(1) πάντες				(5) τῶν ζῴων			
(2) οἱ ἄγγελοι				(6) τὰ πρόσωπα			
(3) τοῦ θρόνου				(7) αὐτῶν			
(4) τῶν πρεσβυτέρων				(8) τῷ θεῷ			

STEP FOUR: **Translate** the text into understandable English.

VOCABULARY

κύκλῳ, around
τέσσαρες, four
ζῷον, τό, living creature

STEP FIVE: **Notice** significant exegetical and syntactical insights.

- **εἰστήκεισαν:** This is a pluperfect form; only 86 pluperfect forms occur in the NT, and this is the only occurrence in Revelation. The verb ἵστημι, the lexical form of this pluperfect verb, occurs several times in Revelation in other tense-forms: future (18:15), aorist (8:3; 11:11; 12:18; 18:17), and perfect (3:20; 8:2; 12:4). Wallace (*GGBB* 586) suggests that some stative verbs (such as ἵστημι) that occur in the pluperfect should be understood as conveying a simple past meaning ("stood").

- **ἔπεσαν:** This verb is a second-aorist form of πίπτω. The stem of this verb is πετ-, with the epsilon (ε) dropping in the present form and the pi (π) reduplicating, similar to a mi verb. In the aorist form, the tau (τ) drops when followed by a sigma (σ).

- **προσεκύνησαν τῷ θεῷ:** Several verbs, such as προσκυνέω, take their direct object in the dative case instead of the expected accusative case (e.g., ἀκολουθέω, ἀποκρίνομαι, and πιστεύω).

FOR THE JOURNEY

John presents a picture of all the hosts of heaven worshiping God. He first mentions that "all the angels" (πάντες οἱ ἄγγελοι) worshiped around the throne. In 5:11 he refers to "many angels" (ἀγγέλων πολλῶν), but in 7:11 he speaks of all the angels, along with the elders and the four living creatures. This worship is added to the vast multitude of the redeemed saints who stand around the throne (7:9). Not only do all the elders and four living creatures fall down to worship God on his throne (see 5:14), but here they fall down "on their faces." John sees an amazing vision of God being worshiped by his creation. People today fail to give God his due praise. This is true not only of unbelievers but also of believers. In heaven, however, God receives the worship that he is due. Our view of who God is should lead us to worship.

ANSWER KEY

1. *Parse:* (1) εἰστήκεισαν (ἵστημι, pluperf. act. ind. 3rd pl.), (2) ἔπεσαν (πίπτω, aor. act. ind. 3rd pl.), (3) προσεκύνησαν (προσκυνέω, aor. act. ind. 3rd pl.).

2. *Identify:* (1) πάντες (masc. nom. pl.), (2) οἱ ἄγγελοι (masc. nom. pl.), (3) τοῦ θρόνου (masc. gen. sg.), (4) τῶν πρεσβυτέρων (masc. gen. pl.), (5) τῶν ζῴων (neut. gen. pl.), (6) τὰ πρόσωπα (neut. acc. pl.), (7) αὐτῶν (gen. pl.), (8) τῷ θεῷ (masc. dat. sg.).

3. *Translate:* "And all the angels stood around the throne and [around] the elders and the four living creatures, and they fell before the throne on their faces and worshiped God."

DAY 18: REVELATION 7:12

STEP ONE: **Read** aloud the text at least five times.

λέγοντες, ἀμήν, ἡ εὐλογία καὶ ἡ δόξα καὶ ἡ σοφία καὶ ἡ εὐχαριστία καὶ ἡ τιμὴ καὶ ἡ δύναμις καὶ ἡ ἰσχὺς τῷ θεῷ ἡμῶν εἰς τοὺς αἰῶνας τῶν αἰώνων· ἀμήν.

STEP TWO: **Parse** any verbs.
There are no verbs.

STEP THREE: **Identify** the gender, case, and number of the following words.

	Gender	Case	Num.		Gender	Case	Num.
(1) ἡ εὐλογία				(7) ἡ ἰσχύς			
(2) ἡ δόξα				(8) τῷ θεῷ			
(3) ἡ σοφία				(9) ἡμῶν			
(4) ἡ εὐχαριστία				(10) τοὺς αἰῶνας			
(5) ἡ τιμή				(11) τῶν αἰώνων			
(6) ἡ δύναμις							

STEP FOUR: **Translate** the text into understandable English.

VOCABULARY

εὐλογία, ἡ, blessing, praise
εὐχαριστία, ἡ, thanksgiving
τιμή, ἡ, honor
ἰσχύς, ἡ, strength, might

STEP FIVE: **Notice** significant exegetical and syntactical insights.

- **λέγοντες:** This form is an adverbial participle (pres. act. ptc. masc. nom. pl. of λέγω) and introduces what the angels, the elders, and the four living creatures are saying.

- **Ἀμήν . . . ἀμήν:** Because the speech is bracketed by the term ἀμήν ("truly" or "let it be so"), it signifies a "strong affirmation of what is declared" (L&N 72.6).

- **ἡ εὐλογία καὶ ἡ δόξα καὶ ἡ σοφία καὶ ἡ εὐχαριστία καὶ ἡ τιμὴ καὶ ἡ δύναμις καὶ ἡ ἰσχὺς:** Notice three features related to these nouns and articles. First, all these nouns are feminine in gender, which is true of most abstract nouns in Greek. Second, all these nouns possess the article, which is common for abstract nouns in Greek (though in English abstract nouns do not usually have articles). Third, the heavenly host praise God, attributing to him precisely seven qualities (cf. 5:12). In Revelation, the number seven is highly symbolic and often constitutes fullness, so this sevenfold ascription conveys the perfections of God's virtues.

- **εἰς τοὺς αἰῶνας τῶν αἰώνων:** This prepositional phrase (literally rendered "into the ages of ages") refers to something unending or that continues forever. Here it refers to the eternal duration of praise being given to God.[2]

FOR THE JOURNEY

This verse reminds us that God is worthy of our praise. The vocalization (internally or out loud) of such attributes is a way in which we honor God for the qualities he possesses. We do not confer these qualities upon him but instead proclaim and celebrate these qualities that he has within himself. All the heavenly host (angels, elders, four living creatures) cry out to God, declaring his blessings and glory and wisdom and thanksgiving and honor and power and strength. This vision of heaven was given to encourage us to remember that God is still on his throne; just as those in heaven fall down and worship God, we should do the same.

2. See David L. Mathewson, *Revelation*, BHGNT (Waco: Baylor University Press, 2016), 101.

ANSWER KEY

1. *Parse:* No verbs to parse.
2. *Identify:* (1) ἡ εὐλογία (fem. nom. sg.), (2) ἡ δόξα (fem. nom. sg.), (3) ἡ σοφία (fem. nom. sg.), (4) ἡ εὐχαριστία (fem. nom. sg.), (5) ἡ τιμή (fem. nom. sg.), (6) ἡ δύναμις (fem. nom. sg.), (7) ἡ ἰσχύς (fem. nom. sg.), (8) τῷ θεῷ (masc. dat. sg.), (9) ἡμῶν (gen. pl.), (10) τοὺς αἰῶνας (masc. acc. pl.), (11) τῶν αἰώνων (masc. gen. pl.).
3. *Translate:* "Saying, 'Amen! Blessing and glory and wisdom and thanksgiving and honor and power and strength to our God forever and ever. Amen.'"

DAY 19: REVELATION 7:13–15

STEP ONE: **Read** aloud the text at least five times.

Καὶ ἀπεκρίθη εἷς ἐκ τῶν πρεσβυτέρων. . . . καὶ εἶπέν μοι, Οὗτοί εἰσιν οἱ ἐρχόμενοι ἐκ τῆς θλίψεως τῆς μεγάλης. . . . διὰ τοῦτό εἰσιν ἐνώπιον τοῦ θρόνου τοῦ θεοῦ καὶ λατρεύουσιν αὐτῷ ἡμέρας καὶ νυκτὸς ἐν τῷ ναῷ αὐτοῦ.

STEP TWO: **Parse** the following verbs.

	Lexical Form	Tense	Voice	Mood	Pers.	Num.	Translation
(1) ἀπεκρίθη							
(2) εἶπέν							
(3) εἰσιν							
(4) λατρεύουσιν							

STEP THREE: **Identify** the gender, case, and number of the following words.

	Gender	Case	Num.		Gender	Case	Num.
(1) εἷς				(7) τοῦ θεοῦ			
(2) τῶν πρεσβυτέρων				(8) αὐτῷ			
(3) μοι				(9) ἡμέρας			
(4) οὗτοι				(10) νυκτός			
(5) τῆς θλίψεως				(11) τῷ ναῷ			
(6) τοῦ θρόνου				(12) αὐτοῦ			

STEP FOUR: **Translate** the text into understandable English.

_____

_____

VOCABULARY

θλῖψις, ἡ, tribulation
λατρεύω, I serve
ναός, ὁ, temple

STEP FIVE: **Notice** significant exegetical and syntactical insights.

- **οἱ ἐρχόμενοι:** This substantival participle (pres. mid. ptc. masc. nom. pl. of ἔρχομαι) is functioning as a predicate nominative ("these are *the ones coming*").

- **λατρεύουσιν αὐτῷ:** This verb is in the present tense but is used to refer to the future. Mathewson notes, "The difference may be that the present tense λατρεύουσιν describes what the people will do to God, while the futures [used later in the context] are used of what God can be expected to do for his people" (*Revelation*, 104). Also note that this verb takes its direct object in the dative (not accusative) case (αὐτῷ).

FOR THE JOURNEY

John is told about the saints who are clothed in white robes and who have endured the great tribulation. Their robes are white because they have been washed in the blood of the Lamb. Consequently, they serve God day and night in his temple. The term that John uses for "serve" (λατρεύω) is a term often associated in the Septuagint with the temple and the service or worship that the priests rendered to God at the temple. Thus, believers will worship God day and night "in his temple" (7:15), a reference to the heavenly temple. Earlier in Revelation, John tells us that Jesus Christ "has . . . made us a kingdom, priests to his God and Father" (1:6). Thus such service and worship of God begins now. Paul writes that we should present our "bodies as a living sacrifice, holy and acceptable to God, which is your spiritual worship" (Rom. 12:1 ESV) and that believers are those "who worship [λατρεύω] by the Spirit of God" (Phil. 3:3).

ANSWER KEY

1. *Parse:* (1) ἀπεκρίθη (ἀποκρίνομαι, aor. mid. ind. 3rd sg.), (2) εἶπέν (λέγω, aor. act. ind. 3rd sg.), (3) εἰσιν (εἰμί, pres. act. ind. 3rd pl.), (4) λατρεύουσιν (λατρεύω, pres. act. ind. 3rd pl.).

2. *Identify:* (1) εἷς (masc. nom. sg.), (2) τῶν πρεσβυτέρων (masc. gen. pl.), (3) μοι (dat. sg.), (4) οὗτοι (masc. nom. pl.), (5) τῆς θλίψεως (fem. gen. sg.), (6) τοῦ θρόνου (masc. gen. sg.), (7) τοῦ θεοῦ (masc. gen. sg.), (8) αὐτῷ (masc. dat. sg.), (9) ἡμέρας (fem. gen. sg.), (10) νυκτός (fem. gen. sg.), (11) τῷ ναῷ (masc. dat. sg.), (12) αὐτοῦ (masc. gen. sg.).

3. *Translate:* "And one of the elders answered. . . . And he said to me, 'These are the ones coming out of the great tribulation; . . . they are before the throne of God and serve him day and night in his temple.'"

DAY 20: REVELATION 7:16–17

STEP ONE: **Read** aloud the text at least five times.

οὐ πεινάσουσιν ἔτι οὐδὲ διψήσουσιν ἔτι . . . , ὅτι τὸ ἀρνίον τὸ ἀνὰ μέσον τοῦ θρόνου ποιμανεῖ αὐτοὺς καὶ ὁδηγήσει αὐτοὺς ἐπὶ ζωῆς πηγὰς ὑδάτων, καὶ ἐξαλείψει ὁ θεὸς πᾶν δάκρυον ἐκ τῶν ὀφθαλμῶν αὐτῶν.

STEP TWO: **Parse** the following verbs.

	Lexical Form	Tense	Voice	Mood	Pers.	Num.	Translation
(1) πεινάσουσιν							
(2) διψήσουσιν							
(3) ποιμανεῖ							
(4) ὁδηγήσει							
(5) ἐξαλείψει							

STEP THREE: **Identify** the gender, case, and number of the following words.

	Gender	Case	Num.		Gender	Case	Num.
(1) τὸ ἀρνίον				(7) ὑδάτων			
(2) τὸ μέσον				(8) θεός			
(3) τοῦ θρόνου				(9) πᾶν			
(4) αὐτούς				(10) δάκρυον			
(5) ζωῆς				(11) τῶν ὀφθαλμῶν			
(6) πηγάς				(12) αὐτῶν			

STEP FOUR: **Translate** the text into understandable English.

63

> VOCABULARY
>
> πεινάω, I am hungry
> διψάω, I am thirsty
> ἀρνίον, τό, lamb
> ἀνά, in the midst
> ποιμαίνω, I shepherd
> ὁδηγέω, I lead, guide
> πηγή, ἡ, spring, fountain
> ἐξαλείφω, I wipe away
> δάκρυον, τό, tear

STEP FIVE: **Notice** significant exegetical and syntactical insights.

- **πεινάσουσιν ... διψήσουσιν ... ποιμανεῖ ... ὁδηγήσει ... ἐξα-
λείψει:** These five verbs are all in the future tense (the first two are 3rd pl.; the last three are 3rd sg.). The signature feature for the future tense is the addition of a sigma (σ) to the stem (πεινάσουσιν, διψήσουσιν, ὁδηγήσει). Two of the forms are slightly irregular. The form ποιμανεῖ does not have a sigma because it is a liquid verb. A liquid verb has a stem ending in λ, μ, ν, or ρ. These consonants reject the sigma, often causing two changes as a result: (1) the stem changes (in this case the stem changes from ποιμαιν- to ποι-μαν-), and (2) the accent becomes a circumflex. The other verb is ἐξαλείψει, with ἐξαλείφω as the lexical form. Because the final consonant of the stem is a phi (φ), the addition of a sigma changes the consonant to a psi (φ + σ = ψ).

- **ἐπὶ ζωῆς πηγὰς ὑδάτων:** This prepositional phrase has two genitive forms that need to be explained. The object of the preposition is the accusative (i.e., πηγάς, "to springs"). The question, then, is the function of the two genitive forms. The second genitive (ὑδάτων) is best understood as genitive of content ("springs containing water"). The first genitive form (ζωῆς), however, functions attributively but could modify either πηγάς (*"living* springs of water") or ὑδάτων ("springs of *living* water"). Based on other uses in Revelation where ζωῆς ("living") modifies "water," the latter is more likely. The up-front placement of ζωῆς conveys emphasis.

FOR THE JOURNEY

These verses offer comfort to weary pilgrims and essentially quote Isa. 49:10 ("They shall not hunger or thirst, neither scorching wind nor sun shall strike them, for he who has pity on them will lead them, and by springs of water will guide them," ESV). All bodily deprivation (hunger and thirst) will be removed, along with all external harm (sun and burning heat). Instead, in the presence of Jesus, his people will experience his abundant sustenance and protection. Jesus is the good Shepherd who leads, knows, and lays down his life for his sheep (John 10). He is "the Shepherd and Overseer of [our] souls" (1 Pet. 2:25), "the chief Shepherd" (1 Pet. 5:4), and the "great Shepherd of the sheep" (Heb. 13:20). This is the Shepherd who will guide his people to springs of living water and will wipe away every tear of pain and suffering from our eyes.

ANSWER KEY

1. *Parse:* (1) πεινάσουσιν (πεινάω, fut. act. ind. 3rd pl.), (2) διψήσουσιν (διψάω, fut. act. ind. 3rd pl.), (3) ποιμανεῖ (ποιμαίνω, fut. act. ind. 3rd sg.), (4) ὁδηγήσει (ὁδηγέω, fut. act. ind. 3rd sg.), (5) ἐξαλείψει (ἐξαλείφω, fut. act. ind. 3rd sg.).

2. *Identify:* (1) τὸ ἀρνίον (neut. nom. sg.), (2) τὸ μέσον (neut. nom. sg.), (3) τοῦ θρόνου (masc. gen. sg.), (4) αὐτούς (masc. acc. pl.), (5) ζωῆς (fem. gen. sg.), (6) πηγάς (fem. acc. pl.), (7) ὑδάτων (neut. gen. pl.), (8) θεός (masc. nom. sg.), (9) πᾶν (neut. acc. sg.), (10) δάκρυον (neut. acc. sg.), (11) τῶν ὀφθαλμῶν (masc. gen. pl.), (12) αὐτῶν (masc. gen. pl.).

3. *Translate:* "They shall hunger no more, neither shall they thirst anymore . . . , because the Lamb in the midst of the throne will shepherd them and will guide them to springs of living water, and God will wipe away every tear from their eyes."

ROUTE 5

Matthew 5:43–48

DAY 21: MATTHEW 5:43

STEP ONE: **Read** aloud the text at least five times.

Ἠκούσατε ὅτι ἐρρέθη, Ἀγαπήσεις τὸν πλησίον σου καὶ μισήσεις τὸν ἐχθρόν σου.

STEP TWO: **Parse** the following verbs.

	Lexical Form	Tense	Voice	Mood	Pers.	Num.	Translation
(1) ἠκούσατε							
(2) ἐρρέθη							
(3) ἀγαπήσεις							
(4) μισήσεις							

STEP THREE: **Identify** the gender, case, and number of the following words.

	Gender	Case	Num.
(1) τὸν πλησίον			
(2) σου			
(3) τὸν ἐχθρόν			

STEP FOUR: **Translate** the text into understandable English.

> VOCABULARY
>
> πλησίον, ό, neighbor
> μισέω, I hate, detest
> ἐχθρός, ό, enemy

STEP FIVE: **Notice** significant exegetical and syntactical insights.

- **Ἠκούσατε ὅτι ἐρρέθη:** This phrase ("you heard that it was said") is contrasted with the phrase ἐγὼ δὲ λέγω ὑμῖν ("but I say to you," 5:44), used six times in Matt. 5:21–48 (known as the six antitheses). This formula contrasts Jesus's interpretation of the OT with common rabbinic interpretations. The form ἐρρέθη is irregular since λέγω uses multiple roots. This form is known as a divine passive since God is the implied agent of communication.

- **Ἀγαπήσεις . . . μισήσεις:** These two verbs are in the future tense but express a command (i.e., the imperatival future). Most of the NT occurrences of the imperatival future are citations of the OT. This usage is most commonly found in the Gospels, especially in Matthew (usually in the second person), and as a prohibition (negated with οὐ). Perhaps the difference between the imperatival future and an imperative-mood verb is that the former is more emphatic or solemn. The first part of the statement is a quote from Lev. 19:18 ("You shall love your neighbor as yourself," ESV); the second part is not found in the OT ("You shall hate your enemy").

FOR THE JOURNEY

Jesus states that he did not come to abolish the Law or the Prophets but to fulfill all that was written in them (Matt. 5:17). Paul tells us that Jesus is the "end/culmination [τέλος] of the law" for all believers (Rom. 10:4 ESV/NIV). Jesus fulfills the law through his life and teaching. As such, he is the ultimate divine interpreter of God's law. Jesus is portrayed as the second and greater Moses (prophet) who clarifies the true intention of the OT. That is, he reveals the ultimate meaning of the law, which includes a "righteousness that exceeds that of the scribes and Pharisees" (Matt. 5:20). The call to love one's neighbor is found in Lev. 19:18. Although the command to hate one's enemies is not found in the OT, perhaps it was assumed that this was a natural corollary. In Jesus's day, it was thought that one's neighbor was a fellow Jew. But in the parable of the Good Samaritan (Luke 10:35–47), Jesus teaches that a neighbor is anyone we come across whose needs we can meet.

ANSWER KEY

1. *Parse:* (1) ἠκούσατε (ἀκούω, aor. act. ind. 2nd pl.), (2) ἐρρέθη (λέγω, aor. pass. ind. 3rd sg.), (3) ἀγαπήσεις (ἀγαπάω, fut. act. ind. 2nd sg.), (4) μισήσεις (μισέω, fut. act. ind. 2nd sg.).
2. *Identify:* (1) τὸν πλησίον (masc. acc. sg.), (2) σου (gen. sg.), (3) τὸν ἐχθρόν (masc. acc. sg.).
3. *Translate:* "You heard that it was said, 'You shall love your neighbor and hate your enemy.'"

DAY 22: MATTHEW 5:44

STEP ONE: **Read** aloud the text at least five times.

ἐγὼ δὲ λέγω ὑμῖν, ἀγαπᾶτε τοὺς ἐχθροὺς ὑμῶν καὶ προσεύχεσθε ὑπὲρ τῶν διωκόντων ὑμᾶς.

STEP TWO: **Parse** the following verbs.

	Lexical Form	Tense	Voice	Mood	Pers.	Num.	Translation
(1) λέγω							
(2) ἀγαπᾶτε							
(3) προσεύχεσθε							

STEP THREE: **Identify** the gender, case, and number of the following words.

	Gender	Case	Num.		Gender	Case	Num.
(1) ἐγώ				(4) ὑμῶν			
(2) ὑμῖν				(5) ὑμᾶς			
(3) τοὺς ἐχθρούς							

STEP FOUR: **Translate** the text into understandable English.

> VOCABULARY
>
> διώκω, I persecute, pursue

STEP FIVE: **Notice** significant exegetical and syntactical insights.

- **ἐγὼ δὲ λέγω ὑμῖν:** This phrase ("but I say to you") provides the contrast of the statement in the previous verse (ἠκούσατε ὅτι ἐρρέθη, "You heard that it was said").

- **ἀγαπᾶτε . . . καὶ προσεύχεσθε:** These two imperatives are both present tense-forms (imperfective aspect), which fits the nature of the action. In other words, because these actions do not have a natural terminus (ending), it would be somewhat unnatural to use the aorist tense-form (which presents the action as a whole or complete). Thus, these are progressive actions ("continue loving . . . and continue praying"). Because ἀγαπᾶτε is an alpha contract verb (ἀγαπάω), a contraction has occurred, causing the epsilon (ε) to drop out and the alpha to lengthen (ἀγαπά̲ετε → ἀγαπᾶτε).

- τῶν διωκόντων: This substantival participle (pres. act. ptc. masc. gen. pl. of διώκω) is functioning as the object of a prepositional phrase ("for *those who persecute* you").

FOR THE JOURNEY

Although the command to love one's enemy is not found in the OT, it is certainly not contradictory to what is written. Leviticus 19:33–34 states, "When a foreigner resides among you in your land, do not mistreat them. The foreigner residing among you must be treated as your native-born. Love them as yourself, for you were foreigners in Egypt. I am the LORD your God" (NIV). Foreigners were not to be hated but to be respected and even loved. Furthermore, Prov. 25:21 says, "If your enemy is hungry, give him food to eat; if he is thirsty, give him water to drink." In the end, Jesus instructs his listeners that hating one's neighbor is inconsistent with holy Scripture. But what does it mean to love one's enemies? Does it mean to have warm feelings for them? Jesus offers a concrete example when he proclaims, "Pray for those who persecute you." When we pray for those who persecute us, we are demonstrating the love of God to them.

ANSWER KEY

1. *Parse:* (1) λέγω (λέγω, pres. act. ind. 1st sg.), (2) ἀγαπᾶτε (ἀγαπάω, pres. act. impv. 2nd pl.), (3) προσεύχεσθε (προσεύχομαι, pres. mid. impv. 2nd pl.).

2. *Identify:* (1) ἐγώ (nom. sg.), (2) ὑμῖν (dat. pl.), (3) τοὺς ἐχθρούς (masc. acc. pl.), (4) ὑμῶν (gen. pl.), (5) ὑμᾶς (acc. pl.).

3. *Translate:* "But I say to you, Love your enemies and pray for those who persecute you."

DAY 23: MATTHEW 5:45

STEP ONE: **Read** aloud the text at least five times.

ὅπως γένησθε υἱοὶ τοῦ πατρὸς ὑμῶν τοῦ ἐν οὐρανοῖς, ὅτι τὸν ἥλιον
αὐτοῦ ἀνατέλλει ἐπὶ πονηροὺς καὶ ἀγαθοὺς καὶ βρέχει ἐπὶ δικαίους
καὶ ἀδίκους.

STEP TWO: **Parse** the following verbs.

	Lexical Form	Tense	Voice	Mood	Pers.	Num.	Translation
(1) γένησθε							
(2) ἀνατέλλει							
(3) βρέχει							

STEP THREE: **Identify** the gender, case, and number of the following
words.

	Gender	Case	Num.		Gender	Case	Num.
(1) υἱοί				(6) αὐτοῦ			
(2) τοῦ πατρός				(7) πονηρούς			
(3) ὑμῶν				(8) ἀγαθούς			
(4) οὐρανοῖς				(9) δικαίους			
(5) τὸν ἥλιον				(10) ἀδίκους			

STEP FOUR: **Translate** the text into understandable English.

VOCABULARY

ἥλιος, ὁ, the sun
ἀνατέλλω, I cause to rise
βρέχω, I send rain
ἄδικος, unrighteous, unjust

STEP FIVE: **Notice** significant exegetical and syntactical insights.

- **ὅπως γένησθε:** The word ὅπως triggers the subjunctive mood and conveys purpose. One purpose of loving our enemies and praying for those who persecute us is *so that* we might prove to be sons and daughters of God.

- **τοῦ πατρὸς ὑμῶν τοῦ ἐν οὐρανοῖς:** The second article (τοῦ) functions as a substantivizer: the article has the ability to take virtually any part of speech and make it into a substantive (i.e., a noun or adjective). In this case, the article takes a prepositional phrase (ἐν οὐρανοῖς) and turns it into an adjective (literally, "the in-the-heavens Father" or "the Father who is in the heavens").

- **ἀνατέλλει . . . βρέχει:** These two verbs convey divine causation related to weather phenomena: "cause to rise" and "cause to rain."

- **πονηροὺς . . . ἀγαθοὺς . . . δικαίους . . . ἀδίκους:** These four terms are substantival adjectives functioning as nouns (e.g., "evil people"). Also note that these four terms form a chiasm:

  A evil
     B good
     B′ righteous
  A′ unrighteous

FOR THE JOURNEY

By loving our enemies and praying for those who persecute us, we become more like our Father in heaven, according to Jesus. One commentator notes, "To return evil for good is devilish; to return good for good is human; to return good for evil is divine."[1] Our natural instinct or desire is not to love or pray for those who seek to harm us. But a loving response mimics God's actions. He brings sunshine and rain on all, not just on those who are good or righteous. Thus, as his children, we are called to display the characteristics of our heavenly Father. And we are able to love others "because he first loved us" (1 John 4:19).

1. Alfred Plummer, *An Exegetical Commentary on the Gospel according to St. Matthew*, 2nd ed. (London: Robert Scott, 1920), 89.

ANSWER KEY

1. *Parse:* (1) γένησθε (γίνομαι, aor. mid. subj. 2nd pl.), (2) ἀνατέλλει (ἀνατέλλω, pres. act. ind. 3rd sg.), (3) βρέχει (βρέχω, pres. act. ind. 3rd sg.).

2. *Identify:* (1) υἱοί (masc. nom. pl.), (2) τοῦ πατρός (masc. gen. sg.), (3) ὑμῶν (gen. pl.), (4) οὐρανοῖς (masc. dat. pl.), (5) τὸν ἥλιον (masc. acc. sg.), (6) αὐτοῦ (masc. gen. sg.), (7) πονηρούς (masc. acc. pl.), (8) ἀγαθούς (masc. acc. pl.), (9) δικαίους (masc. acc. pl.), (10) ἀδίκους (masc. acc. pl.).

3. *Translate:* "so that you may be sons of your Father who is in the heavens. For he makes his sun rise on the evil and the good, and sends rain on the righteous and the unrighteous."

DAY 24: MATTHEW 5:46-47

STEP ONE: **Read** aloud the text at least five times.

ἐὰν γὰρ ἀγαπήσητε τοὺς ἀγαπῶντας ὑμᾶς, τίνα μισθὸν ἔχετε; οὐχὶ
καὶ οἱ τελῶναι τὸ αὐτὸ ποιοῦσιν; καὶ ἐὰν ἀσπάσησθε τοὺς ἀδελ-
φοὺς ὑμῶν μόνον, τί περισσὸν ποιεῖτε; οὐχὶ καὶ οἱ ἐθνικοὶ τὸ αὐτὸ
ποιοῦσιν;

STEP TWO: **Parse** the following verbs.

	Lexical Form	Tense	Voice	Mood	Pers.	Num.	Translation
(1) ἀγαπήσητε							
(2) ἔχετε							
(3) ποιοῦσιν							
(4) ἀσπάσησθε							
(5) ποιεῖτε							

STEP THREE: **Identify** the gender, case, and number of the following words.

	Gender	Case	Num.		Gender	Case	Num.
(1) ὑμᾶς				(6) τοὺς ἀδελφούς			
(2) τίνα				(7) ὑμῶν			
(3) μισθόν				(8) τί			
(4) οἱ τελῶναι				(9) περισσόν			
(5) τὸ αὐτό				(10) οἱ ἐθνικοί			

STEP FOUR: **Translate** the text into understandable English.

_____

_____

VOCABULARY

μισθός, ὁ, reward, wages
τελώνης, ὁ, tax collector
περισσός, abundant, excessive, more
ἐθνικός, Gentile, pagan

STEP FIVE: Notice significant exegetical and syntactical insights.

- ἐὰν . . . ἀγαπήσητε: The word ἐάν triggers the subjunctive mood and introduces a conditional statement ("if . . . you love").

- τοὺς ἀγαπῶντας ὑμᾶς: This substantival participle (pres. act. ptc. masc. acc. pl. of ἀγαπάω) is functioning as the direct object ("if you love *those who love* you").

- οὐχὶ καὶ οἱ τελῶναι τὸ αὐτὸ ποιοῦσιν; . . . οὐχὶ καὶ οἱ ἐθνικοὶ τὸ αὐτὸ ποιοῦσιν; Each of these questions begins with the negative οὐχί, which expects a positive response to the question (e.g., "Is this not so?" suggests that the correct response is "Yes, it is!").

FOR THE JOURNEY

As Christians, we are called to a higher standard of ethics. We don't merely seek to avoid whatever is wrong; we must go beyond and display kindness to those who are not just like us. Tax collectors were despised because they would often charge above what was required so that they could keep more for themselves. But even tax collectors love those who love them. If we express our love only to those who love us, then we have only achieved the status of a tax collector, the lowest of the low. Furthermore, if we are willing to greet only those who are from our family or our people (which is probably the meaning of "brothers" here), then we are no different from the Gentiles. Here "Gentile" means one who is without knowledge of the true God of the Bible (i.e., a pagan). Even the godless express kindness to their own. As Christians, we are called to love the unlovable and receive those who are often rejected by society, which includes our next-door neighbors and the people we work with.

ANSWER KEY

1. *Parse:* (1) ἀγαπήσητε (ἀγαπάω, aor. act. subj. 2nd pl.), (2) ἔχετε (ἔχω, pres. act. ind. 2nd pl.), (3) ποιοῦσιν (ποιέω, pres. act. ind. 3rd pl.), (4) ἀσπάσησθε (ἀσπάζομαι, aor. mid. subj. 2nd pl.), (5) ποιεῖτε (ποιέω, pres. act. ind. 2nd pl.).

2. *Identify:* (1) ὑμᾶς (acc. pl.), (2) τίνα (masc. acc. sg.), (3) μισθόν (masc. acc. sg.), (4) οἱ τελῶναι (masc. nom. pl.), (5) τὸ αὐτό (neut. acc. sg.), (6) τοὺς ἀδελφούς (masc. acc. pl.), (7) ὑμῶν (gen. pl.), (8) τί (neut. acc. sg.), (9) περισσόν (neut. acc. sg.), (10) οἱ ἐθνικοί (masc. nom. pl.).

3. *Translate:* "For if you love those who love you, what reward do you have? Do not even the tax collectors do the same? And if you greet only your brothers, what more are you doing? Do not even the Gentiles do the same?"

DAY 25: MATTHEW 5:48

STEP ONE: **Read** aloud the text at least five times.

Ἔσεσθε οὖν ὑμεῖς τέλειοι ὡς ὁ πατὴρ ὑμῶν ὁ οὐράνιος τέλειός ἐστιν.

STEP TWO: **Parse** the following verbs.

	Lexical Form	Tense	Voice	Mood	Pers.	Num.	Translation
(1) ἔσεσθε							
(2) ἐστιν							

STEP THREE: **Identify** the gender, case, and number of the following words.

	Gender	Case	Num.		Gender	Case	Num.
(1) ὑμεῖς				(4) ὑμῶν			
(2) τέλειοι				(5) ὁ οὐράνιος			
(3) ὁ πατήρ				(6) τέλειος			

STEP FOUR: **Translate** the text into understandable English.

_____

_____

VOCABULARY

τέλειος, perfect, complete

οὐράνιος, heavenly

STEP FIVE: **Notice** significant exegetical and syntactical insights.

- **Ἔσεσθε:** This future form is not a prediction but expresses a command (i.e., the imperatival future).

- **τέλειοι:** The term τέλειος can be rendered "perfect," "complete," or "mature." In this context, it refers to moral perfection.

- **ὁ πατὴρ ὑμῶν ὁ οὐράνιος:** This phrase can be called a "sandwich" construction. The pronoun (ὑμῶν) is sandwiched in between the noun (ὁ πατήρ) and adjective (ὁ οὐράνιος).

FOR THE JOURNEY

This verse not only concludes Matt. 5:43–47 but also concludes the six antitheses (i.e., "You have heard that it was said, . . . but I say to you"; see 5:21–22, 27–28, 31–32, 33–34, 38–39, 43–44). The command to be perfect echoes Lev. 19:2, "You shall be holy, for I the LORD your God am holy" (ESV). Another relevant verse is Deut. 18:13, "You shall be blameless [τέλειος, LXX] before the LORD your God" (ESV). God requires ethical purity or blamelessness. Such purity is related not merely to one's motives or heart but also to one's actions. Jesus exhorts us to love our enemies and to pray for them. God asks for our wholehearted commitment and allegiance. He desires us to seek "his kingdom and his righteousness . . . first" (Matt. 6:33 NIV). Jesus knew we would never reach perfection on this side of the grave. Consequently, he taught us that when we pray, we should ask God to "forgive us our debts//sins" (Matt. 6:12//Luke 11:4). Although God calls us to a standard that we cannot achieve, he has given us his Spirit, who empowers us to walk according to God's will. Apart from Jesus, we "can do nothing" truly good (John 15:5). That is why we walk by the Spirit and not by our own might.

ANSWER KEY

1. *Parse:* (1) ἔσεσθε (εἰμί, fut. mid. ind. 2nd pl.), (2) ἐστιν (εἰμί, pres. act. ind. 3rd sg.).
2. *Identify:* (1) ὑμεῖς (nom. pl.), (2) τέλειοι (masc. nom. pl.), (3) ὁ πατήρ (masc. nom. sg.), (4) ὑμῶν (gen. pl.), (5) ὁ οὐράνιος (masc. nom. sg.), (6) τέλειος (masc. nom. sg.).
3. *Translate:* "Therefore, you shall be perfect as your heavenly Father is perfect."

ROUTE 6

John 8:39–44

STEP ONE: **Read** aloud the text at least five times.

Ἀπεκρίθησαν καὶ εἶπαν αὐτῷ, Ὁ πατὴρ ἡμῶν Ἀβραάμ ἐστιν. λέγει αὐτοῖς ὁ Ἰησοῦς, Εἰ τέκνα τοῦ Ἀβραάμ ἐστε, τὰ ἔργα τοῦ Ἀβραὰμ ἐποιεῖτε.

STEP TWO: **Parse** the following verbs.

	Lexical Form	Tense	Voice	Mood	Pers.	Num.	Translation
(1) ἀπεκρίθησαν							
(2) εἶπαν							
(3) ἐστιν							
(4) λέγει							
(5) ἐστε							
(6) ἐποιεῖτε							

STEP THREE: **Identify** the gender, case, and number of the following words.

	Gender	Case	Num.		Gender	Case	Num.
(1) αὐτῷ				(5) ὁ Ἰησοῦς			
(2) ὁ πατήρ				(6) τέκνα			
(3) ἡμῶν				(7) τοῦ Ἀβραάμ			
(4) αὐτοῖς				(8) τὰ ἔργα			

STEP FOUR: **Translate** the text into understandable English.

STEP FIVE: **Notice** significant exegetical and syntactical insights.

- **Ἀπεκρίθησαν καὶ εἶπαν:** This phrase ("they answered and said") is known as a pleonastic expression, which simply means that it contains redundancy: "answering" implies "saying" without it needing to be explicitly stated. Many modern English versions simplify or eliminate pleonastic constructions (e.g., "they replied," CSB; "they answered him," ESV). Such constructions are common in the Gospels. For example, this particular expression occurs seven times in John's Gospel (2:18; 7:52; 8:39, 48; 9:20, 34; 18:30).

- **Ἀβραάμ ... τοῦ Ἀβραάμ:** In Greek, proper nouns are capitalized. Although most proper names in Greek decline, many foreign names that are brought into Greek are indeclinable. Such is the case with Ἀβραάμ. Without a case ending, there are still two ways to determine the case of the noun: the article and the context. In the second use of the name in 8:39, the genitive article τοῦ conveys the case of the noun. When the article is missing (as in the first use in 8:39), then context is there to help. In the sentence ὁ πατὴρ ἡμῶν Ἀβραάμ ἐστιν, it is clear that ὁ πατήρ is the subject of the sentence, and because the verb is εἰμί, we are expecting a predicate *nominative*.

- **ἐποιεῖτε:** This form is imperfect, but because it is found in the apodosis of a conditional statement, it is normally translated "you would be doing."

FOR THE JOURNEY

The religious leaders claim Abraham as their father or ancestor. In one sense they are correct. They are physical descendants of Abraham. But in another, more important sense, they are gravely mistaken. If they were spiritual children of Abraham, they would act like Abraham. In other words, they would not oppose God and the one whom God has sent. Abraham was the primary patriarch of Israel and was therefore honored above all others. But by their actions, the Jews who opposed Jesus were proving themselves to be outside Abraham's family. As Paul writes, "A person is not a Jew who is one only outwardly, nor is circumcision merely outward and physical" (Rom. 2:28 NIV). What we say and claim must be backed up by our actions. Or as James puts it, "Faith without works is dead" (2:26 NIV).

ANSWER KEY

1. *Parse:* (1) ἀπεκρίθησαν (ἀποκρίνομαι, aor. mid. ind. 3rd pl.), (2) εἶπαν (λέγω, aor. act. ind. 3rd pl.), (3) ἐστιν (εἰμί, pres. act. ind. 3rd sg.), (4) λέγει (λέγω, pres. act. ind. 3rd sg.), (5) ἐστε (εἰμί, pres. act. ind. 2nd pl.), (6) ἐποιεῖτε (ποιέω, impf. act. ind. 2nd pl.).

2. *Identify:* (1) αὐτῷ (masc. dat. sg.), (2) ὁ πατήρ (masc. nom. sg.), (3) ἡμῶν (gen. pl.), (4) αὐτοῖς (masc. dat. pl.), (5) ὁ Ἰησοῦς (masc. nom. sg.), (6) τέκνα (neut. nom. pl.), (7) τοῦ Ἀβραάμ (masc. gen. sg.), (8) τὰ ἔργα (neut. acc. pl.).

3. *Translate:* "They answered and said to him, 'Our father is Abraham.' Jesus said to them, 'If you are children of Abraham, you would be doing the works of Abraham.'"

DAY 27: JOHN 8:40

STEP ONE: **Read** aloud the text at least five times.

νῦν δὲ ζητεῖτέ με ἀποκτεῖναι ἄνθρωπον ὃς τὴν ἀλήθειαν ὑμῖν λελάληκα ἣν ἤκουσα παρὰ τοῦ θεοῦ· τοῦτο Ἀβραὰμ οὐκ ἐποίησεν.

STEP TWO: **Parse** the following verbs.

	Lexical Form	Tense	Voice	Mood	Pers.	Num.	Translation
(1) ζητεῖτε							
(2) λελάληκα							
(3) ἤκουσα							
(4) ἐποίησεν							

STEP THREE: **Identify** the gender, case, and number of the following words.

	Gender	Case	Num.		Gender	Case	Num.
(1) με				(5) ὑμῖν			
(2) ἄνθρωπον				(6) ἥν			
(3) ὅς				(7) τοῦ θεοῦ			
(4) τὴν ἀλήθειαν				(8) τοῦτο			

STEP FOUR: **Translate** the text into understandable English.

_____

_____

STEP FIVE: **Notice** significant exegetical and syntactical insights.

- **ἀποκτεῖναι:** This infinitive (aor. act. inf. of ἀποκτείνω) communicates purpose ("You are seeking *in order to kill* me").

- **ζητεῖτέ . . . λελάληκα . . . ἤκουσα . . . ἐποίησεν:** Three different tense-forms are found in this verse. ζητεῖτε is a present tense-form of an epsilon (ε) contract verb (ζητε + ετε = ζητεετε → ζητεῖτε). λελάληκα is a perfect tense-form that includes the characteristic reduplication (λε) and the kappa (κ) tense formative. Both ἤκουσα and ἐποίησεν are first-aorist forms that include the characteristic epsilon augment (because ἀκούω begins with an alpha, the augment lengthens the alpha [α] to an eta [η]) and the sigma (σ) tense formative.

• ἄνθρωπον ὃς τὴν ἀλήθειαν ὑμῖν λελάληκα ἣν ἤκουσα: A relative pronoun will typically agree with its antecedent in gender and number, but not necessarily in case. In this phrase, the first relative pronoun (ὅς) is masc. *nom.* sg., but its antecedent (ἄνθρωπον) is masc. *acc.* sg.; whereas the second relative pronoun (ἥν) is fem. *acc.* sg. as is its antecedent (τὴν ἀλήθειαν).

FOR THE JOURNEY

Jesus was sent by God and came declaring the truth. The motif of *truth* is a prominent theme in John's Gospel. Jesus is "full of grace and *truth*" (1:14; emphasis added here and below), both of which come through him (1:17). He is "the way, and *the truth*, and the life" (14:6). He sends the Holy Spirit, "the Spirit of *truth*" (14:17), who guides believers "into all the *truth*" (16:13). Believers are sanctified or made holy "by the *truth*," which is God's word (17:17 NIV). Ironically, Pilate asks Jesus "What is truth?" when embodied truth is standing in front of him (18:38). When Jesus speaks the truth that he receives from God, some do not like the truth and seek to kill him. But such action is not like Abraham, who obeyed God (8:39–41; Gen. 26:5). Since Jesus's opponents do not follow the voice of God, they reveal that their father is not God (John 8:44). Again, our actions reveal what we really believe and whom we are following.

ANSWER KEY

1. *Parse:* (1) ζητεῖτε (ζητέω, pres. act. ind. 2nd pl.), (2) λελάληκα (λαλέω, perf. act. ind. 1st sg.), (3) ἤκουσα (ἀκούω, aor. act. ind. 1st sg.), (4) ἐποίησεν (ποιέω, aor. act. ind. 3rd sg.).

2. *Identify:* (1) με (acc. sg.), (2) ἄνθρωπον (masc. acc. sg.), (3) ὅς (masc. nom. sg.), (4) τὴν ἀλήθειαν (fem. acc. sg.), (5) ὑμῖν (dat. pl.), (6) ἥν (fem. acc. sg.), (7) τοῦ θεοῦ (masc. gen. sg.), (8) τοῦτο (neut. acc. sg.).

3. *Translate:* "But now you are seeking to kill me, a man who has spoken the truth to you that I heard from God. Abraham did not do this."

DAY 28: JOHN 8:41

STEP ONE: **Read** aloud the text at least five times.

ὑμεῖς ποιεῖτε τὰ ἔργα τοῦ πατρὸς ὑμῶν. εἶπαν [οὖν] αὐτῷ, Ἡμεῖς ἐκ
πορνείας οὐ γεγεννήμεθα· ἕνα πατέρα ἔχομεν τὸν θεόν.

STEP TWO: **Parse** the following verbs.

	Lexical Form	Tense	Voice	Mood	Pers.	Num.	Translation
(1) ποιεῖτε							
(2) εἶπαν							
(3) γεγεννήμεθα							
(4) ἔχομεν							

STEP THREE: **Identify** the gender, case, and number of the following words.

	Gender	Case	Num.		Gender	Case	Num.
(1) ὑμεῖς				(6) ἡμεῖς			
(2) τὰ ἔργα				(7) πορνείας			
(3) τοῦ πατρός				(8) ἕνα			
(4) ὑμῶν				(9) πατέρα			
(5) αὐτῷ				(10) τὸν θεόν			

STEP FOUR: **Translate** the text into understandable English.

_____

_____

> VOCABULARY
>
> πορνεία, ἡ, immorality, fornication

STEP FIVE: **Notice** significant exegetical and syntactical insights.

- ὑμεῖς ... Ἡμεῖς: Both of these personal pronouns are emphatic since the information about person and number is already conveyed by the accompanying verbs, being embedded in their endings. That is, because the verb ποιεῖτε has a second-person plural ending, the pronoun ὑμεῖς is unnecessary. Likewise, the verb γεγεννήμεθα has a first-person plural ending, so the pronoun ἡμεῖς is unnecessary. We thus conclude that the redundant pronouns are added for emphasis.

- τὰ ἔργα τοῦ πατρὸς ὑμῶν: The referent of πατρός is not Abraham or God, both of whom have been referred to in the context. Instead, as we will soon see, the referent is the devil.

- ἕνα πατέρα ἔχομεν τὸν θεόν: The accusative form τὸν θεόν is in apposition to πατέρα. That is, the "one father" they claim to have is "God."

FOR THE JOURNEY

The Jews fervently deny being born illegitimately. In the OT, God declares Israel to be his son (Exod. 4:22; Hosea 11:1) and God himself to be their father (Jer. 31:9). Thus, these Jews seek to uphold "their heritage and the legitimacy of their birthright and lineage as the people of God."[1] But John has already declared who has the right to be children of God: "But as many as received him, he gave to them the right to be children of God—to those who believe in his name, who were born not from blood nor from the will of the flesh nor from the will of man, but from God" (John 1:12–13). What a contrast! The Jews are claiming their physical birthright, but John earlier told us that the true children of God are those who receive Jesus. Elsewhere in John's Gospel, Nicodemus encounters Jesus and learns that he must be born again to enter God's kingdom (3:3). What matters most is not our physical ancestry but whether God is our Father.

1. Edward W. Klink III, *John*, ZECNT (Grand Rapids: Zondervan, 2016), 418.

ANSWER KEY

1. *Parse:* (1) ποιεῖτε (ποιέω, pres. act. ind. 2nd pl.), (2) εἶπαν (λέγω, aor. act. ind. 3rd pl.), (3) γεγεννήμεθα (γεννάω, perf. pass. ind. 1st pl.), (4) ἔχομεν (ἔχω, pres. act. ind. 1st pl.).

2. *Identify:* (1) ὑμεῖς (nom. pl.), (2) τὰ ἔργα (neut. acc. pl.), (3) τοῦ πατρός (masc. gen. sg.), (4) ὑμῶν (gen. pl.), (5) αὐτῷ (masc. dat. sg.), (6) ἡμεῖς (nom. pl.), (7) πορνείας (fem. gen. sg.), (8) ἕνα (masc. acc. sg.), (9) πατέρα (masc. acc. sg.), (10) τὸν θεόν (masc. acc. sg.).

3. *Translate:* "You are doing the works of your father. Therefore they said to him, 'We have not been born of immorality; we have one father, God.'"

DAY 29: JOHN 8:42-43

STEP ONE: **Read** aloud the text at least five times.

εἶπεν αὐτοῖς ὁ Ἰησοῦς, Εἰ ὁ θεὸς πατὴρ ὑμῶν ἦν ἠγαπᾶτε ἂν ἐμέ, ἐγὼ γὰρ ἐκ τοῦ θεοῦ ἐξῆλθον καὶ ἥκω· οὐδὲ γὰρ ἀπ᾽ ἐμαυτοῦ ἐλήλυθα, ἀλλ᾽ ἐκεῖνός με ἀπέστειλεν.

STEP TWO: **Parse** the following verbs.

	Lexical Form	Tense	Voice	Mood	Pers.	Num.	Translation
(1) εἶπεν							
(2) ἦν			·				
(3) ἠγαπᾶτε							
(4) ἐξῆλθον							
(5) ἥκω							
(6) ἐλήλυθα							
(7) ἀπέστειλεν							

STEP THREE: **Identify** the gender, case, and number of the following words.

	Gender	Case	Num.		Gender	Case	Num.
(1) αὐτοῖς				(6) ἐμέ			
(2) ὁ Ἰησοῦς				(7) ἐγώ			
(3) ὁ θεός				(8) τοῦ θεοῦ			
(4) πατήρ				(9) ἐμαυτοῦ			
(5) ὑμῶν				(10) ἐκεῖνός			

STEP FOUR: **Translate** the text into understandable English.

_____

_____

> **VOCABULARY**
>
> ἥκω, I have come, am present
> ἐμαυτοῦ, myself

STEP FIVE: **Notice** significant exegetical and syntactical insights.

- **Εἰ ὁ θεὸς πατὴρ ὑμῶν ἦν ἠγαπᾶτε ἂν ἐμέ:** This is a second-class conditional sentence, which expresses something as contrary to fact. In other words, Jesus is saying, "If God were your father (but he's not), you would love me (but you don't)." Consequently, the failure of the religious leaders to love Jesus is evidence that God is not their father. The particle ἄν is often used in contexts where a hypothetical or uncertain statement is made.

- **ἀπ' ἐμαυτοῦ ἐλήλυθα:** The theme that Jesus did not come on his own but was sent by God is common in John (see, e.g., 5:43; 7:28; 16:28). He was sent by the Father's initiative and is accomplishing his Father's mission. The form of ἐλήλυθα is a bit tricky. Although the lexical form of the verb ἐλήλυθα is ἔρχομαι, its perfect form is from the root ἐλευθ-. The second epsilon (ἐλ<u>ευ</u>θ) drops, the first two letters are reduplicated (<u>ἐλ</u>έλυθα), and the original beginning epsilon is lengthened (ἐλ<u>ή</u>λυθα).

- **ἀλλ' ἐκεῖνός με ἀπέστειλεν:** The far demonstrative ἐκεῖνος ("that one") is translated "he" by most English versions. Because ἀποστέλλω is a liquid verb (i.e., a verb whose stem ends in λ, μ, ν, or ρ), the sigma (σ) tense formative is rejected. As a result, a lambda (λ) drops out, and compensatory lengthening of the vowel occurs (ἀπέστ<u>ει</u>λεν).

FOR THE JOURNEY

The test for whether someone is a part of God's family is how they relate to Jesus; that is, whether or not they love him. The reason for this connection is because Jesus came from God and was sent by him. In John 5, Jesus states that he does only what the Father does (v. 19), including giving life to some (v. 21). He then adds, "Whoever does not honor the Son does not honor the Father who sent him" (v. 23 ESV). Just as honoring the Son means honoring the Father, so also loving the Son means loving the Father. Conversely, if we fail to love the Son, we fail to love God. One's destiny in life and in death revolves around our response to Jesus: "If we deny him, he also will deny us" (2 Tim. 2:12 ESV). But Jesus says, "Whoever acknowledges me before others, I will also acknowledge before my Father in heaven" (Matt. 10:32 NIV).

ANSWER KEY

1. *Parse:* (1) εἶπεν (λέγω, aor. act. ind. 3rd sg.), (2) ἦν (εἰμί, impf. act. ind. 3rd sg.), (3) ἠγαπᾶτε (ἀγαπάω, impf. act. ind. 2nd pl.), (4) ἐξῆλθον (ἐξέρχομαι, aor. act. ind. 1st sg.), (5) ἥκω (ἥκω, pres. act. ind. 1st sg.), (6) ἐλήλυθα (ἔρχομαι, perf. act. ind. 1st sg.), (7) ἀπέστειλεν (ἀποστέλλω, aor. act. ind. 3rd sg.).

2. *Identify:* (1) αὐτοῖς (masc. dat. pl.), (2) ὁ Ἰησοῦς (masc. nom. sg.), (3) ὁ θεός (masc. nom. sg.), (4) πατήρ (masc. nom. sg.), (5) ὑμῶν (gen. pl.), (6) ἐμέ (acc. sg.), (7) ἐγώ (nom. sg.), (8) τοῦ θεοῦ (masc. gen. sg.), (9) ἐμαυτοῦ (gen. sg.), (10) ἐκεῖνός (masc. nom. sg.).

3. *Translate:* "Jesus said to them, 'If God were your father, you would love me, for I came from God and I am here. For I have not come from myself, but that one sent me.'"

DAY 30: JOHN 8:44

STEP ONE: **Read** aloud the text at least five times.

ὑμεῖς ἐκ τοῦ πατρὸς τοῦ διαβόλου ἐστὲ καὶ τὰς ἐπιθυμίας τοῦ πατρὸς ὑμῶν θέλετε ποιεῖν. ἐκεῖνος ἀνθρωποκτόνος ἦν ἀπ᾽ ἀρχῆς καὶ ἐν τῇ ἀληθείᾳ οὐκ ἔστηκεν, ὅτι οὐκ ἔστιν ἀλήθεια ἐν αὐτῷ. . . . ψεύστης ἐστὶν καὶ ὁ πατὴρ αὐτοῦ.

STEP TWO: **Parse** the following verbs.

	Lexical Form	Tense	Voice	Mood	Pers.	Num.	Translation
(1) ἐστέ							
(2) θέλετε							
(3) ἦν							
(4) ἔστηκεν							
(5) ἔστιν							

STEP THREE: **Identify** the gender, case, and number of the following words.

	Gender	Case	Num.		Gender	Case	Num.
(1) ὑμεῖς				(8) ἀρχῆς			
(2) τοῦ πατρός				(9) τῇ ἀληθείᾳ			
(3) τοῦ διαβόλου				(10) ἀλήθεια			
(4) τὰς ἐπιθυμίας				(11) αὐτῷ			
(5) ὑμῶν				(12) ψεύστης			
(6) ἐκεῖνος				(13) ὁ πατήρ			
(7) ἀνθρωποκτόνος				(14) αὐτοῦ			

STEP FOUR: **Translate** the text into understandable English.

_____

_____

διάβολος, ὁ, devil, adversary
ἐπιθυμία, ἡ, desire, lust
ἀνθρωποκτόνος, ὁ, murderer
ψεύστης, ὁ, liar

STEP FIVE: Notice significant exegetical and syntactical insights.

- **ὑμεῖς ἐκ τοῦ πατρὸς τοῦ διαβόλου ἐστὲ:** Based on its fronted position, the second-person plural pronoun ὑμεῖς is emphatic. The genitive noun τοῦ διαβόλου is in apposition to τοῦ πατρός, further explaining who their father is (i.e., the devil).

- **θέλετε ποιεῖν:** The verb ποιεῖν (pres. act. inf. of ποιέω) is a complementary infinitive since it completes the verbal action ("you want *to do*").

- **ἕστηκεν:** This form could be either imperfect or perfect, depending on whether the breathing mark is smooth (= imperfect) or rough (= perfect).[2] Instead of reduplicating the initial consonant, the perfect form of this verb drops the initial sigma (σ), and a rough breathing mark indicates its absence (σέστηκεν → ἕστηκεν).

- **ὁ πατὴρ αὐτοῦ:** Although this phrase is typically translated "the father of lies," more literally it reads, "the father of it." The pronoun αὐτοῦ is neuter, referring back to ψεῦδος ("lie").

FOR THE JOURNEY

Jesus finally reveals the parenthood of his adversaries: their father is the devil. The contrast between the devil and Jesus cannot be more pronounced. The devil was a "murderer from the beginning." By tempting Adam and Eve, he brought death to the entire human race. Conversely, in Jesus, who has no beginning (1:1), "was life, and the life was the light of men" (1:4). Whereas there is "no truth" in the devil (8:44), Jesus is "the truth" (14:6). The devil not only lies but is the father of lies. In

2. Breathing marks and accents are supplied by modern scholars since early Greek manuscripts lacked them.

contrast, Jesus speaks only the truth that he receives from his father (8:40). Because his opponents desire to kill him and do not embrace the truth that he proclaims, Jesus says that they resemble the devil (their spiritual father) and not God. Later, they retaliate by calling Jesus a Samaritan and claiming that he is demon possessed (8:48). When Jesus claims to have existed before Abraham (and thus is greater than him), they attempt to kill him on the spot (8:58–59). The irony is that they seek to kill the author of life and the one who freely offers them eternal life.

ANSWER KEY

1. *Parse:* (1) ἐστέ (εἰμί, pres. act. ind. 2nd pl.), (2) θέλετε (θέλω, pres. act. ind. 2nd pl.), (3) ἦν (εἰμί, impf. act. ind. 3rd sg.), (4) ἔστηκεν (ἵστημι, impf./perf. act. ind. 3rd sg.), (5) ἔστιν (εἰμί, pres. act. ind. 3rd sg.).

2. *Identify:* (1) ὑμεῖς (nom. pl.), (2) τοῦ πατρός (masc. gen. sg.), (3) τοῦ διαβόλου (masc. gen. sg.), (4) τὰς ἐπιθυμίας (fem. acc. pl.), (5) ὑμῶν (gen. pl.), (6) ἐκεῖνος (masc. nom. sg.), (7) ἀνθρωποκτόνος (masc. nom. sg.), (8) ἀρχῆς (fem. gen. sg.), (9) τῇ ἀληθείᾳ (fem. dat. sg.), (10) ἀλήθεια (fem. nom. sg.), (11) αὐτῷ (fem. dat. sg.), (12) ψεύστης (masc. nom. sg.), (13) ὁ πατήρ (masc. nom. sg.), (14) αὐτοῦ (masc. gen. sg.).

3. *Translate:* "You are of the/your father the devil, and you want to do the desires of your father. That one was a murderer from the beginning and has not stood in the truth, because there is no truth in him. . . . He is a liar and the father of lies."

Journey 2

INTERMEDIATE

ROUTE 7

Luke 2:1–8

STEP ONE: **Read** aloud the text at least five times.

Ἐγένετο δὲ ἐν ταῖς ἡμέραις ἐκείναις ἐξῆλθεν δόγμα παρὰ Καίσαρος Αὐγούστου ἀπογράφεσθαι πᾶσαν τὴν οἰκουμένην. . . . καὶ ἐπορεύοντο πάντες ἀπογράφεσθαι, ἕκαστος εἰς τὴν ἑαυτοῦ πόλιν.

STEP TWO: **Parse** the following verbs.

	Lexical Form	Tense	Voice	Mood	Pers.	Num.	Translation
(1) ἐγένετο							
(2) ἐξῆλθεν							
(3) ἐπορεύοντο							

STEP THREE: **Identify** the gender, case, and number of the following words.

	Gender	Case	Num.		Gender	Case	Num.
(1) ταῖς ἡμέραις				(5) πάντες			
(2) δόγμα				(6) ἕκαστος			
(3) πᾶσαν				(7) τὴν πόλιν			
(4) τὴν οἰκουμένην				(8) ἑαυτοῦ			

STEP FOUR: **Translate** the text into understandable English.

> VOCABULARY
>
> δόγμα, τό, decree
> Καῖσαρ, ὁ, Caesar, emperor
> Αὔγουστος, ὁ, Augustus
> ἀπογράφω, I register
> οἰκουμένη, ἡ, (inhabited) world

STEP FIVE: **Notice** significant exegetical and syntactical insights.

- **Ἐγένετο δέ:** The specific form ἐγένετο occurs 69 times in Luke and 54 times in Acts. Furthermore, the phrase ἐγένετο δέ occurs 37 times, is found only in Luke and Acts, and is often followed by a temporal phrase (e.g., "in those days").

- **ἀπογράφεσθαι:** This infinitive (pres. pass. inf. of ἀπογράφω) occurs both in verse 1 and in verse 3. The first occurrence is probably best labeled epexegetical ("a decree, that is, that all the world register"). The second use communicates purpose ("All were going out in order to be registered").

- **πᾶσαν τὴν οἰκουμένην:** This phrase refers to all the inhabited world. Luke uses this to describe "any event that covered much of the Roman Empire."[1]

FOR THE JOURNEY

The decree referenced by Luke was issued by "Caesar Augustus," who was previously known as Octavian. He was the Roman emperor from 31

1. Darrell L. Bock, *Luke*, vol. 1, *1:1–9:50*, BECNT (Grand Rapids: Baker, 1994), 202.

BC to AD 14, and he was known for his reign of peace. Providentially, God used this ruler for his purposes to usher the true king of peace to Bethlehem, his ancestral home. According to the OT prophecy, the Messiah was to be born in the city of Bethlehem: "But you, O Bethlehem Ephrathah, who are too little to be among the clans of Judah, from you shall come forth for me one who is to be ruler in Israel, whose coming forth is from of old, from ancient days" (Mic. 5:2 ESV). Thus, this unknowing king helps fulfill God's promise to his people. All of God's promises to his people are "Yes" and "Amen" in Christ (2 Cor. 1:20).

ANSWER KEY

1. *Parse:* (1) ἐγένετο (γίνομαι, aor. mid. ind. 3rd sg.), (2) ἐξῆλθεν (ἐξέρχομαι, aor. act. ind. 3rd sg.), (3) ἐπορεύοντο (πορεύομαι, impf. mid. ind. 3rd pl.).

2. *Identify:* (1) ταῖς ἡμέραις (fem. dat. pl.), (2) δόγμα (neut. nom. sg.), (3) πᾶσαν (fem. acc. sg.), (4) τὴν οἰκουμένην (fem. acc. sg.), (5) πάντες (masc. nom. pl.), (6) ἕκαστος (masc. nom. sg.), (7) τὴν πόλιν (fem. acc. sg.), (8) ἑαυτοῦ (masc. gen. sg.).

3. *Translate:* "And it happened in those days a decree went out from Caesar Augustus that all the world be registered. . . . And all were going out to be registered, each to his own town."

DAY 32: LUKE 2:4–5

STEP ONE: **Read** aloud the text at least five times.

Ἀνέβη δὲ καὶ Ἰωσὴφ ἀπὸ τῆς Γαλιλαίας ἐκ πόλεως Ναζαρὲθ εἰς τὴν Ἰουδαίαν εἰς πόλιν Δαυὶδ ἥτις καλεῖται Βηθλέεμ, διὰ τὸ εἶναι αὐτὸν ἐξ οἴκου καὶ πατριᾶς Δαυίδ, ἀπογράψασθαι σὺν Μαριὰμ τῇ ἐμνηστευμένῃ αὐτῷ, οὔσῃ ἐγκύῳ.

STEP TWO: **Parse** the following verbs.

	Lexical Form	Tense	Voice	Mood	Pers.	Num.	Translation
(1) ἀνέβη							
(2) καλεῖται							

STEP THREE: **Identify** the gender, case, and number of the following words.

	Gender	Case	Num.		Gender	Case	Num.
(1) τῆς Γαλιλαίας				(6) αὐτόν			
(2) πόλεως				(7) οἴκου			
(3) τὴν Ἰουδαίαν				(8) πατριᾶς			
(4) πόλιν				(9) αὐτῷ			
(5) ἥτις				(10) ἐγκύῳ			

STEP FOUR: **Translate** the text into understandable English.

VOCABULARY

Ἰωσήφ, ὁ, Joseph
Ναζαρά/Ναζαρέτ(θ), ἡ, Nazareth
Ἰουδαία, ἡ, Judea
Βηθλέεμ, ἡ, Bethlehem

πατριά, ἡ, lineage, family
ἀπογράφω, I register
μνηστεύω, I am engaged
ἔγκυος, pregnant

STEP FIVE: **Notice** significant exegetical and syntactical insights.

- **διὰ τὸ εἶναι αὐτὸν:** The infinitive εἶναι (pres. act. inf. of εἰμί) in construction with διά communicates cause ("*because* he was"). Also, remember that the subject of the infinitive is in the accusative case (αὐτόν).

- **ἀπογράψασθαι:** This infinitive (aor. mid. inf. of ἀπογράφω) communicates purpose ("in order to be registered").

- **σὺν Μαριὰμ τῇ ἐμνηστευμένῃ αὐτῷ, οὔσῃ ἐγκύῳ:** It is probably best to take σὺν Μαριάμ as modifying ἀνέβη and not ἀπογράψασθαι. That is, they traveled together but were not registered together. The entire phrase contains two substantival participles that further describe Mary: τῇ ἐμνηστευμένῃ (perf. pass. ptc. fem. dat. sg. of μνηστεύω) and οὔσῃ (pres. act. ptc. fem. dat. sg. of εἰμί). They are in the dative case because they are linked with Μαριάμ, which must be dative because it follows the preposition σύν. Don't mistake the epsilon (ε) at the beginning of ἐμνηστευμένῃ as an augment; nonindicative verbs do not have augments. Some verbs that begin with a double consonant (such as μνηστεύω) do not fully reduplicate, and only the epsilon of the reduplication remains. As many scholars have noted, this verb indicates that "the marriage had not yet been consummated, although Mary was living as a wife with Joseph (as her going to Bethlehem with him suggests)."[2]

FOR THE JOURNEY

In this passage, Joseph and Mary make a journey. To be obedient to the government (and to fulfill God's purposes), they travel between eighty-five and ninety miles to Bethlehem to register (and thus pay taxes). Luke informs us that Bethlehem is the "city of David," even though it is never explicitly called by that name in the Greek OT (though see 1 Sam. 20:6, τὴν πόλιν αὐτοῦ, "his city"). Earlier the angel told Mary that her son "will be great and will be called the Son of the Most High. And the Lord God will give to him the throne of his father David" (Luke 1:32 ESV). Because Bethlehem is the city of David and because David was the king of Israel, so also Jesus, who comes from the lineage of David, will be born in the city with regal connections.

2. Robert H. Stein, *Luke*, NAC 24 (Nashville: Broadman, 1992), 107.

ANSWER KEY

1. *Parse:* (1) ἀνέβη (ἀναβαίνω, aor. act. ind. 3rd sg.), (2) καλεῖται (καλέω, pres. pass. ind. 3rd sg.).

2. *Identify:* (1) τῆς Γαλιλαίας (fem. gen. sg.), (2) πόλεως (fem. gen. sg.), (3) τὴν Ἰουδαίαν (fem. acc. sg.), (4) πόλιν (fem. acc. sg.), (5) ἥτις (fem. nom. sg.), (6) αὐτόν (masc. acc. sg.), (7) οἴκου (masc. gen. sg.), (8) πατριᾶς (fem. gen. sg.), (9) αὐτῷ (masc. dat. sg.), (10) ἐγκύῳ (fem. dat. sg.).

3. *Translate:* "And Joseph also went up from Galilee, from the town of Nazareth, into Judea, into the city of David, which is called Bethlehem, because he was from the house and lineage of David, to be registered with Mary, who was engaged to him, being pregnant."

DAY 33: LUKE 2:6

STEP ONE: **Read** aloud the text at least five times.

ἐγένετο δὲ ἐν τῷ εἶναι αὐτοὺς ἐκεῖ ἐπλήσθησαν αἱ ἡμέραι τοῦ τεκεῖν αὐτήν,

STEP TWO: **Parse** the following verbs.

	Lexical Form	Tense	Voice	Mood	Pers.	Num.	Translation
(1) ἐγένετο							
(2) ἐπλήσθησαν							

STEP THREE: **Identify** the gender, case, and number of the following words.

	Gender	Case	Num.
(1) αὐτούς			
(2) αἱ ἡμέραι			
(3) αὐτήν			

STEP FOUR: **Translate** the text into understandable English.

_____

_____

VOCABULARY

πίμπλημι, I fill, fulfill

τίκτω, I give birth to

STEP FIVE: **Notice** significant exegetical and syntactical insights.

- **ἐν τῷ εἶναι αὐτοὺς ἐκεῖ:** The infinitive εἶναι (pres. act. inf. of εἰμί) is temporal and communicates a contemporaneous action ("while they were there"). It is important to remember that non-indicative verbs do not convey the time of the action. Because the two indicative verbs are aorist (ἐγένετο and ἐπλήσθησαν), the time of the action is in the past. The action of the infinitive is contemporaneous with the past action of the indicative verbs and therefore is translated as past ("were"). As expected, the subject of the infinitive (αὐτούς) is in the accusative case.

- **ἐπλήσθησαν:** The verb πίμπλημι is another verb that is favored by Luke. In fact, 22 of the 24 NT occurrences are found in Luke (13×) and Acts (9×).

- **τοῦ τεκεῖν αὐτήν:** This infinitive (aor. act. inf. of τίκτω) is epexegetical, further explaining αἱ ἡμέραι ("the days"). The pronoun αὐτήν is the accusative subject of the infinitive.

FOR THE JOURNEY

In one brief verse we learn about the birth of Jesus. Luke communicates it with simplicity, in a style similar to his other accounts. For example, Luke records the birth of John the Baptist as follows: "Now the time came for Elizabeth to give birth, and she bore a son" (Luke 1:57 ESV). Unlike many popular retellings of the story of Jesus's birth, we are not told of a desperate search for lodging in Bethlehem or that Joseph found the last place in town. We are told only that the period of Mary's pregnancy came to completion and she gave birth. No fanfare. No shouts by welcoming crowds. No royal palace. Just a husband and wife and a miracle child who would fulfill the long-awaited hopes of the people of Israel.

ANSWER KEY

1. *Parse:* (1) ἐγένετο (γίνομαι, aor. mid. ind. 3rd sg.), (2) ἐπλήσθησαν (πίμπλημι, aor. pass. ind. 3rd pl.).

2. *Identify:* (1) αὐτούς (masc. acc. pl.), (2) αἱ ἡμέραι (fem. nom. pl.), (3) αὐτήν (fem. acc. sg.).

3. *Translate:* "And it happened that while they were there, the days were fulfilled for her to give birth."

DAY 34: LUKE 2:7

STEP ONE: **Read** aloud the text at least five times.

καὶ ἔτεκεν τὸν υἱὸν αὐτῆς τὸν πρωτότοκον, καὶ ἐσπαργάνωσεν αὐτὸν καὶ ἀνέκλινεν αὐτὸν ἐν φάτνῃ, διότι οὐκ ἦν αὐτοῖς τόπος ἐν τῷ καταλύματι.

STEP TWO: **Parse** the following verbs.

	Lexical Form	Tense	Voice	Mood	Pers.	Num.	Translation
(1) ἔτεκεν							
(2) ἐσπαργάνωσεν							
(3) ἀνέκλινεν							
(4) ἦν							

STEP THREE: **Identify** the gender, case, and number of the following words.

	Gender	Case	Num.		Gender	Case	Num.
(1) τὸν υἱόν				(5) φάτνη			
(2) αὐτῆς				(6) αὐτοῖς			
(3) τὸν πρωτότοκον				(7) τόπος			
(4) αὐτόν				(8) τῷ καταλύματι			

STEP FOUR: **Translate** the text into understandable English.

VOCABULARY

τίκτω, I give birth to
πρωτότοκος, firstborn
σπαργανόω, I wrap in cloths
ἀνακλίνω, I lay (down)

φάτνη, ἡ, manger
διότι, because
κατάλυμα, inn, lodging place

STEP FIVE: **Notice** significant exegetical and syntactical insights.

- **τὸν υἱὸν αὐτῆς τὸν πρωτότοκον:** The order follows the typical article-noun-article-adjective pattern. The only difference is that the pronoun αὐτῆς is sandwiched between the noun and the adjective, clearly demonstrating its syntactical connection.

- **ἔτεκεν . . . καὶ ἐσπαργάνωσεν . . . καὶ ἀνέκλινεν:** It should be remembered that the aorist tense-form is the default tense-form in historical narratives. Each of these verbs includes an augment, but because the final verb is a compound verb, the augment is placed after the prepositional prefix (ἀνέκλινεν). Also, because the final verb (ἀνακλίνω) is a liquid verb (i.e., its stem ends in λ, μ, ν, or ρ), the sigma (σ) is rejected. Consequently, the form could be either aorist (most likely) or imperfect.

- **ἐν τῷ καταλύματι:** The noun κατάλυμα probably does not refer to the commercial accommodations we experience today. In the parable of the good Samaritan, we read that the Samaritan took the injured Jew to an "inn" (πανδοχεῖον, Luke 10:34), referring to a more formal lodging. By contrast, κατάλυμα represents more of a "guest room" (NIV; see also Luke 22:11; Mark 14:14).

FOR THE JOURNEY

What does it mean that Mary gave birth to her "firstborn" (πρωτότο-κος) son? Most likely it does not simply indicate that Jesus was her first child and that Mary had subsequent children. This reference prepares the reader for Luke 2:23–24, which quotes Exod. 13:2 and Lev. 12:8, "'Every male who first opens the womb shall be called holy to the Lord' and to offer a sacrifice according to what is said in the Law of the Lord, 'a pair of turtledoves, or two young pigeons'" (ESV). Yet the term πρωτότοκος also reminds the reader of the special rights of the firstborn. As Bock states, "Jesus has all the rights of a firstborn son, including any regal rights" (*Luke*, 1:207). Jesus's beginnings were simple and humble. He was born in a stable and placed in an empty feed trough (i.e., a manger). "A stable was the Messiah's first throne room" (Bock, *Luke*, 1:209).

ROUTE 7 • Luke 2:1–8

ANSWER KEY

1. *Parse:* (1) ἔτεκεν (τίκτω, aor. act. ind. 3rd sg.), (2) ἐσπαργάνωσεν (σπαργανόω, aor. act. ind. 3rd sg.), (3) ἀνέκλινεν (ἀνακλίνω, aor./impf. act. ind.
3rd sg.), (4) ἦν (εἰμί, impf. act. ind. 3rd sg.).

2. *Identify:* (1) τὸν υἱόν (masc. acc. sg.), (2) αὐτῆς (fem. gen. sg.), (3) τὸν
πρωτότοκον (masc. acc. sg.), (4) αὐτόν (masc. acc. sg.), (5) φάτνῃ (fem. dat.
sg.), (6) αὐτοῖς (masc. dat. pl.), (7) τόπος (masc. nom. sg.), (8) τῷ καταλύματι
(neut. dat. sg.).

3. *Translate:* "And she gave birth to her firstborn son, and wrapped him in cloths
and laid him in a manger, because there was no place for them in the inn."

105

DAY 35: LUKE 2:8

STEP ONE: **Read** aloud the text at least five times.

Καὶ ποιμένες ἦσαν ἐν τῇ χώρᾳ τῇ αὐτῇ ἀγραυλοῦντες καὶ φυλάσσοντες φυλακὰς τῆς νυκτὸς ἐπὶ τὴν ποίμνην αὐτῶν.

STEP TWO: **Parse** the following verb.

	Lexical Form	Tense	Voice	Mood	Pers.	Num.	Translation
ἦσαν							

STEP THREE: **Identify** the gender, case, and number of the following words.

	Gender	Case	Num.		Gender	Case	Num.
(1) ποιμένες				(5) τῆς νυκτός			
(2) τῇ χώρᾳ				(6) τὴν ποίμνην			
(3) τῇ αὐτῇ				(7) αὐτῶν			
(4) φυλακάς							

STEP FOUR: **Translate** the text into understandable English.

_____

_____

VOCABULARY

ποιμήν, ὁ, shepherd

χώρα, ἡ, region

ἀγραυλέω, I live outside

φυλάσσω, I watch, guard

φυλακή, ἡ, a watch, guard

ποίμνη, ἡ, flock

STEP FIVE: **Notice** significant exegetical and syntactical insights.

- ἦσαν . . . ἀγραυλοῦντες καὶ φυλάσσοντες: The imperfect of εἰμί (ἦσαν) is used in a periphrastic construction with two present participles: ἀγραυλοῦντες (pres. act. ptc. masc. nom. pl. of ἀγραυλέω) and φυλάσσοντες (pres. act. ptc. masc. nom. pl. of φυλάσσω). A periphrastic construction involves a finite verb (usually the present, imperfect, or future of εἰμί) plus a participle (present or perfect).

- ἐν τῇ χώρᾳ τῇ αὐτῇ: This represents an example of the identical use of the third-person personal pronoun αὐτός. In this usage, the article directly precedes the pronoun and is translated "same" (i.e., "the same region").

- φυλάσσοντες φυλακάς: These two terms are cognates, meaning that they share the same lexical root. The first form (φυλάσσοντες) is a participle, and the second (φυλακάς) is classified as a cognate accusative. Literally, the text states that they were "watching watches" (notice that the plural form is used).

FOR THE JOURNEY

The good news of Jesus's birth is first proclaimed to shepherds who are attending to their flocks at night. Although some have noted that shepherds were poor, unclean, and often dishonest, in the Bible they are often represented positively. God is our shepherd (Ps. 23), and many of the OT patriarchs were shepherds (e.g., Abraham, Moses, and David). Furthermore, one of the major metaphors that the NT uses for church leaders (elders, overseers, or pastors) is that of shepherd, with the congregation as their flock (see Eph. 4:11; 1 Pet. 5:1–4). Indeed, the term "pastor" is derived from the Latin for a herdsman or one who provides pasture. And yet the imagery of a shepherd does convey the idea of one who is lowly and humble. Throughout his Gospel, Luke highlights how the good news of Jesus is for all people, especially those who are the lowly or despised of society. With Jesus, there is no partiality (Rom. 3:22). All are welcome, all who humble themselves before him.

ANSWER KEY

1. *Parse:* ἦσαν (εἰμί, impf. act. ind. 3rd pl.).

2. *Identify:* (1) ποιμένες (masc. nom. pl.), (2) τῇ χώρᾳ (fem. dat. sg.), (3) τῇ αὐτῇ (fem. dat. sg.), (4) φυλακάς (fem. acc. pl.), (5) τῆς νυκτός (fem. gen. sg.), (6) τὴν ποίμνην (fem. acc. sg.), (7) αὐτῶν (masc. gen. pl.).

3. *Translate:* "And shepherds were in the same region outside [in the field] and keeping watch at night over their flock."

ROUTE 8

Luke 2:9–15

STEP ONE: **Read** aloud the text at least five times.

καὶ ἄγγελος κυρίου ἐπέστη αὐτοῖς καὶ δόξα κυρίου περιέλαμψεν αὐτούς, καὶ ἐφοβήθησαν φόβον μέγαν.

STEP TWO: **Parse** the following verbs.

	Lexical Form	Tense	Voice	Mood	Pers.	Num.	Translation
(1) ἐπέστη							
(2) περιέλαμψεν							
(3) ἐφοβήθησαν							

STEP THREE: **Identify** the gender, case, and number of the following words.

	Gender	Case	Num.		Gender	Case	Num.
(1) ἄγγελος				(5) αὐτούς			
(2) κυρίου				(6) φόβον			
(3) αὐτοῖς				(7) μέγαν			
(4) δόξα							

STEP FOUR: **Translate** the text into understandable English.

> VOCABULARY
>
> ἐφίστημι, I stand (over/at/near)
> περιλάμπω, I shine around
> φόβος, ὁ, fear

STEP FIVE: **Notice** significant exegetical and syntactical insights.

- **ἄγγελος κυρίου ἐπέστη αὐτοῖς:** Who is the "angel of the Lord"? Although some identify the angel of the Lord as a theophanic appearance of God himself or as a preincarnate appearance of Christ, it is better to view this appearance as one of God's angels.[1] The verb ἐπέστη (from ἐφίστημι) describes the angel's arrival, a term that commonly refers to supernatural or angelic appearances. Indeed, this verb (meaning "to stand at or near a specific person," BDAG 418) is favored by Luke: 18 of the 21 NT occurrences are found in Luke-Acts.

- **δόξα κυρίου περιέλαμψεν αὐτούς:** The glory of God represents God's presence with his people. For example, Exod. 40:34 states, "Then the cloud covered the tent of meeting, and the glory of the LORD filled the tabernacle" (ESV; see also Exod. 16:7, 10; 24:17; Ps. 63:2; Isa. 40:5).

- **ἐφοβήθησαν φόβον μέγαν:** The first two terms are cognates—that is, they share the same lexical root. The term φόβον is classified as a cognate accusative and, along with μέγαν, adds emphasis: literally, "they feared a great fear."

---

1. See John R. Gilhooly, *40 Questions about Angels, Demons, and Spiritual Warfare* (Grand Rapids: Kregel, 2018), 45–51.

FOR THE JOURNEY

Bock comments, "The encounter with the divine is initially startling and unsettling."[2] This reality is demonstrated several times in Luke's Gospel. When an angel of the Lord appeared on the altar of incense, "Zechariah was troubled when he saw him, and fear fell upon him. But the angel said to him, 'Do not be afraid, Zechariah, for your prayer has been heard'" (1:12–13 ESV). When the angel Gabriel greeted Mary, "she was greatly troubled. . . . And the angel said to her, 'Do not be afraid, Mary, for you have found favor with God'" (1:29–30 ESV). As a cloud overshadowed some of Jesus's disciples at the transfiguration, they "were afraid as they entered the cloud" (9:34 ESV). The natural response to an encounter with an angelic being or with God's presence is to fear. It is good to have a healthy fear of God. At the same time, God's response to us, as it was to Zechariah, Mary, and John, is often "fear not" (e.g., Rev. 1:17).

ANSWER KEY

1. *Parse:* (1) ἐπέστη (ἐφίστημι, aor. act. ind. 3rd sg.), (2) περιέλαμψεν (περιλάμπω, aor. act. ind. 3rd sg.), (3) ἐφοβήθησαν (φοβέομαι, aor. pass. ind. 3rd pl.).
2. *Identify:* (1) ἄγγελος (masc. nom. sg.), (2) κυρίου (masc. gen. sg.), (3) αὐτοῖς (masc. dat. pl.), (4) δόξα (fem. nom. sg.), (5) αὐτούς (masc. acc. pl.), (6) φόβον (masc. acc. sg.), (7) μέγαν (masc. acc. sg.).
3. *Translate:* "And an angel of the Lord stood by them, and the glory of the Lord shone around them, and they feared a great fear."

2. Darrell L. Bock, *Luke,* vol. 1, *1:1–9:50,* BECNT (Grand Rapids: Baker, 1994), 215.

DAY 37: LUKE 2:10

STEP ONE: **Read** aloud the text at least five times.

καὶ εἶπεν αὐτοῖς ὁ ἄγγελος, Μὴ φοβεῖσθε, ἰδοὺ γὰρ εὐαγγελίζομαι ὑμῖν χαρὰν μεγάλην ἥτις ἔσται παντὶ τῷ λαῷ.

STEP TWO: **Parse** the following verbs.

	Lexical Form	Tense	Voice	Mood	Pers.	Num.	Translation
(1) εἶπεν							
(2) φοβεῖσθε							
(3) εὐαγγελίζομαι							
(4) ἔσται							

STEP THREE: **Identify** the gender, case, and number of the following words.

	Gender	Case	Num.		Gender	Case	Num.
(1) αὐτοῖς				(5) μεγάλην			
(2) ὁ ἄγγελος				(6) ἥτις			
(3) ὑμῖν				(7) παντί			
(4) χαράν				(8) τῷ λαῷ			

STEP FOUR: **Translate** the text into understandable English.

_____

_____

STEP FIVE: **Notice** significant exegetical and syntactical insights.

- **μὴ φοβεῖσθε:** This imperative is classified as a prohibition since it is negated (by μή). The verb φοβέομαι is a contract verb whose stem ends with epsilon (ε), causing the final vowel of the stem to contract with the initial vowel of the ending (φοβε + εσθε = φοβέεσθε → φοβεῖσθε).

- **εὐαγγελίζομαι ὑμῖν χαρὰν μεγάλην:** The verb εὐαγγελίζομαι ("to proclaim good news") occurs 11 times in the Gospels, and 10 of these occur in Luke (Matt. 11:5; Luke 1:19; 2:10; 3:18; 4:18, 43; 7:22; 8:1; 9:6; 16:16; 20:1). The reason (γάρ) that the shepherds should not experience "great fear" (φόβον μέγαν) is because the angel came to proclaim good news of "great joy" (χαρὰν μεγάλην).

• παντὶ τῷ λαῷ: This phrase is classified as a dative of advantage ("for the benefit of all people").

FOR THE JOURNEY

Luke emphasizes the preaching of the good news through his frequent use of the verb εὐαγγελίζομαι in his Gospel. Good news is proclaimed (1) by the angel Gabriel to Zechariah regarding the birth of John the Baptist (1:19); (2) by John the Baptist, who "preached good news to the people" (3:18 ESV); (3) by the twelve disciples (9:1, 6); and (4) especially by Jesus. In the synagogue at Nazareth, Jesus quotes Isa. 61:1–2: "The Spirit of the Lord is upon me, because he has anointed me to proclaim good news to the poor" (Luke 4:18 ESV). He states to the crowds, "I must preach the good news of the kingdom of God to the other towns as well; for I was sent for this purpose" (4:43 ESV). When John's disciples come to Jesus to inquire if he really is the Messiah, Jesus responds, "Go and tell John what you have seen and heard: . . . the poor have good news preached to them" (7:22 ESV). Later, Luke records that Jesus "went on through cities and villages, proclaiming and bringing the good news of the kingdom of God" (8:1 ESV). Near the end of Luke's Gospel, we read that "Jesus was teaching the people in the temple and preaching the gospel" (20:1 ESV). Jesus not only proclaimed the good news; he was the source of the good news.

ANSWER KEY

1. *Parse:* (1) εἶπεν (λέγω, aor. act. ind. 3rd sg.), (2) φοβεῖσθε (φοβέομαι, aor. mid. impv. 2nd pl.), (3) εὐαγγελίζομαι (εὐαγγελίζομαι, pres. mid. ind. 1st sg.), (4) ἔσται (εἰμί, fut. mid. ind. 3rd sg.).

2. *Identify:* (1) αὐτοῖς (masc. dat. pl.), (2) ὁ ἄγγελος (masc. nom. sg.), (3) ὑμῖν (masc. dat. pl.), (4) χαράν (fem. acc. sg.), (5) μεγάλην (fem. acc. sg.), (6) ἥτις (fem. nom. sg.), (7) παντί (masc. dat. sg.), (8) τῷ λαῷ (masc. dat. sg.).

3. *Translate:* "And the angel said to them, 'Do not fear; for behold, I proclaim good news to you of great joy that will be for all the people.'"

DAY 38: LUKE 2:11-12

STEP ONE: **Read** aloud the text at least five times.

ὅτι ἐτέχθη ὑμῖν σήμερον σωτὴρ ὅς ἐστιν Χριστὸς κύριος ἐν πόλει Δαυίδ. καὶ τοῦτο ὑμῖν τὸ σημεῖον, εὑρήσετε βρέφος ἐσπαργανωμένον καὶ κείμενον ἐν φάτνῃ.

STEP TWO: **Parse** the following verbs.

	Lexical Form	Tense	Voice	Mood	Pers.	Num.	Translation
(1) ἐτέχθη							
(2) ἐστιν							
(3) εὑρήσετε							

STEP THREE: **Identify** the gender, case, and number of the following words.

	Gender	Case	Num.		Gender	Case	Num.
(1) ὑμῖν				(6) πόλει			
(2) σωτήρ				(7) τοῦτο			
(3) ὅς				(8) τὸ σημεῖον			
(4) Χριστός				(9) βρέφος			
(5) κύριος				(10) φάτνῃ			

STEP FOUR: **Translate** the text into understandable English.

VOCABULARY

τίκτω, I give birth to
σήμερον, today
σωτήρ, ὁ, savior
βρέφος, τό, baby, infant

σπαργανόω, I wrap in cloths
κεῖμαι, I lie
φάτνη, ἡ, manger

STEP FIVE: **Notice** significant exegetical and syntactical insights.

- **ὑμῖν . . . ὑμῖν:** These two uses of the second-person personal pronouns are classified as datives of advantage ("for you"). Specifically, the shepherds are beneficiaries of Jesus's birth, and a sign will be given to them.

- **ἐν πόλει Δαυίδ:** This prepositional phrase lacks the article although the object of the prepositional phrase is definite ("in *the* city").[3] The preposition ἐν is always followed by a dative complement. The noun πόλει is an irregular third-declension noun. The proper noun Δαυίδ is a loan word and indeclinable. The context, however, makes clear that it is used as a genitive ("of David"). This connection to David draws attention to the messianic role of Jesus.

- **ἐσπαργανωμένον καὶ κείμενον ἐν φάτνῃ:** These two participles, ἐσπαργανωμένον (perf. pass. ptc. neut. acc. sg. from σπαργανόω) and κείμενον (perf. pass. ptc. neut. acc. sg. from κεῖμαι), are attributive, modifying the neuter noun βρέφος.

FOR THE JOURNEY

The angel declared to the shepherds, "Today a Savior who is Christ the Lord" is born: The combination of these three christological titles (σωτήρ, "Savior"; Χριστός, "Christ"; κύριος, "Lord") do not appear together in any other NT text in reference to Jesus. In the OT, "Savior" is often applied to God, who delivers his people from peril. Earlier in Luke, Mary praises God by declaring "My spirit rejoices in God my Savior" (1:47 ESV). But here in 2:11 the title is applied to Jesus (cf. 1:69). The title "Christ" or "Messiah" is not unexpected since Luke has been using language that highlights Jesus's royal connection to the house of David (see 1:27, 32–33, 69; 2:4). Just as God, the absolute sovereign deity, is called "Lord" (1:16–17, 46, 68, 76), so also is it applied to Jesus (cf. 1:43). These three titles emphasize the divine status of Jesus, even at the beginning of Luke's Gospel.

---

3. Wallace states, "There is no need for the article to be used to make the object of a preposition definite" (*GGBB* 247). Another example is found in Luke 2:14: δόξα ἐν ὑψίστοις θεῷ = "Glory to God in *the* highest."

ANSWER KEY

1. *Parse:* (1) ἐτέχθη (τίκτω, aor. pass. ind. 3rd sg.), (2) ἐστιν (εἰμί, pres. act. ind. 3rd sg.), (3) εὑρήσετε (εὑρίσκω, fut. act. ind. 2nd pl.).

2. *Identify:* (1) ὑμῖν (dat. pl.), (2) σωτήρ (masc. nom. sg.), (3) ὅς (masc. nom. sg.), (4) Χριστός (masc. nom. sg.), (5) κύριος (masc. nom. sg.), (6) πόλει (fem. dat. sg.), (7) τοῦτο (neut. nom. sg.), (8) τὸ σημεῖον (neut. nom. sg.), (9) βρέφος (neut. acc. sg.), (10) φάτνῃ (fem. dat. sg.).

3. *Translate:* "that was born for you today a Savior, who is Christ the Lord, in the city of David. And this [will be] the sign for you: you will find a baby wrapped in cloths and lying in a manger."

DAY 39: LUKE 2:13–14

STEP ONE: **Read** aloud the text at least five times.

καὶ ἐξαίφνης ἐγένετο σὺν τῷ ἀγγέλῳ πλῆθος στρατιᾶς οὐρανίου αἰνούντων τὸν θεὸν καὶ λεγόντων, Δόξα ἐν ὑψίστοις θεῷ καὶ ἐπὶ γῆς εἰρήνη ἐν ἀνθρώποις εὐδοκίας.

STEP TWO: **Parse** the following verb.

	Lexical Form	Tense	Voice	Mood	Pers.	Num.	Translation
ἐγένετο							

STEP THREE: **Identify** the gender, case, and number of the following words.

	Gender	Case	Num.		Gender	Case	Num.
(1) τῷ ἀγγέλῳ				(7) ὑψίστοις			
(2) πλῆθος				(8) θεῷ			
(3) στρατιᾶς				(9) γῆς			
(4) οὐρανίου				(10) εἰρήνη			
(5) τὸν θεόν				(11) ἀνθρώποις			
(6) δόξα				(12) εὐδοκίας			

STEP FOUR. Translate the text into understandable English.

VOCABULARY

ἐξαίφνης, suddenly, unexpectedly
πλῆθος, τό, multitude
στρατιά, ἡ, army, host
οὐράνιος, heavenly
αἰνέω, I praise
ὕψιστος, highest
εὐδοκία, ἡ, goodwill

STEP FIVE: **Notice** significant exegetical and syntactical insights.

- **πλῆθος στρατιᾶς οὐρανίου:** πλῆθος ("multitude") is the subject of the verb ἐγένετο. The genitive στρατιᾶς is categorized as a partitive genitive, "which means that the multitude is a select group that comes from the entire heavenly array of angels" (Bock, *Luke*, 1:219). The adjective οὐρανίου modifies στρατιᾶς, indicating that they are a "heavenly army" (or an "army from heaven").

- **αἰνούντων τὸν θεὸν καὶ λεγόντων:** The two participles αἰνούντων (pres. act. ptc. masc. gen. pl. from αἰνέω) and λεγόντων (pres. act. ptc. masc. gen. pl. from λέγω) are attributive participles modifying πλῆθος ("a multitude praising and saying . . ."). This is a *constructio ad sensum* (construction according to sense) since technically the noun πλῆθος is singular (known as a collective singular), but the participles are plural.

- **ἐπὶ γῆς εἰρήνη ἐν ἀνθρώποις εὐδοκίας:** Notice the parallelism with this phrase and the preceding one: glory//peace; in the highest [place]//on earth; to God//to men/humans. The peace that is given rests "on men/people of favor" (ἐν ἀνθρώποις εὐδοκίας). Here the idea is that God's favor rests on his people. As Thompson notes, "The phrase emphasizes God's initiative and purpose in salvation rather than human merit."[4]

FOR THE JOURNEY

The term "praise" (αἰνέω) is common in Luke's writings, with seven of the nine NT occurrences in Luke-Acts. Not only does (1) the heavenly army *praise* God (2:13–14), but also (2) the shepherds return, "glorifying and *praising* God for all they had heard and seen" (2:20 ESV); (3) the multitude of Jesus's disciples "began to rejoice and *praise* God with a loud voice for all the mighty works that they had seen" (19:37); (4) the early church is characterized as "*praising* God and having favor with all the people" (Acts 2:47 ESV); and (5) a disabled beggar healed by Peter was "walking and leaping and *praising* God" (Acts 3:8 ESV; see also 3:9). When the heavenly army cries out "Glory in the highest places to God," they are giving God the praise he deserves.

4. Alan J. Thompson, *Luke*, EGGNT (Nashville: B&H Academic, 2016), 46.

ANSWER KEY

1. *Parse:* ἐγένετο (γίνομαι, aor. mid. ind. 3rd sg.).

2. *Identify:* (1) τῷ ἀγγέλῳ (masc. dat. sg.), (2) πλῆθος (neut. nom. sg.), (3) στρατιᾶς (fem. gen. sg.), (4) οὐρανίου (fem. gen. sg.), (5) τὸν θεόν (masc. acc. sg.),
(6) δόξα (fem. nom. sg.), (7) ὑψίστοις (neut. dat. pl.), (8) θεῷ (masc. dat. sg.),
(9) γῆς (fem. gen. sg.), (10) εἰρήνη (fem. nom. sg.), (11) ἀνθρώποις (masc. dat.
pl.), (12) εὐδοκίας (fem. gen. sg.).

3. *Translate:* "And suddenly there was with the angel a multitude of a heavenly
army, praising God and saying, 'Glory in the highest [place] to God and on
earth peace to men of goodwill.'"

DAY 40: LUKE 2:15

STEP ONE: **Read** aloud the text at least five times.

Καὶ ἐγένετο ὡς ἀπῆλθον ἀπ' αὐτῶν εἰς τὸν οὐρανὸν οἱ ἄγγελοι, οἱ ποιμένες ἐλάλουν πρὸς ἀλλήλους· Διέλθωμεν δὴ ἕως Βηθλέεμ καὶ ἴδωμεν τὸ ῥῆμα τοῦτο τὸ γεγονὸς ὃ ὁ κύριος ἐγνώρισεν ἡμῖν.

STEP TWO: **Parse** the following verbs.

	Lexical Form	Tense	Voice	Mood	Pers.	Num.	Translation
(1) ἐγένετο							
(2) ἀπῆλθον							
(3) ἐλάλουν							
(4) διέλθωμεν							
(5) ἴδωμεν							
(6) ἐγνώρισεν							

STEP THREE: **Identify** the gender, case, and number of the following words.

	Gender	Case	Num.		Gender	Case	Num.
(1) αὐτῶν				(6) τὸ ῥῆμα			
(2) τὸν οὐρανόν				(7) τοῦτο			
(3) οἱ ἄγγελοι				(8) ὅ			
(4) οἱ ποιμένες				(9) ὁ κύριος			
(5) ἀλλήλους				(10) ἡμῖν			

STEP FOUR: **Translate** the text into understandable English.

VOCABULARY

ποιμήν, ὁ, shepherd

διέρχομαι, I go (through)

δή, now, then

Βηθλέεμ, ἡ, Bethlehem

γνωρίζω, I make known, reveal

STEP FIVE: **Notice** significant exegetical and syntactical insights.

- **ὡς ἀπῆλθον ἀπ' αὐτῶν εἰς τὸν οὐρανὸν οἱ ἄγγελοι:** This temporal phrase (ὡς, "as") provides background information. The subject (οἱ ἄγγελοι) is found at the end of the phrase. This word order might be difficult for us but was common in Greek.

- **διέλθωμεν δὴ . . . καὶ ἴδωμεν:** Both the two main verbs, διέλθωμεν and ἴδωμεν, are hortatory subjunctives. Because Greek does not have a first-person imperative, the subjunctive mood is used. Such verbs are usually best translated "let us . . ." (e.g., "let us go" and "let us see"). The particle δή may add emphasis or urgency: "let us *now* go" (NRSVue) or "let us go *straight*" (CSB, NASB1995).

- **τὸ ῥῆμα τοῦτο τὸ γεγονὸς:** The term ῥῆμα can refer to "an event that can be spoken about," and with this meaning is glossed "thing, object, matter, event" (BDAG 905). The phrase τὸ γεγονός is an attributive participle (perf. act. ptc. neut. acc. sg. of γίνομαι) and modifies τὸ ῥῆμα ("the thing *that has happened*").

FOR THE JOURNEY

Shepherds do not normally leave their sheep. Without the shepherd there, the sheep are unprotected and vulnerable. But sometimes it is necessary to leave the flock behind, as when a sheep wanders off and the shepherd needs to go after the lost one. But here the shepherds leave their sheep and travel to Bethlehem, seeking the one who would someday declare himself the "good Shepherd" (John 10:11, 14) and whom Peter would call the "Chief Shepherd" (1 Pet. 5:4) and the "Shepherd and Overseer of [our] souls" (2:25). The shepherds hurry to

Bethlehem and find Joseph and Mary, with the newborn infant in the manger. They leave, "glorifying and praising God" (Luke 2:20). The message reported to them by the angel has come to pass. The Messiah has been born in the city of David!

ANSWER KEY

1. *Parse:* (1) ἐγένετο (γίνομαι, aor. mid. ind. 3rd sg.), (2) ἀπῆλθον (ἀπέρχομαι, aor. act. ind. 3rd pl.), (3) ἐλάλουν (λαλέω, impf. act. ind. 3rd pl.), (4) διέλθωμεν (διέρχομαι, aor. act. subj. 1st pl.), (5) ἴδωμεν (βλέπω/ὁράω, aor. act. subj. 1st pl.), (6) ἐγνώρισεν (γνωρίζω, aor. act. ind. 3rd sg.).

2. *Identify:* (1) αὐτῶν (masc. gen. pl.), (2) τὸν οὐρανόν (masc. acc. sg.), (3) οἱ ἄγγελοι (masc. nom. pl.), (4) οἱ ποιμένες (masc. nom. pl.), (5) ἀλλήλους (masc. acc. pl.), (6) τὸ ῥῆμα (neut. acc. sg.), (7) τοῦτο (neut. acc. sg.), (8) ὅ (neut. acc. sg.), (9) ὁ κύριος (masc. nom. sg.), (10) ἡμῖν (dat. pl.).

3. *Translate:* "And it happened as the angels went away from them into heaven, the shepherds were speaking to one another, 'Let us now go to Bethlehem, and let us see the thing that has happened, which the Lord has made known to us.'"

ROUTE 9

Romans 1:11–17

STEP ONE: **Read** aloud the text at least five times.

ἐπιποθῶ γὰρ ἰδεῖν ὑμᾶς, ἵνα τι μεταδῶ χάρισμα ὑμῖν πνευματικὸν
εἰς τὸ στηριχθῆναι ὑμᾶς, τοῦτο δέ ἐστιν συμπαρακληθῆναι ἐν ὑμῖν
διὰ τῆς ἐν ἀλλήλοις πίστεως ὑμῶν τε καὶ ἐμοῦ.

STEP TWO: **Parse** the following verbs.

	Lexical Form	Tense	Voice	Mood	Pers.	Num.	Translation
(1) ἐπιποθῶ							
(2) μεταδῶ							
(3) ἐστιν							

STEP THREE: **Identify** the gender, case, and number of the following words.

	Gender	Case	Num.		Gender	Case	Num.
(1) ὑμᾶς				(6) τοῦτο			
(2) τι				(7) ἀλλήλοις			
(3) χάρισμα				(8) τῆς πίστεως			
(4) ὑμῖν				(9) ὑμῶν			
(5) πνευματικόν				(10) ἐμοῦ			

STEP FOUR: Translate the text into understandable English.

VOCABULARY

ἐπιποθέω, I desire, long for
μεταδίδωμι, I share, impart
χάρισμα, τό, gift
πνευματικός, spiritual
τηρίζω, I confirm, establish, strengthen
συμπαρακαλέω, I am mutually encouraged

STEP FIVE: Notice significant exegetical and syntactical insights.

- **ἐπιποθῶ γὰρ ἰδεῖν ὑμᾶς:** The verb ἰδεῖν (aor. act. inf. of ὁράω) is a complementary infinitive, completing the verb ἐπιποθῶ ("I desire *to see*"). Although the accusative ὑμᾶς could function as the subject of the infinitive, here it functions as the object ("to see *you*").

- **ἵνα τι μεταδῶ χάρισμα ὑμῖν πνευματικὸν:** The conjunction ἵνα communicates purpose and is followed by the subjunctive μεταδῶ. Interestingly, the words that normally belong together are spaced out: τι . . . χάρισμα . . . πνευματικὸν = "some spiritual gift." It is possible that this type of word order "is a rhetorical technique that gives greater emphasis to the separated elements."[1]

- **εἰς τὸ στηριχθῆναι ὑμᾶς:** Following εἰς τό, the verb στηριχθῆναι (aor. pass. inf. of στηρίζω) is an infinitive of purpose. In contrast to its use in the previous clause, the accusative ὑμᾶς this time functions as the subject of the infinitive ("that *you* might be strengthened").

- **τοῦτο δέ ἐστιν συμπαρακληθῆναι ἐν ὑμῖν:** The verb συμπαρακληθῆναι (aor. pass. inf. of συμπαρακαλέω) is an infinitive of purpose, parallel to στηριχθῆναι.

- **διὰ τῆς ἐν ἀλλήλοις πίστεως ὑμῶν:** The article τῆς is in construction with πίστεως, which brackets the prepositional phrase ἐν ἀλλήλοις.

---

1. John D. Harvey, *Romans*, EGGNT (Nashville: B&H Academic, 2017), 21.

FOR THE JOURNEY

Paul expresses a genuine desire to see and encourage the Christians in Rome. The verb ἐπιποθέω conveys a deep longing such as that of a nursing infant longing for its mother's milk (1 Pet. 2:2) or a deer longing for satisfying water (Ps. 42:1 [41:2 LXX]). Elsewhere, Paul uses this word to describe his desire for the Christians in Philippi (Phil. 1:8), in Thessalonica (1 Thess. 3:6), and for Timothy (2 Tim. 1:4). Specifically, Paul indicates that he longs to see them so that he might share some spiritual gift with them. But Paul is not acting arrogantly, as if he has goodies to offer to others in need. Rather, Paul emphasizes that what he has to offer is not from him but from God, and that he will also be blessed by his visit with them: (1) the verb μεταδίδωμι is best translated "share" and not simply "give"; (2) the passive στηριχθῆναι implies that God is the one who will strengthen them; (3) the prepositional prefix (σύν, "with") on the verb συμπαρακαλέω and (4) the pronoun ἀλλήλων highlight the reciprocal nature of the encouragement; and (5) the conjunction τε emphasizes the equity between "yours" (ὑμῶν) and "mine" (ἐμοῦ). Paul's longing desire for mutual encouragement is a good reminder for us.

ANSWER KEY

1. Parse: (1) ἐπιποθῶ (ἐπιποθέω, pres. act. ind. 1st sg.), (2) μεταδῶ (μεταδίδωμι, aor. act. subj. 1st sg.), (3) ἐστιν (εἰμί, pres. act. ind. 3rd sg.).

2. *Identify:* (1) ὑμᾶς (acc. pl.), (2) τι (neut. acc. sg.), (3) χάρισμα (neut. acc. sg.), (4) ὑμῖν (dat. pl.), (5) πνευματικόν (neut. acc. sg.), (6) τοῦτο (neut. nom. sg.), (7) ἀλλήλοις (masc. dat. pl.), (8) τῆς πίστεως (fem. gen. sg.), (9) ὑμῶν (gen. pl.), (10) ἐμοῦ (gen. sg.).

3. *Translate:* "For I long to see you, that I might share with you some spiritual gift so that you might be strengthened, that is, that we might be mutually encouraged among you through our faith among each other, both yours and mine."

DAY 42: ROMANS 1:13

STEP ONE: **Read** aloud the text at least five times.

οὐ θέλω δὲ ὑμᾶς ἀγνοεῖν, ἀδελφοί, ὅτι πολλάκις προεθέμην ἐλθεῖν πρὸς ὑμᾶς, καὶ ἐκωλύθην ἄχρι τοῦ δεῦρο, ἵνα τινὰ καρπὸν σχῶ καὶ ἐν ὑμῖν καθὼς καὶ ἐν τοῖς λοιποῖς ἔθνεσιν.

STEP TWO: **Parse** the following verbs.

	Lexical Form	Tense	Voice	Mood	Pers.	Num.	Translation
(1) θέλω							
(2) προεθέμην							
(3) ἐκωλύθην							
(4) σχῶ							

STEP THREE: **Identify** the gender, case, and number of the following words.

	Gender	Case	Num.		Gender	Case	Num.
(1) ὑμᾶς				(5) ὑμῖν			
(2) ἀδελφοί				(6) τοῖς ἔθνεσιν			
(3) τινά				(7) λοιποῖς			
(4) καρπόν							

STEP FOUR: **Translate** the text into understandable English.

VOCABULARY

ἀγνοέω, I am ignorant
πολλάκις, often, frequent
προτίθημι, I plan, intend
κωλύω, I hinder, prevent, forbid
ἄχρι, until
δεῦρο, come, until now

STEP FIVE: **Notice** significant exegetical and syntactical insights.

- **οὐ θέλω δὲ ὑμᾶς ἀγνοεῖν:** The verb ἀγνοεῖν (pres. act. inf. of ἀγνοέω) is a complementary infinitive, completing the verb θέλω ("I do not want you *to be ignorant*"). The accusative ὑμᾶς functions as the subject of the infinitive.

- **πολλάκις προεθέμην ἐλθεῖν πρὸς ὑμᾶς:** The infinitive ἐλθεῖν may be categorized as complementary or as conveying purpose ("I planned *to come*").

- **ἵνα τινὰ καρπὸν σχῶ καὶ ἐν ὑμῖν:** The verb σχῶ communicates purpose following ἵνα. The root of ἔχω is σεχ, but the epsilon (ε) drops out in the aorist form. In the present tense-form (ἔχω), the sigma (σ) drops out and is replaced with a rough breathing mark (which also drops out when the following letter is a spirant, such as chi, χ). The rough breathing mark is seen in the future form (ἕξω).

FOR THE JOURNEY

Paul grabs the attention of his readers in two ways: (1) through the phrase "I don't want you to be ignorant," which signals special significance, and (2) by the vocative "brothers." Paul is explaining the purpose of his forthcoming visit and why he has yet to visit the believers in Rome. For some unstated reason, Paul indicates that his plans to visit them were hindered but that such hindrances (in ministry, life, etc.) are now gone. His goal is that he might have some "fruit" (καρπός) among them, just as he had among other Gentiles. This fruit is not primarily referring to new converts but to the benefits and growth that believers receive when they better understand (or understand afresh) the gospel and its implications for our lives. God desires not only that the gospel be brought to all people groups but also that people from all groups grow in the likeness of Christ, deepening their faith and thus producing greater "fruit."

ANSWER KEY

1. *Parse:* (1) θέλω (θέλω, pres. act. ind. 1st sg.), (2) προεθέμην (προτίθημι, aor. mid. ind. 1st sg.), (3) ἐκωλύθην (κωλύω, aor. pass. ind. 1st sg.), (4) σχῶ (ἔχω, aor. act. subj. 1st sg.).

2. *Identify:* (1) ὑμᾶς (acc. pl.), (2) ἀδελφοί (masc. voc. pl.), (3) τινά (masc. acc. sg.), (4) καρπόν (masc. acc. sg.), (5) ὑμῖν (dat. pl.), (6) τοῖς ἔθνεσιν (neut. dat. pl.), (7) λοιποῖς (neut. dat. pl.).

3. *Translate:* "I do not want you to be ignorant, brothers, that often I planned to come to you (and was prevented until now to come), that I might have some fruit among you just as also among the rest of the Gentiles."

DAY 43: ROMANS 1:14–15

STEP ONE: **Read** aloud the text at least five times.

Ἕλλησίν τε καὶ βαρβάροις, σοφοῖς τε καὶ ἀνοήτοις ὀφειλέτης εἰμί,
οὕτως τὸ κατ᾽ ἐμὲ πρόθυμον καὶ ὑμῖν τοῖς ἐν Ῥώμῃ εὐαγγελίσασθαι.

STEP TWO: **Parse** the following verb.

	Lexical Form	Tense	Voice	Mood	Pers.	Num.	Translation
εἰμί							

STEP THREE: **Identify** the gender, case, and number of the following words.

	Gender	Case	Num.		Gender	Case	Num.
(1) Ἕλλησιν				(6) ἐμέ			
(2) βαρβάροις				(7) τὸ πρόθυμον			
(3) σοφοῖς				(8) ὑμῖν			
(4) ἀνοήτοις				(9) Ῥώμῃ			
(5) ὀφειλέτης							

STEP FOUR: **Translate** the text into understandable English.

VOCABULARY

Ἕλλην, ὁ, Greek
βάρβαρος, barbarian
σοφός, wise
ἀνόητος, foolish
ὀφειλέτης, ὁ, debtor
πρόθυμος, eager, ready, willing
Ῥώμη, ἡ, Rome

STEP FIVE: **Notice** significant exegetical and syntactical insights.

- Ἕλλησίν τε καὶ βαρβάροις, σοφοῖς τε καὶ ἀνοήτοις ὀφειλέτης εἰμί: "Greeks" (Ἕλλησίν) were cultured and had influence on society; "barbarians" (βαρβάροις) were the uncultured and could not speak Greek or Latin. The "wise" (σοφοῖς) were educated, and the "unwise" or "foolish" (ἀνοήτοις) were not. Thus Paul felt obligated to the cultured and uncultured, and to the educated and uneducated.

- οὕτως τὸ κατ' ἐμὲ πρόθυμον . . . εὐαγγελίσασθαι: The article (τό) is linked to the adjective πρόθυμον and turns it into a noun, which is then modified by the prepositional phrase κατ' ἐμέ. This phrase functions similar to a genitive construction ("the eagerness according to me" = "my eagerness") and is the subject of the following infinitive εὐαγγελίσασθαι (pres. mid. inf. of εὐαγγελίζομαι), which is epexegetical since it explains Paul's eagerness.

- καὶ ὑμῖν τοῖς ἐν Ῥώμῃ: The article (τοῖς) functions as a substantivizer, turning the prepositional phrase (ἐν Ῥώμῃ) into a noun ("to those in Rome"). This phrase is in apposition to ὑμῖν ("to you, [that is] to those in Rome").

FOR THE JOURNEY

When we think of preaching the gospel (εὐαγγελίζομαι), we often think of evangelistic preaching to unbelievers. And, according to its frequent NT use, that would not be incorrect. For example, in Acts 14:21, Luke uses two different verbs for Paul and Barnabas preaching the gospel (εὐαγγελισάμενοί) and for making disciples (μαθητεύσαντες). But here in Rom. 1:15, Paul uses the verb εὐαγγελίζομαι to refer to ongoing discipleship. John Harvey comments, "The idea of 'preaching the gospel' goes beyond the initial act of winning converts to include challenging believers to live in a manner worthy of the gospel" (*Romans*, 27). Likewise, Moo notes that the term refers "to the ongoing work of teaching and discipleship that builds on the initial evangelization."[2] The gospel is not merely for unbelievers; it is also what believers constantly need to hear and be reminded of in order to bear fruit.

2. Douglas J. Moo, *The Letter to the Romans*, 2nd ed., NICNT (Grand Rapids: Eerdmans, 2018), 66.

ANSWER KEY

1. *Parse:* εἰμί (εἰμί, pres. act. ind. 1st sg.).

2. *Identify:* (1) Ἕλλησίν (masc. dat. pl.), (2) βαρβάροις (masc. dat. pl.), (3) σο-φοῖς (masc. dat. pl.), (4) ἀνοήτοις (masc. dat. pl.), (5) ὀφειλέτης (masc. nom. sg.), (6) ἐμέ (acc. sg.), (7) τὸ πρόθυμον (neut. nom. sg.), (8) ὑμῖν (dat. pl.), (9) Ῥώμη (fem. dat. sg.).

3. *Translate:* "I am a debtor both to Greeks and barbarians, both to the wise and to the foolish, so I am eager to preach the gospel to you also who are in Rome."

DAY 44: ROMANS 1:16

STEP ONE: **Read** aloud the text at least five times.

Οὐ γὰρ ἐπαισχύνομαι τὸ εὐαγγέλιον, δύναμις γὰρ θεοῦ ἐστιν εἰς σωτηρίαν παντὶ τῷ πιστεύοντι, Ἰουδαίῳ τε πρῶτον καὶ Ἕλληνι.

STEP TWO: **Parse** the following verbs.

	Lexical Form	Tense	Voice	Mood	Pers.	Num.	Translation
(1) ἐπαισχύνομαι							
(2) ἐστιν							

STEP THREE: **Identify** the gender, case, and number of the following words.

	Gender	Case	Num.		Gender	Case	Num.
(1) τὸ εὐαγγέλιον				(5) παντί			
(2) δύναμις				(6) Ἰουδαίῳ			
(3) θεοῦ				(7) Ἕλληνι			
(4) σωτηρίαν							

STEP FOUR: **Translate** the text into understandable English.

VOCABULARY

ἐπαισχύνομαι, I am ashamed
σωτηρία, ἡ, salvation
Ἕλλην, ὁ, Greek

STEP FIVE: **Notice** significant exegetical and syntactical insights.

- **Οὐ γὰρ ἐπαισχύνομαι τὸ εὐαγγέλιον:** Moo suggests that the negative statement οὐ ἐπαισχύνομαι ("I am not ashamed") is an example
  of litotes (an understatement used as a rhetorical device). Thus,
  he translates the phrase positively: "I have great confidence in the

gospel" (*Romans*, 68). The article in front of εὐαγγέλιον ("good news") communicates par excellence. The gospel is in a class all by itself. There may be other news that is good, but this news is the best good news!

- **δύναμις γὰρ θεοῦ ἐστιν εἰς σωτηρίαν:** θεοῦ is a genitive of source ("power from God"). Here, εἰς + accusative communicates result ("resulting in salvation").

- **παντὶ τῷ πιστεύοντι:** The participle πιστεύοντι (pres. act. ptc. masc. dat. sg. of πιστεύω) functions substantively ("to everyone who believes").

- **Ἰουδαίῳ τε πρῶτον καὶ Ἕλληνι:** These two nouns (Ἰουδαίῳ and Ἕλληνι) are in apposition to παντὶ τῷ πιστεύοντι. The use of πρῶτος relates both to the Jews being first to receive the gospel in redemptive history (Rom. 3:2; 9:4–5) and to Paul's ministry practice of first evangelizing the Jewish residents of the city before seeking out the Gentiles.

FOR THE JOURNEY

Sometimes the little words are the most important words. Such is often the case with the term γάρ, a word that provides us with the *reason* why something is done. Why is Paul willing to preach the gospel in Rome? Because he is not ashamed of the gospel. And why is Paul not ashamed of the gospel? Because it is the power of God for salvation for everyone who believes. And how is the gospel the power of God (v. 17)? Because in it the righteousness of God is revealed. Paul declares that the gospel leads to salvation for everyone who embraces the good news of Christ. Elsewhere Paul writes that the "message of the cross is foolishness for those who are perishing, but for those who are being saved, it is the power of God" (1 Cor. 1:18). Although in the NT salvation is a past event (Rom. 8:24), present action, and a future hope (5:9–10), here the focus is on the present. Salvation has already been granted to those who believe the gospel. The wrath of God is being revealed against all ungodliness (1:18) and can even now be avoided.

ANSWER KEY

1. *Parse:* (1) ἐπαισχύνομαι (ἐπαισχύνομαι, pres. mid. ind. 1st sg.), (2) ἐστιν (εἰμί, pres. act. ind. 3rd sg.).

2. *Identify:* (1) τὸ εὐαγγέλιον (neut. acc. sg.), (2) δύναμις (fem. nom. sg.), (3) θεοῦ (masc. gen. sg.), (4) σωτηρίαν (fem. acc. sg.), (5) παντί (masc. dat. sg.), (6) Ἰουδαίῳ (masc. dat. sg.), (7) Ἕλληνι (masc. dat. sg.).

3. *Translate:* "For I am not ashamed of the gospel, for it is the power of God for salvation to everyone who believes, to the Jew first and also to the Greek."

DAY 45: ROMANS 1:17

STEP ONE: **Read** aloud the text at least five times.

δικαιοσύνη γὰρ θεοῦ ἐν αὐτῷ ἀποκαλύπτεται ἐκ πίστεως εἰς πίστιν,
καθὼς γέγραπται, Ὁ δὲ δίκαιος ἐκ πίστεως ζήσεται.

STEP TWO: **Parse** the following verbs.

	Lexical Form	Tense	Voice	Mood	Pers.	Num.	Translation
(1) ἀποκαλύπτεται							
(2) γέγραπται							
(3) ζήσεται							

STEP THREE: **Identify** the gender, case, and number of the following words.

	Gender	Case	Num.		Gender	Case	Num.
(1) δικαιοσύνη				(4) πίστεως			
(2) θεοῦ				(5) πίστιν			
(3) αὐτῷ				(6) ὁ δίκαιος			

STEP FOUR: **Translate** the text into understandable English.

VOCABULARY

ἀποκαλύπτω, I reveal

STEP FIVE: **Notice** significant exegetical and syntactical insights.

- **δικαιοσύνη . . . θεοῦ:** The genitive θεοῦ can be interpreted as a genitive of source ("a righteousness *from* God") or as a subjective genitive ("a righteousness that is being shown by God" or "God's saving power"). The former interpretation describes a gift from God (his righteousness), which results in a forensic declaration (a changed status). The latter refers to God's transformative power, which results in a changed life. Some have argued that Paul intends both concepts.[3] This phrase is significant since it occurs seven other times in Romans (3:5, 21, 22, 25, 26; 10:3 [2×]) and in prominent locations (esp. 1:17 and 3:21–26).

- ἐκ πίστεως εἰς πίστιν: Although these prepositional phrases are debated, it is probably best to take the first as conveying source (*"from* faith") and the second as conveying the extent ("*to* faith"; so CSB, KJV, NASB1995, NET, NKJV). For example, the NIV translates it: "from first to last" (cf. "from faith for faith," ESV; "through faith for faith," NRSVue, RSV).

- καθὼς γέγραπται, Ὁ δὲ δίκαιος ἐκ πίστεως ζήσεται: Paul introduces his OT citation with a standard formula (καθὼς γέγραπται), used 13 other times in Romans. The perfect tense is intensive, focusing on the present resulting state of a past action. Consequently, it is appropriate to translate the phrase with an English present ("it is written"). The quotation is from Hab. 2:4, which is also quoted in Gal. 3:11 and Heb. 10:38. The future ζήσεται is gnomic: it conveys a timeless truth.

FOR THE JOURNEY

The great Reformer Martin Luther discusses his remarkable discovery of the gospel related to the meaning of Rom. 1:17. Because of his misunderstanding of the text, he states that he "hated" the phrase "righteousness of God" since, "according to the use and custom of all the teachers, I had been taught to understand philosophically regarding the formal or active righteousness, as they called it, with which God is righteous and punishes the unrighteous sinner."[4] For Luther, the gospel of God's righteousness was not good news but was utterly terrifying since it declares that God will punish sinners. He continues, "I did not love, yes, I hated the righteous God who punishes sinners. . . . Thus I raged with a fierce and troubled conscience" (*LW* 34:336–37). Thankfully, Luther did not give

---

3. See Thomas R. Schreiner, *Romans*, BECNT (Grand Rapids: Baker, 1998), 64–66. Schreiner now leans toward the forensic position in the 2nd (2018) edition of his commentary. See also Frank Thielman, *Romans*, ZECNT (Grand Rapids: Zondervan, 2018), 82.

4. Luther, "Preface to the Complete Edition of Luther's Latin Writings," in *LW* 34:336.

up seeking to find the truth: he continued to study the Scriptures. He reflects, "At last, by the mercy of God, meditating day and night, I gave heed to the context of the words. . . . There I began to understand that the righteousness of God is that by which the righteous lives by a gift of God, namely by faith. And this is the meaning: the righteousness of God is revealed by the gospel, namely, the passive righteousness with which merciful God justifies us by faith, as it is written, 'He who through faith is righteous shall live.' Here I felt that I was altogether born again and had entered paradise itself through open gates" (*LW* 34:337).

ANSWER KEY

1. *Parse:* (1) ἀποκαλύπτεται (ἀποκαλύπτω, pres. pass. ind. 3rd sg.), (2) γέγραπται (γράφω, perf. pass. ind. 3rd sg.), (3) ζήσεται (ζάω, fut. mid. ind. 3rd sg.).

2. *Identify:* (1) δικαιοσύνη (fem. nom. sg.), (2) θεοῦ (masc. gen. sg.), (3) αὐτῷ (masc. dat. sg.), (4) πίστεως (fem. gen. sg.), (5) πίστιν (fem. acc. sg.), (6) ὁ δίκαιος (masc. nom. sg.).

3. *Translate:* "For in it the righteousness of God is revealed from faith to/for faith, as it has been written, 'The righteous will live by faith.'"

ROUTE 10

Ephesians 2:1–10

STEP ONE: **Read** aloud the text at least five times.

Καὶ ὑμᾶς ὄντας νεκροὺς τοῖς παραπτώμασιν καὶ ταῖς ἁμαρτίαις ὑμῶν, ἐν αἷς ποτε περιεπατήσατε· . . . καὶ ἤμεθα τέκνα φύσει ὀργῆς ὡς καὶ οἱ λοιποί.

STEP TWO: **Parse** the following verbs.

	Lexical Form	Tense	Voice	Mood	Gender	Pers.	Num.
(1) περιεπατήσατε							
(2) ἤμεθα							

STEP THREE: **Identify** the gender, case, and number of the following words.

	Gender	Case	Num.		Gender	Case	Num.
(1) ὑμᾶς				(6) αἷς			
(2) νεκρούς				(7) τέκνα			
(3) τοῖς παραπτώμασιν				(8) φύσει			
(4) ταῖς ἁμαρτίαις				(9) ὀργῆς			
(5) ὑμῶν				(10) οἱ λοιποί			

STEP FOUR: **Translate** the text into understandable English.

VOCABULARY

παράπτωμα, τό, trespass, offense
ποτέ, once, formerly
φύσις, ἡ, nature
ὀργή, ἡ, wrath

STEP FIVE: **Notice** significant exegetical and syntactical insights.

- **Καὶ ὑμᾶς ὄντας νεκρούς:** The pronoun ὑμᾶς functions as the accusative direct object of the main verb (συνεζωοποίησε) found in verse 5 ("He made *you* alive together"). The participle ὄντας (pres. act. ptc. masc. acc. pl. of εἰμί) is adverbial and functions concessively ("*although* you were dead"). The adjective νεκρούς is the predicate accusative of ὄντας and is a metaphor for spiritual death.

- **τοῖς παραπτώμασιν καὶ ταῖς ἁμαρτίαις ὑμῶν:** The datives τοῖς παραπτώμασιν and ταῖς ἁμαρτίαις are best understood as datives of sphere ("dead *in* your transgressions and sins"). The two terms are essentially synonymous.

- **καὶ ἤμεθα τέκνα φύσει ὀργῆς ὡς καὶ οἱ λοιποί:** The noun φύσει is either a dative of means ("*by means of* your natural condition") or cause ("*because of* your natural condition"). The noun ὀργῆς is a genitive of destination ("children *destined for wrath*"; Wallace, *GGBB* 100–101).

FOR THE JOURNEY

Apart from the saving power of the gospel, all humanity is in bondage to sin. But it is actually worse. Paul indicates that all are "dead" in their trespasses and sins. We are not merely sick or ailing but are spiritually bankrupt. Thus, we cannot improve our standing before God because we have neither the ability nor the desire to do so. Instead, as Paul writes in verses 2–3, we were influenced by the world, the devil, and the flesh. The "world" refers to all that is opposed to God: the cultural, social, political, and economic ideologies and forces that are hostile to God and his ways. The devil or "Satan" and his minions also influence unbelievers. But the battle is not merely external: the problem also lies within our own hearts. The "flesh" is the sinful nature that is actively opposed to God and his will. The result of living in our sins is that we are deserving of God's wrath. God is holy and therefore must punish sin. Thankfully, this is not where the story ends. Because of his mercy, grace, and love, God has provided a way of escape through his Son. *Soli Deo gloria!* Glory to God alone!

ANSWER KEY

1. *Parse:* (1) περιεπατήσατε (περιπατέω, aor. act. ind. 2nd pl.), (2) ἤμεθα (εἰμί, impf. mid. ind. 1st pl.).

2. *Identify:* (1) ὑμᾶς (acc. pl.), (2) νεκρούς (masc. acc. pl.), (3) τοῖς παραπτώμασιν (masc. dat. pl.), (4) ταῖς ἁμαρτίαις (fem. dat. pl.), (5) ὑμῶν (gen. pl.), (6) αἷς (fem. dat. pl.), (7) τέκνα (neut. nom. pl.), (8) φύσει (fem. dat. sg.), (9) ὀργῆς (fem. gen. sg.), (10) οἱ λοιποί (masc. nom. pl.).

3. *Translate:* "And you, being dead in your trespasses and sins, in which you once walked . . . ; and we were by nature children of wrath even as the rest."

DAY 47: EPHESIANS 2:4–5

STEP ONE: **Read** aloud the text at least five times.

ὁ δὲ θεὸς πλούσιος ὢν ἐν ἐλέει, διὰ τὴν πολλὴν ἀγάπην αὐτοῦ ἣν ἠγάπησεν ἡμᾶς, καὶ ὄντας ἡμᾶς νεκροὺς τοῖς παραπτώμασιν συνεζωοποίησεν τῷ Χριστῷ,—χάριτί ἐστε σεσῳσμένοι—

STEP TWO: **Parse** the following verbs.

	Lexical Form	Tense	Voice	Mood	Pers.	Num.	Translation
(1) ἠγάπησεν							
(2) συνεζωοποίησεν							
(3) ἐστε							

STEP THREE: **Identify** the gender, case, and number of the following words.

	Gender	Case	Num.		Gender	Case	Num.
(1) ὁ θεός				(6) ἡμᾶς			
(2) πλούσιος				(7) νεκρούς			
(3) ἐλέει				(8) τοῖς παραπτώμασιν			
(4) τὴν ἀγάπην				(9) τῷ Χριστῷ			
(5) αὐτοῦ				(10) χάριτι			

STEP FOUR: **Translate** the text into understandable English.

VOCABULARY

πλούσιος, rich
ἔλεος, τό, mercy, compassion
παράπτωμα, τό, trespass, offense
συζωοποιέω, I make alive with

STEP FIVE: **Notice** significant exegetical and syntactical insights.

- **ὁ δὲ θεὸς πλούσιος ὢν ἐν ἐλέει:** The participle ὢν (pres. act. ptc. masc. nom. sg. of εἰμί) is an adverbial causal participle (*"because* he is rich in mercy"*).

- **καὶ ὄντας ἡμᾶς νεκροὺς τοῖς παραπτώμασιν:** The participle ὄντας (pres. act. ptc. masc. acc. pl. of εἰμί) is adverbial and functions concessively (*"although* we were dead") or perhaps temporally (*"when* we were dead").

- **συνεζωοποίησεν τῷ Χριστῷ:** The verb συνεζωοποίησεν is the first main verb of this passage (beginning in v. 1). The three compound συν- verbs (<u>συνε</u>ζωοποίησεν, <u>συν</u>ήγειρεν, and <u>συν</u>εκάθισεν) emphasize the union between Christ and believers.

- **χάριτί ἐστε σεσῳσμένοι:** The addition of the em dashes in the Greek NT (functioning like parentheses) indicates that the editors think this phrase is parenthetical (though important!). The phrase anticipates what Paul will say in verse 8, so its repetition demonstrates emphasis. The noun χάριτι is best categorized as a dative of cause (*"because of* grace" or *"on the basis of* grace"). The participle σεσῳσμένοι (perf. pass. ptc. masc. nom. pl. of σῴζω) is periphrastic in construction with the verb ἐστε, emphasizing the resulting state.

FOR THE JOURNEY

In verses 1–3 Paul details the spiritual situation of fallen humanity apart from God's intervening grace. All of humanity is not simply spiritually sick but also spiritually dead. The result of following the world, the flesh, and the devil is that we are "sons of disobedience" (2:2) and "children of wrath" (2:3). The cure for this grim description, however, is not obedience to God and his commands since such a feat is impossible for those who are spiritually dead and therefore lack the desire or ability to obey God. Rather, the remedy begins with God: "but God . . . made us alive together with Christ" (2:4–5). Before we are able to obey God's commands, we must experience new life (regeneration) through God's intervening grace. We were dead in our trespasses and sins, . . . but God. We pursued the ways of the world, the flesh, and the devil, . . . but God. We were all children of disobedience and wrath, . . . but God. God took the initiative to rescue sinners from the wrath to come.

ANSWER KEY

1. *Parse:* (1) ἠγάπησεν (ἀγαπάω, aor. act. ind. 3rd sg.), (2) συνεζωοποίησεν (συ-ζωοποιέω, aor. act. ind. 3rd sg.), (3) ἐστε (εἰμί, pres. act. ind. 2nd pl.).

2. *Identify:* (1) ὁ θεός (masc. nom. sg.), (2) πλούσιος (masc. nom. sg.), (3) ἐλέει (neut. dat. sg.), (4) τὴν ἀγάπην (fem. acc. sg.), (5) αὐτοῦ (masc. gen. sg.), (6) ἡμᾶς (acc. pl.), (7) νεκρούς (masc. acc. pl.), (8) τοῖς παραπτώμασιν (neut. dat. pl.), (9) τῷ Χριστῷ (masc. dat. sg.), (10) χάριτι (fem. dat. sg.).

3. *Translate:* "But God, being rich in mercy, because of his great love with which he loved us, even when we were dead in our trespasses, made us alive together with Christ (by grace you have been saved)."

DAY 48: EPHESIANS 2:6–7

STEP ONE: **Read** aloud the text at least five times.

καὶ συνήγειρεν καὶ συνεκάθισεν ἐν τοῖς ἐπουρανίοις ἐν Χριστῷ Ἰησοῦ,
ἵνα ἐνδείξηται ἐν τοῖς αἰῶσιν τοῖς ἐπερχομένοις τὸ ὑπερβάλλον
πλοῦτος τῆς χάριτος αὐτοῦ ἐν χρηστότητι ἐφ' ἡμᾶς ἐν Χριστῷ Ἰησοῦ.

STEP TWO: **Parse** the following verbs.

	Lexical Form	Tense	Voice	Mood	Pers.	Num.	Translation
(1) συνήγειρεν							
(2) συνεκάθισεν							
(3) ἐνδείξηται							

STEP THREE: **Identify** the gender, case, and number of the following words.

	Gender	Case	Num.		Gender	Case	Num.
(1) τοῖς ἐπουρανίοις				(5) τῆς χάριτος			
(2) Χριστῷ Ἰησοῦ				(6) αὐτοῦ			
(3) τοῖς αἰῶσιν				(7) χρηστότητι			
(4) τὸ πλοῦτος				(8) ἡμᾶς			

STEP FOUR: **Translate** the text into understandable English.

___

___

VOCABULARY

συνεγείρω, I raise with
συγκαθίζω, I cause to sit with
ἐπουράνιος, heavenly
ἐνδείκνυμι, I show, demonstrate

ἐπέρχομαι, I come about, happen
ὑπερβάλλω, I surpass, go beyond
πλοῦτος, ὁ/τό, riches, wealth
χρηστότης, ἡ, kindness, goodness

STEP FIVE: **Notice** significant exegetical and syntactical insights.

- **καὶ συνήγειρεν καὶ συνεκάθισεν ἐν τοῖς ἐπουρανίοις ἐν Χριστῷ Ἰησοῦ:** By far the majority of prepositional phrases modify verbs (i.e., are adverbial as opposed to adjectival). Such is the case with the two prepositional phrases (ἐν τοῖς ἐπουρανίοις and ἐν Χριστῷ Ἰησοῦ) that modify the second verb (συνεκάθισεν).

- **ἵνα ἐνδείξηται ἐν τοῖς αἰῶσιν τοῖς ἐπερχομένοις:** ἵνα communicates purpose (and possibly also result) and is followed by the subjunctive ἐνδείξηται. The participle ἐπερχομένοις (pres. mid. ptc. masc. dat. pl. of ἐπέρχομαι) is attributive, modifying τοῖς αἰῶσιν ("the *coming* ages").

- **τὸ ὑπερβάλλον πλοῦτος τῆς χάριτος αὐτοῦ ἐν χρηστότητι ἐφ' ἡμᾶς ἐν Χριστῷ Ἰησοῦ:** The participle ὑπερβάλλον (pres. act. ptc. neut. acc. sg. of ὑπερβάλλω) is attributive, modifying πλοῦτος ("*surpassing* riches"). Again, all three prepositional phrases (ἐν χρηστότητι, ἐφ' ἡμᾶς, and ἐν Χριστῷ Ἰησοῦ) are adverbial, modifying the verb ἐνδείξηται.

FOR THE JOURNEY

Paul uses three verbs to describe the regenerating and saving work of God—and all three of these terms underscore the believers' union with Christ: God made us alive together with (συνεζωοποίησεν) Christ, raised us up with (συνήγειρεν) him, and seated us with (συνεκάθισεν) him (Eph. 2:4–6). Each of these verbs in Greek is a compound verb that includes a prepositional prefix (συν-) meaning "together with." Believers partake in the threefold blessing of regeneration ("made alive"), exaltation ("raised"), and coronation ("seated") that was first accomplished by God in Christ. But what would move God to take fallen, broken, and sinful humanity and grant them such blessings? Paul emphasizes the origin of God's saving decision to rescue his people with a variety of phrases: He is "rich in mercy" (2:4), loves us with a "great love" (2:4), and demonstrates the "immeasurable riches of his grace" (2:7) and his "kindness" (2:7). God's mercy and love are the causes that propel him to awaken sinners by the regenerating work of the Spirit, to bring new life to dead hearts.

ANSWER KEY

1. *Parse:* (1) συνήγειρεν (συνεγείρω, aor. act. ind. 3rd sg.), (2) συνεκάθισεν (συγκαθίζω, aor. act. ind. 3rd sg.), (3) ἐνδείξηται (ἐνδείκνυμι, aor. mid. subj. 3rd sg.).

2. *Identify:* (1) τοῖς ἐπουρανίοις (neut. dat. pl.), (2) Χριστῷ Ἰησοῦ (masc. dat. sg.), (3) τοῖς αἰῶσιν (masc. dat. pl.), (4) τὸ πλοῦτος (neut. acc. sg.), (5) τῆς χάριτος (fem. gen. sg.), (6) αὐτοῦ (masc. gen. sg.), (7) χρηστότητι (fem. dat. sg.), (8) ἡμᾶς (acc. pl.).

3. *Translate:* "And he raised [us] up and seated [us] in the heavenly places in Christ Jesus, so that he might show in the coming ages the surpassing riches of his grace in kindness to us in Christ Jesus."

DAY 49: EPHESIANS 2:8–9

STEP ONE: **Read** aloud the text at least five times.

τῇ γὰρ χάριτί ἐστε σεσῳσμένοι διὰ πίστεως· καὶ τοῦτο οὐκ ἐξ ὑμῶν,
θεοῦ τὸ δῶρον· οὐκ ἐξ ἔργων, ἵνα μή τις καυχήσηται.

STEP TWO: **Parse** the following verbs.

	Lexical Form	Tense	Voice	Mood	Pers.	Num.	Translation
(1) ἐστε							
(2) καυχήσηται							

STEP THREE: **Identify** the gender, case, and number of the following words.

	Gender	Case	Num.		Gender	Case	Num.
(1) τῇ χάριτι				(5) θεοῦ			
(2) πίστεως				(6) τὸ δῶρον			
(3) τοῦτο				(7) ἔργων			
(4) ὑμῶν				(8) τις			

STEP FOUR: **Translate** the text into understandable English.

VOCABULARY

δῶρον, τό, gift
καυχάομαι, I boast

STEP FIVE: **Notice** significant exegetical and syntactical insights.

- **τῇ γὰρ χάριτί ἐστε σεσῳσμένοι διὰ πίστεως:** The conjunction γάρ introduces the explanation of Paul's statement about the nature of God's gracious salvation in verse 7. In verse 5, Paul states χάριτί ἐστε σεσῳσμένοι, and now he adds that our salvation is διὰ πίστεως.

147

The noun χάριτι is a dative of cause (*"because of* grace" or *"on the basis of* grace"); then διὰ πίστεως communicates the means by which someone is saved (*"by* faith"). The participle σεσῳσμένοι (perf. pass. ptc. masc. nom. pl. of σῴζω) is in a periphrastic construction with the verb ἐστε.

* **καὶ τοῦτο οὐκ ἐξ ὑμῶν, θεοῦ τὸ δῶρον· οὐκ ἐξ ἔργων:** The demonstrative pronoun τοῦτο is the subject of an implied equative verb (e.g., ἐστιν). Because τοῦτο is neuter and the two previous possible antecedents are feminine (χάριτι and πίστεως), the antecedent is the entire clause that includes both grace and faith. The three genitive nouns (ἐξ ὑμῶν, θεοῦ, and ἐξ ἔργων) are all genitives of source ("from you," "from God," and "from works"). Notice the chiastic construction:

A οὐκ ἐξ ὑμῶν
   B θεοῦ τὸ δῶρον
A′ οὐκ ἐξ ἔργων

* **ἵνα μή τις καυχήσηται:** The conjunction ἵνα introduces a negative purpose clause and is followed by the subjunctive verb καυχήσηται.

FOR THE JOURNEY

Salvation is attained by grace through faith and not by works. More specifically, the grace that results in new life is received *by* faith. Take note: we are saved *because of* grace, which is received *by means of* or *through* faith. In other words, we are not saved because of or on the basis of faith. Faith does not save. God's grace based on Christ's atonement saves. Rather, faith is merely the instrument by which grace is received. Consequently, faith is not viewed as a meritorious work but trusts in Christ's life, death, and resurrection. Paul states negatively that salvation is "not of yourselves" or "not a result of works," but positively it is "the gift of God" (2:8–9). If it is a gift, it is (by definition) not earned but is freely received. Furthermore, if it is freely received as a gift and is not dependent on good works, it precludes any boasting before God.

ANSWER KEY

1. *Parse:* (1) ἐστε (εἰμί, pres. act. ind. 2nd pl.), (2) καυχήσηται (καυχάομαι, aor. mid. subj. 3rd sg.).

2. *Identify:* (1) τῇ χάριτι (fem. dat. sg.), (2) πίστεως (fem. gen. sg.), (3) τοῦτο (neut. nom. sg.), (4) ὑμῶν (gen. pl.), (5) θεοῦ (masc. gen. sg.), (6) τὸ δῶρον (neut. nom. sg.), (7) ἔργων (neut. gen. pl.), (8) τις (masc. nom. sg.).

3. *Translate:* "For by grace you have been saved through faith, and this is not of yourselves; [it is] a gift of God, not from works, so that no one might boast."

DAY 50: EPHESIANS 2:10

STEP ONE: **Read** aloud the text at least five times.

αὐτοῦ γάρ ἐσμεν ποίημα, κτισθέντες ἐν Χριστῷ Ἰησοῦ ἐπὶ ἔργοις ἀγαθοῖς οἷς προητοίμασεν ὁ θεός, ἵνα ἐν αὐτοῖς περιπατήσωμεν.

STEP TWO: **Parse** the following verbs.

	Lexical Form	Tense	Voice	Mood	Pers.	Num.	Translation
(1) ἐσμεν							
(2) προητοίμασεν							
(3) περιπατήσωμεν							

STEP THREE: **Identify** the gender, case, and number of the following words.

	Gender	Case	Num.		Gender	Case	Num.
(1) αὐτοῦ				(5) ἀγαθοῖς			
(2) ποίημα				(6) οἷς			
(3) Χριστῷ Ἰησοῦ				(7) ὁ θεός			
(4) ἔργοις				(8) αὐτοῖς			

STEP FOUR: **Translate** the text into understandable English.

_____

_____

> VOCABULARY
>
> ποίημα, τό, workmanship
> κτίζω, I create
> προετοιμάζω, I prepare beforehand

STEP FIVE: Notice significant exegetical and syntactical insights.

- **αὐτοῦ γάρ ἐσμεν ποίημα:** The conjunction γάρ provides the reason why salvation is by grace and not by works. The noun ποίημα functions as the predicate nominative of ἐσμεν. In the NT, ποίημα occurs only here and in Rom. 1:20, where it refers to God's works at and in creation. Here, it refers to God's work of the new creation. The term has been variously translated into English: "workmanship" (CSB, ESV, NASB1995, NET, NKJV, RSV), "handiwork" (NIV), "masterpiece" (NLT), "work of art" (NJB), and "what he has made" (NRSVue).

- **κτισθέντες ἐν Χριστῷ ᾿Ιησοῦ:** The participle κτισθέντες (aor. pass. ptc. masc. nom. pl. of κτίζω) is a causal adverbial participle ("*because* we were created in Christ Jesus"). This is an example of a divine passive (God is the implied subject of the verb).

- **ἵνα ἐν αὐτοῖς περιπατήσωμεν:** The conjunction ἵνα introduces a purpose followed by the subjunctive verb περιπατήσωμεν. The verb περιπατέω forms an *inclusio* that frames this paragraph: ἐν αἷς ποτε περιεπατήσατε (2:2) . . . ἐν αὐτοῖς περιπατήσωμεν (2:10).

FOR THE JOURNEY

Paul is adamant that good works do not save someone (2:8–9). But he does not shy away from affirming the importance of good works. In fact, believers were "created in Christ Jesus for good works." Yet, as we notice, Paul does not state that their new-creation status is *based on* good works: such a declaration would contradict the earlier statement about salvation being a free gift and not a result of works. Instead, believers are created for the purpose of good works. Additionally, God has preordained believers to perform good works. The free and gracious nature of salvation does not lead to complacency or passivity. Thus, believers are no longer counted among the walking dead (2:1) but are to walk in the good works that God has prepared for them. Salvation, from beginning to end, is a result of God's grace—even the good works that believers perform. Any boasting before God is ruled out since he is the author and perfecter of our faith.

ANSWER KEY

1. *Parse:* (1) ἐσμεν (εἰμί, pres. act. ind. 1st pl.), (2) προητοίμασεν (προετοιμάζω, aor. act. ind. 3rd sg.), (3) περιπατήσωμεν (περιπατέω, aor. act. subj. 1st pl.).

2. *Identify:* (1) αὐτοῦ (masc. gen. sg.), (2) ποίημα (neut. nom. sg.), (3) Χριστῷ Ἰησοῦ (masc. dat. sg.), (4) ἔργοις (neut. dat. pl.), (5) ἀγαθοῖς (neut. dat. pl.), (6) οἷς (neut. dat. pl.), (7) ὁ θεός (masc. nom. sg.), (8) αὐτοῖς (neut. dat. pl.).

3. *Translate:* "For we are his workmanship, created in Christ Jesus for good works, which God prepared beforehand, that we should walk in them."

ROUTE 11

Ephesians 2:11–18

DAY 51: EPHESIANS 2:11–12

STEP ONE: **Read** aloud the text at least five times.

Διὸ μνημονεύετε . . . ὅτι ἦτε τῷ καιρῷ ἐκείνῳ χωρὶς Χριστοῦ, ἀπηλλοτριωμένοι τῆς πολιτείας τοῦ Ἰσραὴλ καὶ ξένοι τῶν διαθηκῶν τῆς ἐπαγγελίας, ἐλπίδα μὴ ἔχοντες καὶ ἄθεοι ἐν τῷ κόσμῳ.

STEP TWO: **Parse** the following verbs.

	Lexical Form	Tense	Voice	Mood	Pers.	Num.	Translation
(1) μνημονεύετε							
(2) ἦτε							

STEP THREE: **Identify** the gender, case, and number of the following words.

	Gender	Case	Num.		Gender	Case	Num.
(1) τῷ καιρῷ				(6) τῶν διαθηκῶν			
(2) Χριστοῦ				(7) τῆς ἐπαγγελίας			
(3) τῆς πολιτείας				(8) ἐλπίδα			
(4) τοῦ Ἰσραήλ				(9) ἄθεοι			
(5) ξένοι				(10) τῷ κόσμῳ			

STEP FOUR: **Translate** the text into understandable English.

> VOCABULARY
>
> μνημονεύω, I remember
> χωρίς, without, apart from
> ἀπαλλοτριόω, I alienate, estrange
> πολιτεία, ἡ, citizenship
> ξένος, strange (substantive: stranger)
> διαθήκη, ἡ, covenant
> ἄθεος, without God, godless

STEP FIVE: **Notice** significant exegetical and syntactical insights.

- **Διὸ μνημονεύετε:** The verb μνημονεύω occurs as an imperative nine times in the NT, each in the present tense-form. This is also the only imperative in the first three chapters of the epistle. The remaining section of verse 11 (that was skipped) elaborates on the background of the recipients: they were formerly Gentiles in the flesh and were called "the uncircumcised" by those called "the circumcised" (a circumcision made in the flesh by hands).

- **ἀπηλλοτριωμένοι τῆς πολιτείας τοῦ Ἰσραὴλ:** The participle ἀπηλλοτριωμένοι (perf. pass. ptc. masc. nom. pl. of ἀπαλλοτριόομαι; see also 4:18; Col. 1:21) functions substantively. The noun τῆς πολιτείας is a genitive of separation ("*from* the citizenship"), which is common following a compound verb beginning with the preposition ἀπό; in the next phrase, τῶν διαθηκῶν is also a genitive of separation: "strangers *from* the covenants."

- **ἐλπίδα μὴ ἔχοντες καὶ ἄθεοι ἐν τῷ κόσμῳ:** The participle ἔχοντες (pres. act. ptc. masc. nom. pl. of ἔχω) functions substantively. The adjective ἄθεοι ("without God") is plural, *not* because it refers to multiple gods, but because it modifies the Gentile believers (i.e., a plurality of people).

FOR THE JOURNEY

In the OT, the Israelites were often exhorted to remember the past deeds of God, especially their slavery in Egypt and subsequent exodus (Deut. 5:15; 15:15; 16:12; 24:18, 22). Similarly, the Ephesians were urged to remember their former separation and alienation from God. Such recollection is not simply a mental activity but involves both evaluation and subsequent action. In other words, it is not about gaining new information but about reminding ourselves of what we already know in order to make us more cognizant of it and to cause us to respond appropriately. It will do us well to slow down and reflect on the faithfulness of God in taking us from those who were not a people and making us his people.

ANSWER KEY

1. *Parse:* (1) μνημονεύετε (μνημονεύω, pres. act. impv. 2nd pl.), (2) ἦτε (εἰμί, impf. act. ind. 2nd pl.).
2. *Identify:* (1) τῷ καιρῷ (masc. dat. sg.), (2) Χριστοῦ (masc. gen. sg.), (3) τῆς πολιτείας (fem. gen. sg.), (4) τοῦ Ἰσραήλ (masc. gen. sg.), (5) ξένοι (masc. nom. pl.), (6) τῶν διαθηκῶν (fem. gen. pl.), (7) τῆς ἐπαγγελίας (fem. gen. sg.), (8) ἐλπίδα (fem. acc. sg.), (9) ἄθεοι (masc. nom. pl.), (10) τῷ κόσμῳ (masc. dat. sg.).
3. *Translate:* "Therefore, remember . . . that you were at that time without Christ, being alienated from the citizenship of Israel and strangers to the covenants of promise, having no hope and godless in the world."

DAY 52: EPHESIANS 2:13

STEP ONE: **Read** aloud the text at least five times.

νυνὶ δὲ ἐν Χριστῷ Ἰησοῦ ὑμεῖς οἵ ποτε ὄντες μακρὰν ἐγενήθητε
ἐγγὺς ἐν τῷ αἵματι τοῦ Χριστοῦ.

STEP TWO: **Parse** the following verb.

	Lexical Form	Tense	Voice	Mood	Pers.	Num.	Translation
ἐγενήθητε							

STEP THREE: **Identify** the gender, case, and number of the following words.

	Gender	Case	Num.		Gender	Case	Num.
(1) Χριστῷ Ἰησοῦ				(3) τῷ αἵματι			
(2) ὑμεῖς				(4) τοῦ Χριστοῦ			

STEP FOUR: **Translate** the text into understandable English.

> VOCABULARY
>
> νυνί, now
> ποτέ, once, formerly
> μακράν, far (away)
> ἐγγύς, near

STEP FIVE: **Notice** significant exegetical and syntactical insights.

- **νυνὶ δὲ ἐν Χριστῷ Ἰησοῦ ὑμεῖς οἵ ποτε ὄντες μακρὰν ἐγενήθητε ἐγγὺς:** The conjunction δέ is adversative (i.e., best translated "but"), which offers a contrast similar to that found in 2:4 (ὁ δὲ θεός, "but God"). The participle οἵ ὄντες (pres. act. ptc. masc. nom. pl. of εἰμί) functions substantively and is in apposition to ὑμεῖς.

- ἐν τῷ αἵματι τοῦ Χριστοῦ: This prepositional phrase is a dative of means ("*by* his blood"), and the phrase τοῦ Χριστοῦ is a possessive genitive ("by *Christ's* blood").

FOR THE JOURNEY

The metaphors μακράν ("far [away/off]") and ἐγγύς ("near") most likely originated from Isa. 57:19: Εἰρήνην ἐπ᾿ εἰρήνην τοῖς μακρὰν καὶ τοῖς ἐγγὺς οὖσιν· καὶ εἶπεν κύριος Ἰάσομαι αὐτούς (LXX, "Peace upon peace to those far and to those near"; and said the Lord, "I will heal them"). The expression οἵ ποτε ὄντες μακράν ("those who once were far") is a euphemism for Gentile believers. In the OT, Gentile nations are described as being "far off" (Deut. 28:49; 29:22; 1 Kings 8:41; Isa. 5:26; Jer. 5:15) while Israel is described as being "near" (Ps. 148:14). This eschatological inclusion that the Gentiles are now experiencing is "by the blood of Christ." That is, our acceptance into the people of God comes through the sacrificial death of Christ. In Eph. 1:7 Paul indicates that *redemption* is possible through Jesus's "blood." Based on their knowledge, belief, and union with Christ, Gentiles now have been *brought near* to God and to his people.

ANSWER KEY

1. *Parse:* ἐγενήθητε (γίνομαι, aor. pass. ind. 2nd pl.).
2. *Identify:* (1) Χριστῷ Ἰησοῦ (masc. dat. sg.), (2) ὑμεῖς (nom. pl.), (3) τῷ αἵματι (neut. dat. sg.), (4) τοῦ Χριστοῦ (masc. gen. sg.).
3. *Translate:* "But now in Christ Jesus you who were once far have been brought near by the blood of Christ."

DAY 53: EPHESIANS 2:14

STEP ONE: **Read** aloud the text at least five times.

Αὐτὸς γάρ ἐστιν ἡ εἰρήνη ἡμῶν, ὁ ποιήσας τὰ ἀμφότερα ἓν καὶ τὸ μεσότοιχον τοῦ φραγμοῦ λύσας, τὴν ἔχθραν ἐν τῇ σαρκὶ αὐτοῦ.

STEP TWO: **Parse** the following verb.

	Lexical Form	Tense	Voice	Mood	Pers.	Num.	Translation
ἐστιν							

STEP THREE: **Identify** the gender, case, and number of the following words.

	Gender	Case	Num.		Gender	Case	Num.
(1) αὐτός				(6) τὸ μεσότοιχον			
(2) ἡ εἰρήνη				(7) τοῦ φραγμοῦ			
(3) ἡμῶν				(8) τὴν ἔχθραν			
(4) τὰ ἀμφότερα				(9) τῇ σαρκί			
(5) ἕν				(10) αὐτοῦ			

STEP FOUR: **Translate** the text into understandable English.

VOCABULARY

ἀμφότεροι, both
μεσότοιχον, τό, dividing wall
φραγμός, ὁ, wall, fence
λύω, I loose, destroy
ἔχθρα, ἡ, enmity

STEP FIVE: **Notice** significant exegetical and syntactical insights.

- **ὁ ποιήσας τὰ ἀμφότερα ἕν:** The participle ὁ ποιήσας (aor. act. ptc. masc. nom. sg. of ποιέω) functions substantively and is in apposition to αὐτός.

- **καὶ τὸ μεσότοιχον τοῦ φραγμοῦ λύσας:** The term μεσότοιχον ("dividing wall") is used only here in biblical Greek. The term φραγμός ("fence") is in apposition to μεσότοιχον ("the dividing wall, *that is, the fence*"). The participle λύσας (aor. act. ptc. masc. nom. sg. of λύω) functions substantively and is parallel to ὁ ποιήσας through the connective καί.

- **τὴν ἔχθραν ἐν τῇ σαρκὶ αὐτοῦ:** The expression τὴν ἔχθραν is in apposition to τὸ μεσότοιχον ("he destroyed the dividing wall, *that is, the enmity*). It is possible that the prepositional phrase ἐν τῇ σαρκὶ αὐτοῦ modifies either the preceding participle λύσας ("he destroyed *in his flesh* the dividing wall," 2:14) *or* the following participle καταργήσας ("he destroyed the dividing wall . . . by abolishing *in his flesh* the law," 2:15).

FOR THE JOURNEY

Paul declares that Christ has broken down the wall that divides Jew and Gentile. The wall to which Paul is referring here is most likely metaphorical, though outside the NT the term μεσότοιχον is used of a literal wall or fence (see BDAG 635; cf. φραγμός here and in Matt. 21:33; Mark 12:1; Luke 14:23). That is, this wall signifies the Mosaic law, which divided Jews and Gentiles, specifically food laws, Sabbath restrictions, and circumcision. Some have also suggested that Paul has in mind a specific example of this "dividing wall," namely, the wall around the temple separating the Court of Gentiles from the inner courts and the sanctuary. The Jewish historian Josephus describes this wall as being about four and a half feet tall, with warning signs posted all along the wall in both Latin and Greek. Two of the warning signs have been discovered and read as follows: "No foreigner is to enter within the railing and enclosure around the temple. Whoever is caught shall have himself to blame for his consequent death."[1] Paul himself was accused of bringing a Gentile into the inner court (Acts 21:28–29). But because there is doubt as to whether the Gentile Ephesians would have been familiar with the inner wall at the temple that restricted Gentiles to an outer court, and because Paul uses φραγμός, a different term from the one that refers to the wall in the temple inscriptions (τρυφακτός), it is difficult to establish a clear link between Paul's statement in Ephesians and the physical wall at the temple.

ANSWER KEY

1. *Parse:* ἐστιν (εἰμί, pres. act. ind. 3rd sg.).
2. *Identify:* (1) αὐτός (masc. nom. sg.), (2) ἡ εἰρήνη (fem. nom. sg.), (3) ἡμῶν (gen. pl.), (4) τὰ ἀμφότερα (neut. acc. pl.), (5) ἕν (neut. acc. sg.), (6) τὸ μεσότοιχον (neut. acc. sg.), (7) τοῦ φραγμοῦ (masc. gen. sg.), (8) τὴν ἔχθραν (fem. acc. sg.), (9) τῇ σαρκί (fem. dat. sg.), (10) αὐτοῦ (masc. gen. sg.).
3. *Translate:* "For he himself is our peace, who made both one and destroyed the dividing wall, the enmity in his flesh."

1. See Josephus, *Jewish Antiquities* 15.11.5; *Jewish War* 5.5.2. For a photo of the temple warning and its transcription, see https://www.newtestamentredux.com/museum/warning-sign-to-greeks-on-the-temple-mount.

DAY 54: EPHESIANS 2:15–16

STEP ONE: **Read** aloud the text at least five times.

τὸν νόμον τῶν ἐντολῶν ἐν δόγμασιν καταργήσας, ἵνα τοὺς δύο κτίσῃ
ἐν αὐτῷ εἰς ἕνα καινὸν ἄνθρωπον ποιῶν εἰρήνην καὶ ἀποκαταλλάξῃ
τοὺς ἀμφοτέρους ἐν ἑνὶ σώματι τῷ θεῷ διὰ τοῦ σταυροῦ, ἀποκτείνας
τὴν ἔχθραν ἐν αὐτῷ.

STEP TWO: **Parse** the following verbs.

	Lexical Form	Tense	Voice	Mood	Pers.	Num.	Translation
(1) κτίσῃ							
(2) ἀποκαταλλάξῃ							

STEP THREE: **Identify** the gender, case, and number of the following words.

	Gender	Case	Num.		Gender	Case	Num.
(1) τὸν νόμον				(7) εἰρήνην			
(2) τῶν ἐντολῶν				(8) τοὺς ἀμφοτέρους			
(3) δόγμασιν				(9) σώματι			
(4) τοὺς δύο				(10) τῷ θεῷ			
(5) ἕνα				(11) τοῦ σταυροῦ			
(6) ἄνθρωπον				(12) τὴν ἔχθραν			

STEP FOUR: **Translate** the text into understandable English.

VOCABULARY

δόγμα, τό, ordinance, command
καταργέω, I abolish
κτίζω, I create
καινός, new

ἀποκαταλλάσσω, I reconcile
ἀμφότεροι, both
σταυρός, ὁ, cross
ἔχθρα, ἡ, enmity

STEP FIVE: **Notice** significant exegetical and syntactical insights.

* **τὸν νόμον τῶν ἐντολῶν ἐν δόγμασιν καταργήσας:** The noun τῶν ἐντολῶν is in apposition to τὸν νόμον ("the law, *that is*, the commandments") or is a genitive of content ("the law *that contains* commandments"). The participle καταργήσας (aor. act. ptc. masc. nom. sg. of καταργέω) is an adverbial participle of means ("*by* abolishing the law").

* **ἵνα τοὺς δύο κτίσῃ ἐν αὐτῷ εἰς ἕνα καινὸν ἄνθρωπον ποιῶν εἰρήνην:** ἵνα introduces a purpose clause and is followed by the subjunctives κτίσῃ (v. 15) and ἀποκαταλλάξῃ (v. 16). The participle ποιῶν (pres. act. ptc. masc. nom. sg. of ποιέω) is an adverbial participle communicating result ("*resulting in* peace" or "*thereby making* peace").

* **ἀποκτείνας τὴν ἔχθραν ἐν αὐτῷ:** The participle ἀποκτείνας (aor. act. ptc. masc. nom. sg. of ἀποκτείνω) is an adverbial parallel to ποιῶν in verse 15 and communicates result ("*thereby* killing the enmity") or means ("*by means of* killing the enmity"). The prepositional phrase ἐν αὐτῷ communicates means and most likely refers to the cross ("by it") rather than to Christ himself ("by him").

FOR THE JOURNEY

Paul indicates that Christ has abolished the law, but he is not claiming that the law is completely useless or destroyed. Earlier Paul wrote, "Do we then overthrow [καταργέω] the law by this faith? By no means! On the contrary, we uphold the law" (Rom. 3:31 ESV). Instead, Paul is claiming that the Mosaic law, which was tied up with the Mosaic covenant, is set aside. As Thielman rightly notes, "The Mosaic law was still authoritative Scripture with the new people of God, but in a different way than it had been for Israel. It revealed the character of God, the nature of humanity, and the centrality of faith to a right relationship with God, but its commandments no longer governed the behavior of God's people without first passing through the filter of the gospel."[2] Although some have tried to limit Paul's comment to merely the "ceremonial" or

2. Frank Thielman, *Ephesians*, BECNT (Grand Rapids: Baker Academic, 2010), 170.

"civil" aspects of the Mosaic law, it is better to take Paul's reference to the law in its entirety. The author of Hebrews writes, "For when there is a change in the priesthood, there is necessarily a change in the law as well" (Heb. 7:12 ESV). With the coming of Christ, the new high priest, the old law is set aside for "the law of Christ" (Gal. 6:2). The twofold result is the creation of one new person and our reconciliation to God.

ANSWER KEY

1. *Parse:* (1) κτίσῃ (κτίζω, aor. act. subj. 3rd sg.), (2) ἀποκαταλλάξῃ (ἀποκα-ταλλάσσω, aor. act. subj. 3rd sg.).

2. *Identify:* (1) τὸν νόμον (masc. acc. sg.), (2) τῶν ἐντολῶν (fem. gen. pl.), (3) δόγμασιν (neut. dat. pl.), (4) τοὺς δύο (masc. acc. pl.), (5) ἕνα (masc. acc. sg.), (6) ἄνθρωπον (masc. acc. sg.), (7) εἰρήνην (fem. acc. sg.), (8) τοὺς ἀμφοτέρους (masc. acc. pl.), (9) σώματι (neut. dat. sg.), (10) τῷ θεῷ (masc. dat. sg.), (11) τοῦ σταυροῦ (masc. gen. sg.), (12) τὴν ἔχθραν (fem. acc. sg.).

3. *Translate:* ". . . abolishing the law of commands expressed in ordinances, that he might create the two into one new person in himself, making peace, and might reconcile both in one body to God through his cross, killing the enmity by it."

DAY 55: EPHESIANS 2:17–18

STEP ONE: **Read** aloud the text at least five times.

καὶ ἐλθὼν εὐηγγελίσατο εἰρήνην ὑμῖν τοῖς μακρὰν καὶ εἰρήνην τοῖς ἐγγύς· ὅτι δι᾽ αὐτοῦ ἔχομεν τὴν προσαγωγὴν οἱ ἀμφότεροι ἐν ἑνὶ πνεύματι πρὸς τὸν πατέρα.

STEP TWO: **Parse** the following verbs.

	Lexical Form	Tense	Voice	Mood	Pers.	Num.	Translation
(1) εὐηγγελίσατο							
(2) ἔχομεν							

STEP THREE: **Identify** the gender, case, and number of the following words.

	Gender	Case	Num.		Gender	Case	Num.
(1) εἰρήνην				(6) τὴν προσαγωγήν			
(2) ὑμῖν				(7) οἱ ἀμφότεροι			
(3) τοῖς μακράν				(8) πνεύματι			
(4) τοῖς ἐγγύς				(9) τὸν πατέρα			
(5) αὐτοῦ							

STEP FOUR: **Translate** the text into understandable English.

VOCABULARY

μακράν, far (away)
ἐγγύς, near
προσαγωγή, ἡ, access
ἀμφότεροι, both

STEP FIVE: **Notice** significant exegetical and syntactical insights.

- **καὶ ἐλθὼν εὐηγγελίσατο:** The participle ἐλθών (aor. act. ptc. masc. nom. sg. of ἔρχομαι) is either a temporal adverbial participle ("And *when he came*, he preached") or, more likely, a participle of attendant circumstance ("And *he came* and preached").

- **εἰρήνην τοῖς μακρὰν καὶ εἰρήνην τοῖς ἐγγύς:** Paul likely draws from Isa. 52:7 (εὐαγγελιζομένου ἀκοὴν εἰρήνης) and 57:19 (εἰρήνην ἐπ' εἰρήνην τοῖς μακρὰν καὶ τοῖς ἐγγύς). Originally referring to the Jewish people who were far (in exile) and near (in the land), Paul interprets these texts christologically to include the Gentiles. The phrase τοῖς μακρὰν καὶ εἰρήνην τοῖς ἐγγύς is in apposition to ὑμῖν. The article (τοῖς) before the adverbs μακράν and ἐγγύς serves as a substantivizer, turning them into virtual nouns, the first a metaphor for "Gentiles" and the second a metaphor for "Jews."

- **οἱ ἀμφότεροι ἐν ἑνὶ πνεύματι πρὸς τὸν πατέρα:** The phrase οἱ ἀμφότεροι refers to Jews and Gentiles together. Given that the subject of the verb is embedded in the verb ἔχομεν (1st pl., "we"), οἱ ἀμφότεροι is technically in apposition to the implied subject.

FOR THE JOURNEY

In verse 18, Paul offers the reason why peace can be proclaimed to Jews and Gentiles. He states, "For through him we both have access in one Spirit to the Father." In the OT, access was severely restricted. But now, through Christ's atoning death and reconciling work, believers can enter the presence of God. Later in Ephesians, Paul states that in Christ, "we have boldness and access with confidence through our faith in him" (3:12 ESV). A similar passage in Romans connects both "peace" and "access": "Therefore, since we have been justified by faith, we have peace with God through our Lord Jesus Christ. Through him we have also obtained access by faith into this grace in which we stand, and we rejoice in hope of the glory of God" (Rom. 5:1–2 ESV). We should also notice the trinitarian formulation that Paul uses: believers have access through Christ, in the Spirit, with the Father.

ANSWER KEY

1. *Parse:* (1) εὐηγγελίσατο (εὐαγγελίζομαι, aor. mid. ind. 3rd sg.), (2) ἔχομεν (ἔχω, pres. act. ind. 1st pl.).

2. *Identify:* (1) εἰρήνην (fem. acc. sg.), (2) ὑμῖν (dat. pl.), (3) τοῖς μακράν (masc. dat. pl.), (4) τοῖς ἐγγύς (masc. dat. pl.), (5) αὐτοῦ (masc. gen. sg.), (6) τὴν προσαγωγήν (fem. acc. sg.), (7) οἱ ἀμφότεροι (masc. nom. pl.), (8) πνεύματι (neut. dat. sg.), (9) τὸν πατέρα (masc. acc. sg.).

3. *Translate:* "And he came and preached peace to you who were far and peace to those who were near. For through him we both have access in one Spirit to the Father."

ROUTE 12

1 Timothy 2:1–7

STEP ONE: **Read** aloud the text at least five times.

Παρακαλῶ οὖν πρῶτον πάντων ποιεῖσθαι δεήσεις προσευχὰς ἐντεύξεις εὐχαριστίας ὑπὲρ πάντων ἀνθρώπων.

STEP TWO: **Parse** the following verb.

	Lexical Form	Tense	Voice	Mood	Pers.	Num.	Translation
παρακαλῶ							

STEP THREE: **Identify** the gender, case, and number of the following words.

	Gender	Case	Num.		Gender	Case	Num.
(1) πάντων				(4) ἐντεύξεις			
(2) δεήσεις				(5) εὐχαριστίας			
(3) προσευχάς				(6) ἀνθρώπων			

STEP FOUR: **Translate** the text into understandable English.

VOCABULARY

δέησις, ἡ, petition, request

προσευχή, ἡ, prayer

ἔντευξις, ἡ, intercession

εὐχαριστία, ἡ, thanksgiving

STEP FIVE: **Notice** significant exegetical and syntactical insights.

- **Παρακαλῶ οὖν πρῶτον πάντων ποιεῖσθαι:** The infinitive ποιεῖσθαι (pres. mid./pass. inf. of ποιέω) conveys indirect discourse, which is often the case for infinitives after a verb of speech (such as παρακαλέω). "If it is passive, the four accusative nouns would be the subjects of the infinitive; if it is middle, an implied τοὺς ἀνθρώπους would be the subject, and the four nouns would be the objects of the infinitive."[1] The adverb πρῶτον indicates something of first importance and therefore draws attention to what follows.

- **δεήσεις προσευχὰς ἐντεύξεις εὐχαριστίας:** These four terms are either the subject of the infinitive ποιεῖσθαι (if it is passive) or the direct objects (if it is middle). They are near synonyms, but all convey a slightly different nuance: (1) δέησις refers to making requests for specific needs; (2) προσευχή is a general term for all prayers; (3) ἔντευξις involves appealing to an authority on behalf of someone else; and (4) εὐχαριστία is a prayer of thanksgiving. The piling up of these terms is a rhetorical feature that emphasizes the importance of prayer.

- **ὑπὲρ πάντων ἀνθρώπων:** In the context, ἄνθρωπος refers to human beings (not only males) and is inclusive, denoting all people without distinction (not all people without exception).

---

1. Larry J. Perkins, *The Pastoral Letters*, BHGNT (Waco: Baylor University Press, 2017), 30.

FOR THE JOURNEY

Prayer is emphasized throughout the Bible. Old Testament saints often engaged in prayer, especially in the Psalms. Prayer was central in the synagogue. The Gospels likewise highlight the importance of prayer. The Jews prayed regularly, John the Baptist taught his disciples to pray (Luke 11:1), and Jesus often prayed. Paul prays for others (Phil. 1:9; Col. 1:3, 9; 2 Thess. 1:11) and requests that others pray for him (Eph. 6:18–20; Col. 4:3; 2 Thess. 3:1). In today's verse, Paul emphasizes prayer in several ways. First, Paul does not use the imperative of προσεύχομαι (as in 1 Thess. 5:25; 2 Thess. 3:1; cf. Eph. 6:18); instead, he uses a verb of exhortation plus an infinitive (παρακαλῶ + ποιεῖσθαι; cf. 1 Tim. 2:8, βούλομαι + προσεύχεσθαι). This construction adds urgency to the request. Second, the adverb πρῶτον conveys something of utmost importance. Third, the fourfold types of prayer further indicate that Christians should be fervent in prayer. Furthermore, our prayers should never be restricted so that certain groups are not included in our prayers. Prayers with the characteristics listed here please God.

ANSWER KEY

1. *Parse:* παρακαλῶ (παρακαλέω, pres. act. ind. 1st sg.).
2. *Identify:* (1) πάντων (neut. gen. pl.), (2) δεήσεις (fem. acc. pl.), (3) προσευχάς (fem. acc. pl.), (4) ἐντεύξεις (fem. acc. pl.), (5) εὐχαριστίας (fem. acc. pl.), (6) ἀνθρώπων (masc. gen. pl.).
3. *Translate:* "Therefore, I urge first of all that petitions, prayers, intercessions, and thanksgivings be made for all people."

DAY 57: 1 TIMOTHY 2:2

STEP ONE: **Read** aloud the text at least five times.

ὑπὲρ βασιλέων καὶ πάντων τῶν ἐν ὑπεροχῇ ὄντων, ἵνα ἤρεμον καὶ ἡσύχιον βίον διάγωμεν ἐν πάσῃ εὐσεβείᾳ καὶ σεμνότητι.

STEP TWO: **Parse** the following verb.

	Lexical Form	Tense	Voice	Mood	Pers.	Num.	Translation
διάγωμεν							

STEP THREE: **Identify** the gender, case, and number of the following words.

	Gender	Case	Num.		Gender	Case	Num.
(1) βασιλέων				(6) βίον			
(2) πάντων				(7) πάσῃ			
(3) ὑπεροχῇ				(8) εὐσεβείᾳ			
(4) ἤρεμον				(9) σεμνότητι			
(5) ἡσύχιον							

STEP FOUR: **Translate** the text into understandable English.

_____

_____

VOCABULARY

ὑπεροχή, ἡ, authority
ἤρεμος, tranquil, peaceful
ἡσύχιος, quiet
βίος, ὁ, life
διάγω, I live
εὐσέβεια, ἡ, godliness
σεμνότης, ἡ, holiness, dignity

STEP FIVE: **Notice** significant exegetical and syntactical insights.

- **ὑπὲρ βασιλέων καὶ πάντων τῶν ἐν ὑπεροχῇ ὄντων:** This prepositional phrase is an explanation (subset) of the previous prepositional phrase in verse 1 (ὑπὲρ πάντων ἀνθρώπων). In other words, the "all people" includes "kings and all those who are in authority." The participle ὄντων (pres. act. ptc. masc. gen. pl. of εἰμί) functions substantively (the article τῶν modifies ὄντων with the prepositional phrase ἐν ὑπεροχῇ sandwiched in between).

- **ἵνα ἤρεμον καὶ ἡσύχιον βίον διάγωμεν:** ἵνα introduces a purpose clause and is followed by the subjunctive mood (διάγωμεν). The adjective ἤρεμος is a NT *hapax legomenon* (i.e., occurs only once), and ἡσύχιος occurs only here and in 1 Pet. 3:4 (referring to a woman's quiet spirit). Regarding the first term, George Knight helpfully comments, "An evaluation of Paul's own life leads one to realize that this 'quiet' does not mean a sheltered life but rather freedom from the turmoil that threatened to thwart his ministry."[2]

- **ἐν πάσῃ εὐσεβείᾳ καὶ σεμνότητι:** The noun εὐσέβεια occurs 15 times in the NT, with 10 of these occurring in the Pastoral Epistles (and 8 in 1 Timothy). "It includes the active, daily decision to pursue a life of godliness in conformity with the gospel" (Perkins, *Pastoral Letters*, 32). The noun σεμνότης occurs less frequently (only 3 times in the NT, all in the Pastoral Epistles: 1 Tim. 3:4; Titus 2:7).

FOR THE JOURNEY

Paul exhorts Christians to pray for all types of people, including kings and those in authority. Both Paul (Rom. 13:1; Titus 3:1) and Peter (2 Pet. 2:13–17) encourage obedience and respect to governing authorities. At the time when Paul wrote 1 Timothy, it is likely that Nero (AD 54–68) was emperor of Rome. But we are not only called to obey and respect our leaders; we are also called to pray for them. Although we may call some "kings," there is only one "King of kings and Lord of lords" who reigns supreme over all (1 Tim. 6:15). As Proverbs reminds us, "By

2. George W. Knight III, *The Pastoral Epistles*, NIGTC (Grand Rapids: Eerdmans, 1992), 117.

[God] kings reign, and rulers decree what is just" (Prov. 8:15 ESV), and "The king's heart is a stream of water in the hand of the LORD; he turns it wherever he will" (Prov. 21:1 ESV). We need to engage the world to fulfill the commission that Jesus gave to his church, to "make disciples of all nations" (Matt. 28:19–20). In doing so, we need to pray for God's favor so that the gospel can go forth unhindered.

ANSWER KEY

1. *Parse:* διάγωμεν (διάγω, pres. act. subj. 1st pl.).
2. *Identify:* (1) βασιλέων (masc. gen. pl.), (2) πάντων (masc. gen. pl.), (3) ὑπεροχῇ (fem. dat. sg.), (4) ἤρεμον (masc. acc. sg.), (5) ἡσύχιον (masc. acc. sg.), (6) βίον (masc. acc. sg.), (7) πάσῃ (fem. dat. sg.), (8) εὐσεβείᾳ (fem. dat. sg.), (9) σεμνότητι (fem. dat. sg.).
3. *Translate:* ". . . for kings and all who are in authority, that we might lead a peaceful and quiet life, with all godliness and dignity."

DAY 58: 1 TIMOTHY 2:3–4

STEP ONE: **Read** aloud the text at least five times.

τοῦτο καλὸν καὶ ἀπόδεκτον ἐνώπιον τοῦ σωτῆρος ἡμῶν θεοῦ, ὃς πάντας ἀνθρώπους θέλει σωθῆναι καὶ εἰς ἐπίγνωσιν ἀληθείας ἐλθεῖν.

STEP TWO: **Parse** the following verb.

	Lexical Form	Tense	Voice	Mood	Pers.	Num.	Translation
θέλει							

STEP THREE: **Identify** the gender, case, and number of the following words.

	Gender	Case	Num.		Gender	Case	Num.
(1) τοῦτο				(7) ὅς			
(2) καλόν				(8) πάντας			
(3) ἀπόδεκτον				(9) ἀνθρώπους			
(4) τοῦ σωτῆρος				(10) ἐπίγνωσιν			
(5) ἡμῶν				(11) ἀληθείας			
(6) θεοῦ							

STEP FOUR: **Translate** the text into understandable English.

VOCABULARY
ἀπόδεκτος, acceptable
σωτήρ, ὁ, savior
ἐπίγνωσις, ἡ, knowledge

STEP FIVE: **Notice** significant exegetical and syntactical insights.

- **τοῦτο καλὸν καὶ ἀπόδεκτον ἐνώπιον τοῦ σωτῆρος ἡμῶν θεοῦ:** The near demonstrative pronoun τοῦτο ("this") refers back to verse

1 and the exhortation to pray for all people (which is pleasing to God). The verb εἰμί is implied ("This [is] good").

- **ὃς πάντας ἀνθρώπους θέλει σωθῆναι:** The phrase πάντας ἀνθρώπους ("all men") corresponds to verse 1 (ὑπὲρ πάντων ἀνθρώπων) and refers to all categories of people (all without distinction, not all without exception) and is the accusative subject of the two following infinitives. The verb σωθῆναι (aor. pass. inf. of σῴζω) is a complementary infinitive, completing the verb θέλει ("he desires *to save*").

- **καὶ εἰς ἐπίγνωσιν ἀληθείας ἐλθεῖν:** It is possible that the conjunction καί functions epexegetically (and thus translated "that is"), meaning that the two phrases essentially state the same truth ("to be saved, that is, to come to a knowledge of the truth"). The verb ἐλθεῖν (aor. act. inf. of ἔρχομαι) is a complementary infinitive, completing the verb θέλει ("He [God] desires all people *to come* to a knowledge of the truth").

FOR THE JOURNEY

In these verses, Paul offers the first of two reasons why we should pray for all types of peoples: (1) because it is pleasing to God and (2) because God desires them to be saved. First, praying for all peoples is good and pleasing to God. God delights in saving sinners, even the worst of sinners, like Paul himself (1 Tim. 1:15). Later, Paul states that God "is the Savior of all people, especially of those who believe" (1 Tim. 4:10 ESV). In Titus he states that "the grace of God has appeared, bringing salvation for all people" (2:11 ESV). Second, praying for all peoples is fitting because God desires all types of peoples to be saved. Robert Yarbrough comments, "With respect to 'all people' . . . being saved, one likely stress, given the history of Paul's missionary efforts, is that God's saving promise fulfilled in Christ is not just for this or that people group but for all people, Jew and Gentile and any other people that could be named."[3] It is possible that some in the Ephesian church were purposefully limiting their prayers and not praying for some groups, but Paul's response is that such limitations do not line up with God's desire.

3. Robert W. Yarbrough, *The Letters to Timothy and Titus*, PNTC (Grand Rapids: Eerdmans, 2018), 152.

ANSWER KEY

1. *Parse:* θέλει (θέλω, pres. act. ind. 3rd sg.).

2. *Identify:* (1) τοῦτο (neut. nom. sg.), (2) καλόν (neut. nom. sg.), (3) ἀπόδε-κτον (neut. nom. sg.), (4) τοῦ σωτῆρος (masc. gen. sg.), (5) ἡμῶν (gen. pl.), (6) θεοῦ (masc. gen. sg.), (7) ὅς (masc. nom. sg.), (8) πάντας (masc. acc. pl.), (9) ἀνθρώπους (masc. acc. pl.), (10) ἐπίγνωσιν (fem. acc. sg.), (11) ἀληθείας (fem. gen. sg.).

3. *Translate:* "This is good and pleasing before God our Savior, who desires all people to be saved and to come to a knowledge of the truth."

175

DAY 59: 1 TIMOTHY 2:5–6

STEP ONE: **Read** aloud the text at least five times.

εἷς γὰρ θεός, εἷς καὶ μεσίτης θεοῦ καὶ ἀνθρώπων, ἄνθρωπος Χριστὸς Ἰησοῦς, ὁ δοὺς ἑαυτὸν ἀντίλυτρον ὑπὲρ πάντων, τὸ μαρτύριον καιροῖς ἰδίοις.

STEP TWO: **Parse** any verbs.
There are no verbs.

STEP THREE: **Identify** the gender, case, and number of the following words.

	Gender	Case	Num.		Gender	Case	Num.
(1) εἷς				(7) ἑαυτόν			
(2) θεός				(8) ἀντίλυτρον			
(3) μεσίτης				(9) πάντων			
(4) θεοῦ				(10) τὸ μαρτύριον			
(5) ἀνθρώπων				(11) καιροῖς			
(6) Χριστὸς Ἰησοῦς				(12) ἰδίοις			

STEP FOUR: **Translate** the text into understandable English.

_____

_____

VOCABULARY

μεσίτης, ὁ, mediator
ἀντίλυτρον, τό, ransom
μαρτύριον, τό, testimony

STEP FIVE: **Notice** significant exegetical and syntactical insights.

- **εἷς καὶ μεσίτης θεοῦ καὶ ἀνθρώπων, ἄνθρωπος Χριστὸς Ἰησοῦς:** The noun μεσίτης requires the following noun to be the genitive case ("one mediator *between God* and *men*"). The noun ἄνθρωπος is in apposition to μεσίτης, emphasizing the human nature of the mediator (and Χριστὸς Ἰησοῦς is in apposition to ἄνθρωπος).

- **ὁ δοὺς ἑαυτὸν ἀντίλυτρον ὑπὲρ πάντων:** The participle δούς (aor. act. ptc. masc. nom. sg. of δίδωμι) functions substantively ("the one who gave"). The noun ἀντίλυτρον functions as a double accusative along with ἑαυτόν ("the one who gave himself *as a ransom*"). "δίδωμι is one of many verbs in Greek that can take a double accusative, in which one is the direct object and the other the complement that adds information about the object" (Perkins, *Pastoral Letters*, 35).

- **τὸ μαρτύριον καιροῖς ἰδίοις:** This phrase (in particular, τὸ μαρτύριον) is in apposition to Christ's ransom (ἀντίλυτρον) for all people. Although the phrase καιροῖς ἰδίοις is plural, this idiomatic usage can refer to a specific time frame. Consequently, it is often translated as a singular form ("the proper time").

FOR THE JOURNEY

Paul offers two more reasons why we should pray for all types of peoples: (1) because God is one and (2) because there is only one mediator. First, we should pray for all peoples because there is one God. The opening phrase of verse 5 (εἷς γὰρ θεός) is reminiscent of the OT Shema: "Hear, O Israel: The LORD our God, the LORD is one" (Deut. 6:4 NIV; see also Rom. 3:29–30; 1 Cor. 8:6). We pray for all peoples because salvation is only by the God of Israel. Second, the only way to be reconciled to this one God is through the atonement secured by Christ. Because he is the only mediator between sinful humanity and a holy God, it is imperative that believers extend their prayers to include all peoples. Knight helpfully summarizes, "So step-by-step from monotheism to the gospel itself Paul has argued that it is self-evident that God desires all people, Jew and Gentile, slave and free, ruled and ruler, etc., to be saved, and that such a perspective should elicit our prayers for all people" (*Pastoral Epistles*, 121).

ANSWER KEY

1. *Parse:* No verbs to parse.
2. *Identify:* (1) εἷς (masc. nom. sg.), (2) θεός (masc. nom. sg.), (3) μεσίτης (masc. nom. sg.), (4) θεοῦ (masc. gen. sg.), (5) ἀνθρώπων (masc. gen. pl.), (6) Χριστὸς Ἰησοῦς (masc. nom. sg.), (7) ἑαυτόν (masc. acc. sg.), (8) ἀντίλυτρον (neut. acc. sg.), (9) πάντων (masc. gen. pl.), (10) τὸ μαρτύριον (neut. nom. sg.), (11) καιροῖς (masc. dat. pl.), (12) ἰδίοις (masc. dat. pl.).
3. *Translate:* "For there is one God, and one mediator between God and men, the man Christ Jesus, who gave himself as a ransom for all, the testimony at the proper time."

DAY 60: 1 TIMOTHY 2:7

STEP ONE: **Read** aloud the text at least five times.

εἰς ὃ ἐτέθην ἐγὼ κῆρυξ καὶ ἀπόστολος, ἀλήθειαν λέγω οὐ ψεύδομαι,
διδάσκαλος ἐθνῶν ἐν πίστει καὶ ἀληθείᾳ.

STEP TWO: **Parse** the following verbs.

	Lexical Form	Tense	Voice	Mood	Pers.	Num.	Translation
(1) ἐτέθην							
(2) λέγω							
(3) ψεύδομαι							

STEP THREE: **Identify** the gender, case, and number of the following words.

	Gender	Case	Num.		Gender	Case	Num.
(1) ὅ				(6) διδάσκαλος			
(2) ἐγώ				(7) ἐθνῶν			
(3) κῆρυξ				(8) πίστει			
(4) ἀπόστολος				(9) ἀληθείᾳ			
(5) ἀλήθειαν							

STEP FOUR: **Translate** the text into understandable English.

VOCABULARY

κῆρυξ, ὁ, herald
ψεύδομαι, I lie

STEP FIVE: **Notice** significant exegetical and syntactical insights.

- εἰς ὃ ἐτέθην ἐγὼ κῆρυξ καὶ ἀπόστολος: The verb ἐτέθην is a divine passive, with the implied agent being God or, more specifically, Jesus Christ (see 1 Tim. 1:1). The term κῆρυξ ("herald") appears only here and in 2 Tim. 1:11 (εἰς ὃ ἐτέθην ἐγὼ κῆρυξ καὶ ἀπόστολος καὶ διδάσκαλος) and in 2 Pet. 2:5 (referring to Abraham, "a herald of righteousness"). A κῆρυξ "was the crier of the public sales and of official actions such as taxes; he announced the beginning of the public games, the name of each participant, and the name of the winner's father. He announced the orders of the king and the king's arrival."[4]

- ἀλήθειαν λέγω οὐ ψεύδομαι: This phrase could support Paul's claim that he is a herald and apostle (looking back) or his claim that he is a teacher to the Gentiles (looking forward). If the latter is the case,[5] then Paul is again emphasizing the need for the church to pray for all, including Gentiles. God desires their salvation, Christ died for them and is their mediator, and Paul is appointed by God to preach the gospel to them.

- διδάσκαλος ἐθνῶν ἐν πίστει καὶ ἀληθείᾳ: The noun ἐθνῶν is an objective genitive (a teacher of the Gentiles = Paul teaches the Gentiles).

FOR THE JOURNEY

In this verse we are given the final argument as to why Christians should pray for all peoples: because God himself has appointed Paul to the task of reaching the various groups of Gentiles. Although Paul preaches the gospel "to the Jew first and also to the Greek" (Rom. 1:16 ESV), he concentrates his efforts on reaching Gentiles. Through Christ, he "received grace and apostleship to bring about the obedience of faith for the sake of his name among all the nations" (1:5 ESV). He wants to visit the (mostly Gentile) Christians in Rome so that he may "reap some harvest among you as well as among the rest of the Gentiles" (1:13 ESV). He calls himself "an apostle to the Gentiles" (11:13 ESV)

---

4. William D. Mounce, *Pastoral Epistles*, WBC 46 (Nashville: Nelson, 2000), 92.
5. This is the view of Mounce, *Pastoral Epistles*, 91–92.

and confesses that God's grace was given to him "to be a minister of Christ Jesus to the Gentiles" (15:16 ESV). Through Christ, Paul was able "to bring the Gentiles to obedience" (15:18 ESV) and "to bring about the obedience of faith" (16:26 ESV). Finally, at the end of his life, Paul reminds Timothy how "the Lord stood by me and strengthened me, so that through me the message might be fully proclaimed and all the Gentiles might hear it" (2 Tim. 4:17 ESV). Believers should pray for all peoples, as witnessed in the life and ministry of the apostle Paul.

ANSWER KEY

1. *Parse:* (1) ἐτέθην (τίθημι, aor. pass. ind. 1st sg.), (2) λέγω (λέγω, pres. act. ind. 1st sg.), (3) ψεύδομαι (ψεύδομαι, pres. mid. ind. 1st sg.).

2. *Identify:* (1) ὅ (neut. acc. sg.), (2) ἐγώ (nom. sg.), (3) κῆρυξ (masc. nom. sg.), (4) ἀπόστολος (masc. nom. sg.), (5) ἀλήθειαν (fem. acc. sg.), (6) διδάσκαλος (masc. nom. sg.), (7) ἐθνῶν (neut. gen. pl.), (8) πίστει (fem. dat. sg.), (9) ἀληθείᾳ (fem. dat. sg.).

3. *Translate:* ". . . for which I was appointed a herald and apostle—I am speaking the truth, I am not lying—a teacher of the Gentiles in faith and truth."

Journey 3

DIFFICULT

ROUTE 13

Mark 8:31–37

DAY 61: MARK 8:31

STEP ONE: **Read** aloud the text at least five times.

Καὶ ἤρξατο διδάσκειν αὐτοὺς ὅτι δεῖ τὸν υἱὸν τοῦ ἀνθρώπου πολλὰ παθεῖν καὶ ἀποδοκιμασθῆναι ὑπὸ τῶν πρεσβυτέρων καὶ τῶν ἀρχιερέων καὶ τῶν γραμματέων καὶ ἀποκτανθῆναι καὶ μετὰ τρεῖς ἡμέρας ἀναστῆναι.

STEP TWO: **Parse** the following verbs.

	Lexical Form	Tense	Voice	Mood	Pers.	Num.	Translation
(1) ἤρξατο							
(2) δεῖ							

STEP THREE: **Identify** the gender, case, and number of the following words.

	Gender	Case	Num.		Gender	Case	Num.
(1) αὐτούς				(5) τῶν πρεσβυτέρων			
(2) τὸν υἱόν				(6) τῶν ἀρχιερέων			
(3) τοῦ ἀνθρώπου				(7) τῶν γραμματέων			
(4) πολλά				(8) ἡμέρας			

STEP FOUR: **Translate** the text into understandable English.

VOCABULARY

πάσχω, I suffer, endure
ἀποδοκιμάζω, I reject

STEP FIVE: **Notice** significant exegetical and syntactical insights.

- **Καὶ ἤρξατο διδάσκειν αὐτούς:** Mark's use of ἤρξατο (from ἄρχομαι) grabs the reader's attention and signals a transition in Jesus's teaching as he begins to predict his suffering and death in Jerusalem. The verb διδάσκειν (pres. act. inf. of διδάσκω) is a complementary infinitive since it completes the thought of the previous verb ("he began *to teach*").

- **δεῖ τὸν υἱὸν τοῦ ἀνθρώπου πολλὰ παθεῖν καὶ ἀποδοκιμασθῆναι . . . καὶ ἀποκτανθῆναι καὶ . . . ἀναστῆναι:** This phrase contains a series of complementary infinitives, with the accusative τὸν υἱόν functioning as the subject of the infinitives: "The Son of Man must suffer [παθεῖν, pres. act. inf. of πάσχω] . . . and be rejected [ἀποδοκιμασθῆναι, aor. pass. inf. of ἀποδοκιμάζω] and be killed [ἀποκτανθῆναι, aor. pass. inf. of ἀποκτείνω] . . . and to rise [ἀναστῆναι, aor. act. inf. of ἀνίστημι]." It is also possible to view the τὸν υἱόν as an accusative of respect (reference) and the infinitives as the subjects of δεῖ: "For the Son of Man to suffer . . . and be rejected . . . and be killed . . . and to rise *is necessary.*"

186

FOR THE JOURNEY

In this verse, Jesus predicts his suffering, death, and resurrection. This reference is the first of three times that he speaks to his disciples this "passion prediction" (see also 9:31; 10:33–34). It was not accidental or a series of unfortunate events that caused Jesus's crucifixion. Mark's use of the word δεῖ ("must," "it is necessary") indicates that this was part of God's divine plan and predicted in the OT. Although other passages are significant (see Pss. 22; 69; 118:22; Zech. 9–14), Isa. 52:13–53:12 is perhaps the clearest. Isaiah prophesies regarding a messianic servant of God who would suffer and even die to restore God's people. And so here in Mark, Jesus announces to his confused disciples that he will allow himself to be rejected, beaten, crucified, and killed. But Jesus leaves his disciples on a note of hope (even if they don't fully comprehend his words). He continues by mentioning his resurrection on the third day. Jesus was faithful to obey his heavenly Father, to suffer for the sins of others, to die as a substitute for his people. And all of that was purposeful because death could not keep him, and the grave could not hold him.

ANSWER KEY

1. *Parse:* (1) ἤρξατο (ἄρχομαι, aor. mid. ind. 3rd sg.), (2) δεῖ (δεῖ, pres. act. ind. 3rd sg.).

2. *Identify:* (1) αὐτοῖς (masc. acc. pl.), (2) τὸν υἱὸν (masc. acc. sg.), (3) τοῦ ἀνθρώπου (masc. gen. sg.), (4) πολλά (neut. acc. pl.), (5) τῶν πρεσβυτέρων (masc. gen. pl.), (6) τῶν ἀρχιερέων (masc. gen. pl.), (7) τῶν γραμματέων (masc. gen. pl.), (8) ἡμέρας (fem. acc. pl.).

3. *Translate:* "And he began to teach them that the Son of Man must suffer many things and be rejected by the elders and the chief priests and the scribes and be killed and after three days to rise."

187

DAY 62: MARK 8:32–33

STEP ONE: **Read** aloud the text at least five times.

καὶ παρρησίᾳ τὸν λόγον ἐλάλει. καὶ προσλαβόμενος ὁ Πέτρος αὐτὸν ἤρξατο ἐπιτιμᾶν αὐτῷ. ὁ δὲ ἐπιστραφεὶς καὶ ἰδὼν τοὺς μαθητὰς αὐτοῦ ἐπετίμησεν Πέτρῳ καὶ λέγει, Ὕπαγε ὀπίσω μου, Σατανᾶ, ὅτι οὐ φρονεῖς τὰ τοῦ θεοῦ ἀλλὰ τὰ τῶν ἀνθρώπων.

STEP TWO: **Parse** the following verbs.

	Lexical Form	Tense	Voice	Mood	Pers.	Num.	Translation
(1) ἐλάλει							
(2) ἤρξατο							
(3) ἐπετίμησεν							
(4) λέγει							
(5) ὕπαγε							
(6) φρονεῖς							

STEP THREE: **Identify** the gender, case, and number of the following words.

	Gender	Case	Num.		Gender	Case	Num.
(1) παρρησίᾳ				(7) αὐτοῦ			
(2) τὸν λόγον				(8) Πέτρῳ			
(3) ὁ Πέτρος				(9) μου			
(4) αὐτόν				(10) τά			
(5) αὐτῷ				(11) τοῦ θεοῦ			
(6) τοὺς μαθητάς				(12) τῶν ἀνθρώπων			

STEP FOUR: **Translate** the text into understandable English.

STEP FIVE: Notice significant exegetical and syntactical insights.

• **καὶ προσλαβόμενος ὁ Πέτρος αὐτὸν ἤρξατο ἐπιτιμᾶν αὐτῷ:** The adverbial participle προσλαβόμενος (aor. mid. ptc. masc. nom. sg. of προσλαμβάνω) is used temporally ("and after taking him aside . . ."). The verb ἐπιτιμᾶν (pres. act. inf. of ἐπιτιμάω) is a complementary infinitive ("he began *to rebuke*"). The pronoun αὐτῷ is a dative direct object since the verb ἐπιτιμάω takes its objects in the dative (not accusative) case (see also Πέτρῳ in the following sentence).

• **ὁ δὲ ἐπιστραφεὶς καὶ ἰδὼν τοὺς μαθητὰς αὐτοῦ:** The adverbial participles ἐπιστραφείς (aor. pass. ptc. masc. nom. sg. of ἐπιστρέφω) and ἰδών (aor. act. ptc. masc. nom. sg. of βλέπω/ὁράω) are used temporally ("and after/when he turned and saw his disciples").

• **ὅτι οὐ φρονεῖς τὰ τοῦ θεοῦ ἀλλὰ τὰ τῶν ἀνθρώπων:** The article τά functions as a substantivizer, turning the following genitive constructions into substantives ("the things of God . . . the things of men").

FOR THE JOURNEY

The "word" (λόγος) that Jesus begins to speak to his disciples is his shocking pronouncement that he will suffer, be killed, and rise on the third day—a message that Jesus now speaks "plainly" (παρρησίᾳ) with his disciples, no longer in parables. Thinking that Jesus must be misguided or confused, Peter "rebukes" (ἐπιτιμάω) Jesus. But Jesus turns the tables on Peter (and the rest of the disciples) and "rebukes" him (ἐπιτιμάω). Such thinking, according to Jesus, is not just indifferent to God's plan but actually contrary to it. "By opposing the will of God (δεῖ) for his Messiah, Peter and those with him are acting as spokesmen of God's ultimate enemy" (i.e., Satan).[1] God's ways are not our ways, and his thoughts are not our thoughts (cf. Isa. 55:8). Jesus establishes his kingdom through his sufferings.

ANSWER KEY

1. *Parse:* (1) ἐλάλει (λαλέω, impf. act. ind. 3rd sg.), (2) ἤρξατο (ἄρχομαι, aor. mid. ind. 3rd sg.), (3) ἐπετίμησεν (ἐπιτιμάω, aor. act. ind. 3rd sg.), (4) λέγει (λέγω, pres. act. ind. 3rd sg.), (5) ὕπαγε (ὑπάγω, pres. act. impv. 2nd sg.), (6) φρονεῖς (φρονέω, pres. act. ind. 2nd sg.).

2. *Identify:* (1) παρρησίᾳ (fem. dat. sg.), (2) τὸν λόγον (masc. acc. sg.), (3) ὁ Πέτρος (masc. nom. sg.), (4) αὐτόν (masc. acc. sg.), (5) αὐτῷ (masc. dat. sg.), (6) τοὺς μαθητάς (masc. acc. pl.), (7) αὐτοῦ (masc. gen. sg.), (8) Πέτρῳ (masc. dat. sg.), (9) μου (gen. sg.), (10) τά (neut. acc. pl.), (11) τοῦ θεοῦ (masc. gen. sg.), (12) τῶν ἀνθρώπων (masc. gen. pl.).

3. *Translate:* "And he was speaking the word with boldness (openly). And taking him aside, Peter began to rebuke him. But turning and seeing his disciples, he rebuked Peter and said, 'Go behind me, Satan, because you are not thinking about the things of God but the things of men.'"

1. R. T. France, *The Gospel of Mark*, NIGTC (Grand Rapids: Eerdmans, 2002), 338.

DAY 63: MARK 8:34

STEP ONE: **Read** aloud the text at least five times.

Καὶ προσκαλεσάμενος τὸν ὄχλον σὺν τοῖς μαθηταῖς αὐτοῦ εἶπεν αὐτοῖς, Εἴ τις θέλει ὀπίσω μου ἀκολουθεῖν, ἀπαρνησάσθω ἑαυτὸν καὶ ἀράτω τὸν σταυρὸν αὐτοῦ καὶ ἀκολουθείτω μοι.

STEP TWO: **Parse** the following verbs.

	Lexical Form	Tense	Voice	Mood	Pers.	Num.	Translation
(1) εἶπεν							
(2) θέλει							
(3) ἀπαρνησάσθω							
(4) ἀράτω							
(5) ἀκολουθείτω							

STEP THREE: **Identify** the gender, case, and number of the following words.

	Gender	Case	Num.		Gender	Case	Num.
(1) τὸν ὄχλον				(6) μου			
(2) τοῖς μαθηταῖς				(7) ἑαυτόν			
(3) αὐτοῦ				(8) τὸν σταυρόν			
(4) αὐτοῖς				(9) μοι			
(5) τις							

STEP FOUR: **Translate** the text into understandable English.

VOCABULARY

προσκαλέω, I call, summon
ὀπίσω, behind, after

ἀπαρνέομαι, I deny
σταυρός, ὁ, cross

STEP FIVE: **Notice** significant exegetical and syntactical insights.

- **Καὶ προσκαλεσάμενος τὸν ὄχλον:** The adverbial participle προσ-καλεσάμενος (aor. mid. ptc. masc. nom. sg. of προσκαλέω) is used temporally ("and after he called the crowd . . .").

- **Εἴ τις θέλει ὀπίσω μου ἀκολουθεῖν:** The verb ἀκολουθεῖν (pres. act. inf. of ἀκολουθέω) is a complementary infinitive ("wants *to follow*").

- **ἀπαρνησάσθω ἑαυτὸν καὶ ἀράτω τὸν σταυρὸν αὐτοῦ καὶ ἀκο-λουθείτω μοι:** Why is there a change in tense-form for the three imperatives: ἀπαρνησάσθω (aor.) . . . ἀράτω (aor.) . . . ἀκολουθείτω (present)?[2] Based on their lexical meanings, some verbs naturally prefer one tense-form over another. If a verb typically takes a short time to complete or has a natural ending, it prefers the aorist, such as with the verb ἀπαρνέομαι ("deny") and αἴρω ("take up"). Conversely, if a verb has no natural ending point, then it prefers the present. The evidence bears this out: ἀπαρνέομαι occurs twice as an aorist imperative and never as a present imperative, and αἴρω occurs 22 times as an aorist imperative and only 4 times as a present imperative. In contrast, verbs of motion occur almost exclusively in the present tense-form in the imperative mood. For instance, ἀκολουθέω occurs 16 times as a present imperative and only twice as an aorist imperative. Thus, the tense-form of the verbs used are the expected ones that carry no special nuance. The pronoun μοι is a dative of direct object since the verb ἀκολουθέω takes its direct object in the dative case.

---

2. For a more detailed explanation of this question, see Benjamin L. Merkle, *Exegetical Gems from Biblical Greek: A Refreshing Guide to Grammar and Interpretation* (Grand Rapids: Baker Academic, 2019), 53–56.

FOR THE JOURNEY

Speaking to his disciples and to the crowd, Jesus explains what it means to follow him: a person must (1) deny himself, (2) take up his cross, and (3) follow Jesus. To deny oneself "does not mean to live a life of self-denial or self-discipline. It is to renounce your claim to yourself—desires, ambitions, personal goals—and to submit to Christ as his slave."[3] It is not merely the denial of certain things but the denial of one's very self. The metaphor "take up one's cross" also means more than just enduring hardship patiently: it is primarily a call to be willing to follow Jesus in suffering and even death. This is a radical call of discipleship. The call is great, but the One we follow is even greater!

ANSWER KEY

1. *Parse:* (1) εἶπεν (λέγω, aor. act. ind. 3rd sg.), (2) θέλει (θέλω, pres. act. ind. 3rd sg.), (3) ἀπαρνησάσθω (ἀπαρνέομαι, aor. mid. impv. 3rd sg.), (4) ἀράτω (αἴρω, aor. act. impv. 3rd sg.), (5) ἀκολουθείτω (ἀκολουθέω, pres. act. impv. 3rd sg.).

2. *Identify:* (1) τὸν ὄχλον (masc. acc. sg.), (2) τοῖς μαθηταῖς (masc. dat. pl.), (3) αὐτοῦ (masc. gen. sg.), (4) αὐτοῖς (masc. dat. pl.), (5) τις (masc. nom. sg.), (6) μου (gen. sg.), (7) ἑαυτόν (masc. acc. sg.), (8) τὸν σταυρόν (masc. acc. sg.), (9) μοι (dat. sg.).

3. *Translate:* "And calling the crowd along with his disciples, he said to them, 'If anyone wants to follow after me, he must deny himself and take (up) his cross and follow me.'"

3. Mark L. Strauss, *Mark*, ZECNT (Grand Rapids: Zondervan, 2014), 372.

DAY 64: MARK 8:35

STEP ONE: **Read** aloud the text at least five times.

ὃς γὰρ ἐὰν θέλῃ τὴν ψυχὴν αὐτοῦ σῶσαι ἀπολέσει αὐτήν· ὃς δ᾽ ἂν ἀπολέσει τὴν ψυχὴν αὐτοῦ ἕνεκεν ἐμοῦ καὶ τοῦ εὐαγγελίου σώσει αὐτήν.

STEP TWO: **Parse** the following verbs.

	Lexical Form	Tense	Voice	Mood	Pers.	Num.	Translation
(1) θέλῃ							
(2) ἀπολέσει							
(3) σώσει							

STEP THREE: **Identify** the gender, case, and number of the following words.

	Gender	Case	Num.		Gender	Case	Num.
(1) ὅς				(4) αὐτήν			
(2) τὴν ψυχήν				(5) ἐμοῦ			
(3) αὐτοῦ				(6) τοῦ εὐαγγελίου			

STEP FOUR: **Translate** the text into understandable English.

_____

_____

> VOCABULARY
>
> ἕνεκα, because of, on account of

STEP FIVE: **Notice** significant exegetical and syntactical insights.

- **ὃς γὰρ ἐὰν θέλῃ τὴν ψυχὴν αὐτοῦ σῶσαι:** The relative pronoun ὅς followed by the indefinite marker ἐάν makes it an indefinite relative pronoun ("whoever") and triggers the subjunctive mood (θέλῃ). The verb σῶσαι (pres. act. inf. of σῴζω) is a complementary infinitive ("wants *to save*").

- ὃς δ' ἂν ἀπολέσει τὴν ψυχὴν αὐτοῦ: The postpositive conjunction δέ dropped the epsilon (ε) because the next word (ἂν) begins with a vowel. To mark that change, an apostrophe is added. One would expect the subjunctive case following an indefinite relative pronoun (ὃς ἂν), but instead the future is used (ἀπολέσει). Such use is somewhat common, demonstrating the affinity between the future tense and the subjunctive mood, which often communicates something that could potentially occur *in the future*.

- ἕνεκεν ἐμοῦ καὶ τοῦ εὐαγγελίου σώσει αὐτήν: Notice that the future form of σῴζω (σώσει) and the previous aorist infinitive (σῶσαι) do not have the zeta (ζ) that is part of the present (and only the present) form. From this we can conclude that it is not part of the verb's root form.

FOR THE JOURNEY

Jesus's teaching is both poetic and penetrating (maybe it's penetrating because it is so poetic). These verses display a chiastic arrangement:

A For whoever wants *to save* his life
  B will *lose* it,
  B′ but whoever *loses* his life for my sake and the gospel's
A′ will *save* it.

The irony is that to gain true life, one must be willing to give up one's life. Those who attempt to gain life on their own in this world will end up losing everything when they die. But those who are willing to surrender to the messianic king and proclaim his good news will be granted life, eternal life. Jesus encouraged the church at Smyrna to "be faithful unto death" with the promise that he would give them "the crown of life" (Rev. 2:10). Such a promise would be difficult to grasp if Jesus himself had not conquered death through his resurrection from the grave.

ANSWER KEY

1. *Parse:* (1) θέλῃ (θέλω, pres. act. subj. 3rd sg.), (2) ἀπολέσει (ἀπόλλυμι, fut. act. ind. 3rd sg.), (3) σώσει (σῴζω, fut. act. ind. 3rd sg.).

2. *Identify:* (1) ὅς (masc. nom. sg.), (2) τὴν ψυχήν (fem. acc. sg.), (3) αὐτοῦ (masc. gen. sg.), (4) αὐτήν (fem. acc. sg.), (5) ἐμοῦ (gen. sg.), (6) τοῦ εὐαγγελίου (neut. gen. sg.).

3. *Translate:* "For whoever wants to save his life will lose it, but whoever loses his life because of me and the gospel will save it."

DAY 65: MARK 8:36–37

STEP ONE: **Read** aloud the text at least five times.

τί γὰρ ὠφελεῖ ἄνθρωπον κερδῆσαι τὸν κόσμον ὅλον καὶ ζημιωθῆναι τὴν ψυχὴν αὐτοῦ; τί γὰρ δοῖ ἄνθρωπος ἀντάλλαγμα τῆς ψυχῆς αὐτοῦ;

STEP TWO: **Parse** the following verbs.

	Lexical Form	Tense	Voice	Mood	Pers.	Num.	Translation
(1) ὠφελεῖ							
(2) δοῖ							

STEP THREE: **Identify** the gender, case, and number of the following words.

	Gender	Case	Num.		Gender	Case	Num.
(1) τί				(5) αὐτοῦ			
(2) ἄνθρωπον				(6) ἄνθρωπος			
(3) τὸν κόσμον				(7) ἀντάλλαγμα			
(4) τὴν ψυχήν				(8) τῆς ψυχῆς			

STEP FOUR: **Translate** the text into understandable English.

VOCABULARY

ὠφελέω, I profit
κερδαίνω, I gain
ζημιόω, I lose, suffer loss
ἀντάλλαγμα, τό, an exchange

STEP FIVE: **Notice** significant exegetical and syntactical insights.

- **τί γὰρ ὠφελεῖ ἄνθρωπον κερδῆσαι . . . καὶ ζημιωθῆναι:** Verses 36 and 37 contain rhetorical questions that tease out the implications of verse 35. The verbs κερδῆσαι (aor. act. inf. of κερδαίνω) and ζημιωθῆναι (aor. pass. inf. of ζημιόω) are infinitives that introduce a conditional idea ("What does it profit *if* a person gains the whole world and *if* he loses his life?"). This interpretation is confirmed by Matthew's version of the saying where ἐάν + subjunctive is used (Matt. 16:26: τί γὰρ ὠφεληθήσεται ἄνθρωπος ἐὰν τὸν κόσμον ὅλον κερδήσῃ τὴν δὲ ψυχὴν αὐτοῦ ζημιωθῇ;).

- **τί γὰρ δοῖ ἄνθρωπος ἀντάλλαγμα τῆς ψυχῆς αὐτοῦ:** The verb δοῖ is a deliberative subjunctive that introduces a rhetorical question. Wallace comments, "The implication is that 'there is nothing that would compensate for such a loss.' Although the question appears to be asking whether such an exchange is possible, it is really an indictment against gaining the world and losing one's life in the process" (*GGBB* 467). The noun τῆς ψυχῆς is a genitive of price ("for his soul").

FOR THE JOURNEY

As a master teacher, Jesus knew how to ask the right question at the right time. Upon reflection, we all know that gaining the whole world only to lose our soul is foolishness. And yet, many are willing to lose their souls for only a small crumb of the world. Is the passing pleasure of sin (Heb. 11:25) worth losing our relationship with our maker and creator? Indeed, the world itself "is passing away" (1 Cor. 7:31; 1 John 2:17). Even if we can gain the whole world, it will not last long. Or put differently, what are we willing to exchange for our souls? Obviously, our souls/lives are our most valuable "possession." Without it, we don't exist. So a sane person would not trade anything for their soul (except perhaps to help others). Jesus is worth following, but he demands our very lives. Because he is Lord of heaven and earth, he requires that we make him the center of our lives in order to be his disciple. But he promises that, in the end, it will all be worth it. Paul puts it this way, "He who did not spare his own Son but gave him up for us all, how will he not also with him graciously give us all things?" (Rom. 8:32).

ANSWER KEY

1. *Parse:* (1) ὠφελεῖ (ὠφελέω, pres. act. ind. 3rd sg.), (2) δοῖ (δίδωμι, aor. act. subj. 3rd sg.).

2. *Identify:* (1) τί (neut. nom. sg.), (2) ἄνθρωπον (masc. acc. sg.), (3) τὸν κόσμον (masc. acc. sg.), (4) τὴν ψυχήν (fem. acc. sg.), (5) αὐτοῦ (masc. gen. sg.), (6) ἄνθρωπος (masc. nom. sg.), (7) ἀντάλλαγμα (neut. acc. sg.), (8) τῆς ψυχῆς (fem. gen. sg.).

3. *Translate:* "For what does it profit a person to gain the whole world and lose his life? For what would a person give in exchange for his life?"

ROUTE 14

James 2:18–26

STEP ONE: **Read** aloud the text at least five times.

Ἀλλ' ἐρεῖ τις, Σὺ πίστιν ἔχεις, κἀγὼ ἔργα ἔχω· δεῖξόν μοι τὴν πίστιν σου χωρὶς τῶν ἔργων, κἀγώ σοι δείξω ἐκ τῶν ἔργων μου τὴν πίστιν.

STEP TWO: **Parse** the following verbs.

	Lexical Form	Tense	Voice	Mood	Pers.	Num.	Translation
(1) ἐρεῖ							
(2) ἔχεις							
(3) ἔχω							
(4) δεῖξον							
(5) δείξω							

STEP THREE: **Identify** the gender, case, and number of the following words.

	Gender	Case	Num.		Gender	Case	Num.
(1) τις				(6) τὴν πίστιν			
(2) σύ				(7) σου			
(3) πίστιν				(8) τῶν ἔργων			
(4) ἔργα				(9) σοι			
(5) μοι				(10) μου			

200

STEP FOUR: **Translate** the text into understandable English.

VOCABULARY

δείκνυμι, I show

χωρίς, without, apart from

STEP FIVE: **Notice** significant exegetical and syntactical insights.

- Ἀλλ' ἐρεῖ τις: The indefinite pronoun τις and the future form ἐρεῖ together function similar to a subjunctive construction. Again, this demonstrates the close usage of the future and the subjunctive mood.

- Σὺ πίστιν ἔχεις, κἀγὼ ἔργα ἔχω: Notice the emphatic position of the pronouns σύ and ἐγώ (actually, the form is κἀγώ, a crasis [contraction] formed from καί + ἐγώ): "*You* have faith, and *I* have works."

- δεῖξόν μοι τὴν πίστιν σου χωρὶς τῶν ἔργων: The aorist imperative (δεῖξον) is the expected tense-form since (1) the verb is telic (has a natural ending) and does not normally take long to complete (thus making it difficult to portray as an ongoing action). This is confirmed by the actual usage of the verb. As an imperative, it occurs eight times as an aorist and never as a present.

- κἀγώ σοι δείξω ἐκ τῶν ἔργων μου τὴν πίστιν: Again, notice the emphatic position of the pronouns σοι and μου. Normally, these pronouns are placed after the noun to which they are related (see, e.g., τὴν πίστιν σου in the previous phrase).

FOR THE JOURNEY

In the previous verses (2:14–17), James has been defending true faith as a faith that is accompanied by works. It is not sufficient for someone to claim to have faith since a workless faith is not saving faith. True faith clothes the poor and gives food to the hungry. Workless faith, by itself, is dead. To this claim (to have workless faith), James raises the voice of an objector (interlocutor): "But what if some have faith and if others have works?" After all, we can't do everything; sometimes it is better to specialize. Some are good at faith, and others are good at works. To this claim, James replies, "Nice try, but the only way we know that a person has faith is by the things that they do" (my paraphrase). That is, faith and works are inseparable. As McCartney states, "One cannot show faith by any means other than works, and thus faith and works cannot be separated."[1] The things that we do reflect what we believe.

ANSWER KEY

1. *Parse:* (1) ἐρεῖ (λέγω, fut. act. ind. 3rd sg.), (2) ἔχεις (ἔχω, pres. act. ind. 2nd sg.), (3) ἔχω (ἔχω, pres. act. ind. 1st sg.), (4) δεῖξον (δείκνυμι, aor. act. impv. 2nd sg.), (5) δείξω (δείκνυμι, fut. act. ind. 1st sg.).

2. *Identify:* (1) τις (masc. nom. sg.), (2) σύ (nom. sg.), (3) πίστιν (fem. acc. sg.), (4) ἔργα (neut. acc. pl.), (5) μοι (dat. sg.), (6) τὴν πίστιν (fem. acc. sg.), (7) σου (gen. sg.), (8) τῶν ἔργων (neut. gen. pl.), (9) σοι (dat. sg.), (10) μου (gen. sg.).

3. *Translate:* "But someone will say, 'You have faith, and I have works.' Show me your faith without works, and I will show you faith by my works."

1. Dan G. McCartney, *James*, BECNT (Grand Rapids: Baker Academic, 2009), 160.

DAY 67: JAMES 2:19–20

STEP ONE: **Read** aloud the text at least five times.

σὺ πιστεύεις ὅτι εἷς ἐστιν ὁ θεός, καλῶς ποιεῖς· καὶ τὰ δαιμόνια πιστεύουσιν καὶ φρίσσουσιν. θέλεις δὲ γνῶναι, ὦ ἄνθρωπε κενέ, ὅτι ἡ πίστις χωρὶς τῶν ἔργων ἀργή ἐστιν;

STEP TWO: **Parse** the following verbs.

	Lexical Form	Tense	Voice	Mood	Pers.	Num.	Translation
(1) πιστεύεις							
(2) ἐστιν							
(3) ποιεῖς							
(4) πιστεύουσιν							
(5) θέλεις							

STEP THREE: **Identify** the gender, case, and number of the following words.

	Gender	Case	Num.		Gender	Case	Num.
(1) σύ				(5) ἄνθρωπε			
(2) εἷς				(6) ἡ πίστις			
(3) ὁ θεός				(7) τῶν ἔργων			
(4) τὰ δαιμόνια				(8) ἀργή			

STEP FOUR: **Translate** the text into understandable English.

VOCABULARY

καλῶς, well

φρίσσω, I shudder

ὦ, O

κενός, empty, vain

χωρίς, without, apart from

ἀργός, useless, worthless

STEP FIVE: **Notice** significant exegetical and syntactical insights.

- **σὺ πιστεύεις ὅτι εἷς ἐστιν ὁ θεός, καλῶς ποιεῖς:** The pronoun σύ is added for emphasis (it is not needed because that information is embedded in the verb itself). Although there is some uncertainty as to whether the verb πιστεύεις should be taken as a statement ("You believe that God is one") or as a question ("Do you believe that God is one?"), based on the following phrase ("You do well"), the former is more likely. Notice that the type of "faith" that James addresses "is not personal 'believe *in*,' but creedal, 'believe *that*.'"[2]

- **καὶ τὰ δαιμόνια πιστεύουσιν καὶ φρίσσουσιν:** The two present-tense verbs (πιστεύουσιν and φρίσσουσιν) are gnomic, meaning that they are characteristically true.

- **θέλεις δὲ γνῶναι, ὦ ἄνθρωπε κενέ:** The verb γνῶναι (aor. act. inf. of γινώσκω) is a complementary infinitive ("Do you want *to know?*" or "Do you wish *to be shown?*"). This rhetorical question functions as a rebuke. The interjection ὦ is somewhat rare (it occurs 20 times in the NT) and often indicates strong emotion.

- **ὅτι ἡ πίστις χωρὶς τῶν ἔργων ἀργή ἐστιν:** The use of the article before πίστις is anaphoric, referring back to the type of faith (i.e., a workless faith) first mentioned in 2:14. Interestingly, the term ἀργός literally means "without work" and comes from the term ἔργον ("work") with the addition of an alpha privative: ἀ + ἔργον = ἀργός. Thus, a workless faith does not work.

---

2. Chris A. Vlachos, *James*, EGGNT (Nashville: B&H Academic, 2013), 93.

FOR THE JOURNEY

The importance of the Shema (Deut. 6:4) in the OT can hardly be overstated: "Hear, O Israel: The LORD our God, the LORD is one" (ESV). It is cited by Jesus when he was asked by a scribe what the most important command is (Mark 12:29). To believe such a statement is good. James's imaginary dialogue partner even believes such a statement. But while such belief is necessary, it is not sufficient for salvation, for even the demons have such belief. Knowledge and intellectual assent to truths do not result in salvation. In fact, such belief doesn't put someone on par with the demons but actually *below* them, since the demons respond to such belief with trembling and shuddering. We must not only believe *that* God is one: we must also believe *in* the God who is one. Works, by themselves, are useless. Faith, by itself, is useless. True and saving faith is a faith that responds with works.

ANSWER KEY

1. *Parse:* (1) πιστεύεις (πιστεύω, pres. act. ind. 2nd sg.), (2) ἐστιν (εἰμί, pres. act. ind. 3rd sg.), (3) ποιεῖς (ποιέω, pres. act. ind. 2nd sg.), (4) πιστεύουσιν (πιστεύω, pres. act. ind. 3rd pl.), (5) θέλεις (θέλω, pres. act. ind. 2nd sg.).

2. *Identify:* (1) σύ (nom. sg.), (2) εἷς (masc. nom. sg.), (3) ὁ θεός (masc. nom. sg.), (4) τὰ δαιμόνια (neut. nom. pl.), (5) ἄνθρωπε (masc. voc. sg.), (6) ἡ πίστις (fem. nom. sg.), (7) τῶν ἔργων (neut. gen. pl.), (8) ἀργή (fem. nom. sg.).

3. *Translate:* "You believe that God is one; you do well. Even the demons believe and shudder. Do you want to know, O foolish person, that faith without works is useless?"

DAY 68: JAMES 2:21–22

STEP ONE: **Read** aloud the text at least five times.

Ἀβραὰμ ὁ πατὴρ ἡμῶν οὐκ ἐξ ἔργων ἐδικαιώθη ἀνενέγκας Ἰσαὰκ
τὸν υἱὸν αὐτοῦ ἐπὶ τὸ θυσιαστήριον; βλέπεις ὅτι ἡ πίστις συνήργει
τοῖς ἔργοις αὐτοῦ καὶ ἐκ τῶν ἔργων ἡ πίστις ἐτελειώθη,

STEP TWO: **Parse** the following verbs.

	Lexical Form	Tense	Voice	Mood	Pers.	Num.	Translation
(1) ἐδικαιώθη							
(2) βλέπεις							
(3) συνήργει							
(4) ἐτελειώθη							

STEP THREE: **Identify** the gender, case, and number of the following words.

	Gender	Case	Num.		Gender	Case	Num.
(1) ὁ πατήρ				(5) αὐτοῦ			
(2) ἡμῶν				(6) τὸ θυσιαστήριον			
(3) ἔργων				(7) ἡ πίστις			
(4) τὸν υἱόν				(8) τοῖς ἔργοις			

STEP FOUR: **Translate** the text into understandable English.

VOCABULARY

δικαιόω, I vindicate
ἀναφέρω, I offer up
Ἰσαάκ, ὁ, Isaac
θυσιαστήριον, τό, altar
συνεργέω, I work together with
τελειόω, I make perfect, complete

STEP FIVE: **Notice** significant exegetical and syntactical insights.

- **Ἀβραὰμ ὁ πατὴρ ἡμῶν οὐκ ἐξ ἔργων ἐδικαιώθη:** The particle οὐκ expects a positive answer to the question ("Abraham our father was justified by works, wasn't he?").

- **ἀνενέγκας Ἰσαὰκ τὸν υἱὸν αὐτοῦ ἐπὶ τὸ θυσιαστήριον:** The adverbial participle ἀνενέγκας (aor. act. ptc. masc. nom. sg. of ἀναφέρω) functions temporally ("*when* he offered . . .") or possibly instrumentally ("*by* offering") or causally ("*because* he offered").

- **βλέπεις ὅτι ἡ πίστις συνήργει τοῖς ἔργοις αὐτοῦ:** The verb συνήργει is imperfect. The augment comes after the prepositional prefix (συνήργει). The noun τοῖς ἔργοις is a dative of association ("with works").

- **καὶ ἐκ τῶν ἔργων ἡ πίστις ἐτελειώθη:** The instrument of the passive verb ἐτελειώθη is ἐκ τῶν ἔργων ("*by means of works* faith is completed/perfected"). A similar meaning of the verb τελειόω is found in 1 John 4:12: "If we love one another, God remains in us and his love *is perfected/made complete* in us" (cf. versions). That is, it reaches its intended goal.

FOR THE JOURNEY

James appeals to the examples of Abraham (and later Rahab) to demonstrate that works are a natural fruit of true faith. That is, Abraham's faith was validated because he put his faith into action when he willingly offered up his only son of promise on the altar. Abraham didn't just say that he believed the promises of God; he proved it by accepting God's command to offer up Isaac. Ultimately, it was Abraham's faith that justified him before God (Gen. 15:6), and he was justified before he even offered up Isaac (Gen. 22). Thus, "the offering of Isaac was not the basis for Abraham's righteousness or even for God's recognition of Abraham as righteous; rather, it was the necessary and proper outworking and manifestation of Abraham's inward righteousness that came by a working faith, so that his faith and works together resulted in a genuinely righteous life" (McCartney, *James*, 163). Abraham demonstrated that he had been justified by God through his faith, which was evidenced by his works.

ANSWER KEY

1. *Parse:* (1) ἐδικαιώθη (δικαιόω, aor. pass. ind. 3rd sg.), (2) βλέπεις (βλέπω, pres. act. ind. 2nd sg.), (3) συνήργει (συνεργέω, impf. act. ind. 3rd sg.), (4) ἐτελειώθη (τελειόω, aor. pass. ind. 3rd sg.).

2. *Identify:* (1) ὁ πατήρ (masc. nom. sg.), (2) ἡμῶν (gen. pl.), (3) ἔργων (neut. gen. pl.), (4) τὸν υἱόν (masc. acc. sg.), (5) αὐτοῦ (masc. gen. sg.), (6) τὸ θυσιαστήριον (neut. acc. sg.), (7) ἡ πίστις (fem. nom. sg.), (8) τοῖς ἔργοις (neut. dat. pl.).

3. *Translate:* "Was not Abraham, our father, justified by works when he offered up Isaac, his son, on the altar? You see that faith was working together with his works, and by works faith was perfected."

208

DAY 69: JAMES 2:23–24

STEP ONE: **Read** aloud the text at least five times.

καὶ ἐπληρώθη ἡ γραφὴ ἡ λέγουσα, Ἐπίστευσεν δὲ Ἀβραὰμ τῷ θεῷ, καὶ ἐλογίσθη αὐτῷ εἰς δικαιοσύνην καὶ φίλος θεοῦ ἐκλήθη. ὁρᾶτε ὅτι ἐξ ἔργων δικαιοῦται ἄνθρωπος καὶ οὐκ ἐκ πίστεως μόνον.

STEP TWO: **Parse** the following verbs.

	Lexical Form	Tense	Voice	Mood	Pers.	Num.	Translation
(1) ἐπληρώθη							
(2) ἐπίστευσεν							
(3) ἐλογίσθη							
(4) ἐκλήθη							
(5) ὁρᾶτε							
(6) δικαιοῦται							

STEP THREE: **Identify** the gender, case, and number of the following words.

	Gender	Case	Num.		Gender	Case	Num.
(1) ἡ γραφή				(6) θεοῦ			
(2) τῷ θεῷ				(7) ἔργων			
(3) αὐτῷ				(8) ἄνθρωπος			
(4) δικαιοσύνην				(9) πίστεως			
(5) φίλος							

STEP FOUR: **Translate** the text into understandable English.

___

___

VOCABULARY

λογίζομαι, I reckon
φίλος, ὁ, friend
δικαιόω, I vindicate, justify

STEP FIVE: **Notice** significant exegetical and syntactical insights.

- **καὶ ἐπληρώθη ἡ γραφὴ ἡ λέγουσα:** The participle λέγουσα (pres. act. ptc. fem. nom. sg. of λέγω) functions attributively, modifying ἡ γραφή ("the Scripture, *which says*").

- **Ἐπίστευσεν δὲ Ἀβραὰμ τῷ θεῷ, καὶ ἐλογίσθη αὐτῷ εἰς δικαιοσύνην:** James offers a verbatim citation of Gen. 15:6, minus the connective δέ (LXX). The verb πιστεύω usually takes a dative direct object, as it does here (i.e., τῷ θεῷ). In contrast to the interlocutor who merely believes something *about* God ("that God is one"), Abraham placed his faith *in* God (he "believed in God").

- **καὶ φίλος θεοῦ ἐκλήθη:** The noun φίλος is a predicate nominative, with the verb καλέω functioning similar to the copulative verb εἰμί. Because of Colwell's Rule,[3] the anarthrous noun should be considered definite ("the friend of God").

- **ὁρᾶτε ὅτι ἐξ ἔργων δικαιοῦται ἄνθρωπος καὶ οὐκ ἐκ πίστεως μόνον:** Because James offers a truism ("a person is justified by works and not by faith alone"), the present-tense verb δικαιοῦται is gnomic (axiomatic), and the noun ἄνθρωπος is generic ("a person").

FOR THE JOURNEY

With the phrase "You [pl.] see," James shifts from speaking to the imaginary disputant to addressing his readers. James 2:24 ("A person is justified by works and not by faith alone") is sometimes seen as contradictory to Rom. 3:28 (a person "is justified by faith apart from the works of the law"). But at least two distinctions must be remembered: (1) James and Paul are addressing different issues and therefore (2) use terminology differently. Throughout the history of the church, theologians have helped clarify these distinctions. For example, Martin Luther stated: "For those who glory that they are Christians and do not show this faith by such good works . . . are not Christians at all. . . . Works only reveal faith, just as fruits only show the tree, whether it is

---

3. Colwell's Rule states that when a predicate nominative precedes the verb, the lack of article is a matter of style, and only context can determine whether the noun is definite.

a good tree. I say, therefore, that works justify, that is, they show that we have been justified. . . . True faith is not idle. Works are necessary to salvation, but they do not cause salvation, because faith alone gives life" (Martin Luther, *The Disputation concerning Justification*, in *LW* 34:161, 165). Thus, "works are necessary in order to prove that we are righteous" (*LW* 34:166). So, although James and Paul appear to disagree, on closer examination they are compatible.

ANSWER KEY

1. *Parse:* (1) ἐπληρώθη (πληρόω, aor. pass. ind. 3rd sg.), (2) ἐπίστευσεν (πι-στεύω, aor. act. ind. 3rd sg.), (3) ἐλογίσθη (λογίζομαι, aor. pass. ind. 3rd sg.), (4) ἐκλήθη (καλέω, aor. pass. ind. 3rd sg.), (5) ὁρᾶτε (ὁράω, pres. act. ind. 2nd pl.), (6) δικαιοῦται (δικαιόω, pres. pass. ind. 3rd sg.).

2. *Identify:* (1) ἡ γραφή (fem. nom. sg.), (2) τῷ θεῷ (masc. dat. sg.), (3) αὐτῷ (masc. dat. sg.), (4) δικαιοσύνην (fem. acc. sg.), (5) φίλος (masc. nom. sg.), (6) θεοῦ (masc. gen. sg.), (7) ἔργων (neut. gen. pl.), (8) ἄνθρωπος (masc. nom. sg.), (9) πίστεως (fem. gen. sg.).

3. *Translate:* "And the Scripture was fulfilled that says, 'And Abraham believed God, and it was credited to him for righteousness,' and he was called the friend of God. You see that a person is justified by works and not by faith alone."

DAY 70: JAMES 2:25–26

STEP ONE: **Read** aloud the text at least five times.

ὁμοίως δὲ καὶ Ῥαὰβ ἡ πόρνη οὐκ ἐξ ἔργων ἐδικαιώθη ὑποδεξαμένη τοὺς ἀγγέλους καὶ ἑτέρᾳ ὁδῷ ἐκβαλοῦσα; ὥσπερ γὰρ τὸ σῶμα χωρὶς πνεύματος νεκρόν ἐστιν, οὕτως καὶ ἡ πίστις χωρὶς ἔργων νεκρά ἐστιν.

STEP TWO: **Parse** the following verbs.

	Lexical Form	Tense	Voice	Mood	Pers.	Num.	Translation
(1) ἐδικαιώθη							
(2) ἐστιν							

STEP THREE: **Identify** the gender, case, and number of the following words.

	Gender	Case	Num.		Gender	Case	Num.
(1) ἡ πόρνη				(6) πνεύματος			
(2) ἔργων				(7) νεκρόν			
(3) τοὺς ἀγγέλους				(8) ἡ πίστις			
(4) ὁδῷ				(9) νεκρά			
(5) τὸ σῶμα							

STEP FOUR: **Translate** the text into understandable English.

> VOCABULARY
>
> ὁμοίως, likewise, similarly
> Ῥαάβ, ἡ, Rahab
> πόρνη, ἡ, prostitute, whore
> δικαιόω, I vindicate, justify
> ὑποδέχομαι, I welcome, receive
> ὥσπερ, (just) as
> χωρίς, without, apart from

STEP FIVE: **Notice** significant exegetical and syntactical insights.

- **ὁμοίως δὲ καὶ Ῥαὰβ ἡ πόρνη οὐκ ἐξ ἔργων ἐδικαιώθη:** As with verse 21 and the example of Abraham, the particle οὐκ expects a positive answer to the question ("Rahab the prostitute was justified by works, wasn't she?").

- **ὑποδεξαμένη τοὺς ἀγγέλους καὶ ἑτέρᾳ ὁδῷ ἐκβαλοῦσα:** The two adverbial participles ὑποδεξαμένη (aor. mid. ptc. fem. nom. sg. of ὑποδέχομαι) and ἐκβαλοῦσα (aor. act. ptc. fem. nom. sg. of ἐκβάλλω) function temporally ("*when* she welcomed" and "*when* she sent out") or possibly instrumentally ("*by* welcoming" or "*by* sending out") or causally ("because she welcomed" or "because she sent out").

- **ὥσπερ γὰρ τὸ σῶμα χωρὶς πνεύματος νεκρόν ἐστιν:** Because adjectives do not have a gender of their own but take on the case of the noun they modify, νεκρόν in this phrase is neuter (because it is linked to the neuter πνεύματος) but it changes to νεκρά in the following phrase (because it modifies the feminine πίστις).

- **οὕτως καὶ ἡ πίστις χωρὶς ἔργων νεκρά ἐστιν:** This concluding phrase sums up the main point that James has been making in this passage as it repeats for emphasis almost exactly the phrase found in verse 20:

ἡ πίστις χωρὶς τῶν ἔργων ἀργή ἐστιν (v. 20b)
ἡ πίστις χωρὶς ἔργων νεκρά ἐστιν (v. 26b)

FOR THE JOURNEY

James not only uses the example of Abraham to illustrate a work-producing type of faith, but he also uses Rahab. She is also mentioned in Heb. 11:31: "By faith Rahab the prostitute did not perish with those who were disobedient because she had given a friendly welcome to the spies" (ESV). In one sense the two could not be more different. Abraham was the father of the Jewish nation whereas Rahab was an outcast from a Canaanite nation. Abraham was a wealthy, moral man whereas Rahab was a poor, immoral woman. Abraham was a prominent figure in his society whereas Rahab was a lowly prostitute. Such a use of polar extremes is called a *merism*, a literary device presenting extremes and thereby indicating that everyone (or everything) in between is included. Everyone who is justified before God must have a faith that is alive and not dead, and a dead faith is a workless faith. In contrast, a living faith (i.e., true, authentic, saving faith) is a faith that is accompanied by works. Christ alone saves, but the faith that saves is never alone!

ANSWER KEY

1. *Parse:* (1) ἐδικαιώθη (δικαιόω, aor. pass. ind. 3rd sg.), (2) ἐστιν (εἰμί, pres. act. ind. 3rd sg.).

2. *Identify:* (1) ἡ πόρνη (fem. nom. sg.), (2) ἔργων (neut. gen. pl.), (3) τοὺς ἀγγέλους (masc. acc. pl.), (4) ὁδῷ (fem. dat. sg.), (5) τὸ σῶμα (neut. nom. sg.), (6) πνεύματος (neut. gen. sg.), (7) νεκρόν (neut. nom. sg.), (8) ἡ πίστις (fem. nom. sg.), (9) νεκρά (fem. nom. sg.).

3. *Translate:* "And in the same way, was not also Rahab the prostitute justified by works when she welcomed the messengers and sent them out a different way? Just as the body without the spirit is dead, so also faith without works is dead."

ROUTE 15

1 Peter 4:12–19

STEP ONE: **Read** aloud the text at least five times.

Ἀγαπητοί, μὴ ξενίζεσθε τῇ ἐν ὑμῖν πυρώσει πρὸς πειρασμὸν ὑμῖν γινομένῃ ὡς ξένου ὑμῖν συμβαίνοντος, ἀλλὰ καθὸ κοινωνεῖτε τοῖς τοῦ Χριστοῦ παθήμασιν, χαίρετε, ἵνα καὶ ἐν τῇ ἀποκαλύψει τῆς δόξης αὐτοῦ χαρῆτε ἀγαλλιώμενοι.

STEP TWO: **Parse** the following verbs.

	Lexical Form	Tense	Voice	Mood	Pers.	Num.	Translation
(1) ξενίζεσθε							
(2) κοινωνεῖτε							
(3) χαίρετε							
(4) χαρῆτε							

STEP THREE: **Identify** the gender, case, and number of the following words.

	Gender	Case	Num.		Gender	Case	Num.
(1) ἀγαπητοί				(6) τοῖς παθήμασιν			
(2) τῇ πυρώσει				(7) τοῦ Χριστοῦ			
(3) ὑμῖν				(8) τῇ ἀποκαλύψει			
(4) πειρασμόν				(9) τῆς δόξης			
(5) ξένου				(10) αὐτοῦ			

STEP FOUR: **Translate** the text into understandable English.

VOCABULARY

ξενίζω, I am surprised
πύρωσις, ἡ, burning
πειρασμός, ὁ, test, trial
ξένος, strange
συμβαίνω, I happen, come about
καθό, insofar as
κοινωνέω, I share
πάθημα, τό, suffering
ἀποκάλυψις, ἡ, revelation
ἀγαλλιάω, I rejoice, am glad

STEP FIVE: **Notice** significant exegetical and syntactical insights.

- **μὴ ξενίζεσθε τῇ ἐν ὑμῖν πυρώσει πρὸς πειρασμὸν ὑμῖν γινομένῃ:**
  The prohibition μὴ ξενίζεσθε functions more as an entreaty than
  a command. The verb ξενίζω is often followed by a dative noun
  that causes the surprise (e.g., τῇ πυρώσει). Notice the sandwich
  construction where the prepositional phrase ἐν ὑμῖν is put inside
  the dative phrase τῇ . . . πυρώσει. This demonstrates that the prepositional phrase is adjectival and modifies τῇ πυρώσει. The participle
  γινομένῃ (pres. mid. ptc. fem. dat. sg. of γίνομαι) could be taken as
  attributive ("the fiery ordeal *that is coming* among you to test you")
  or as a causal adverbial participle ("the fiery trial that is among
  you, *because it is happening* to test you").[1] Because the participle is
  anarthrous (lacks an article), the second option seems best (though
  most commentators and English versions opt for the former).

- **ὡς ξένου ὑμῖν συμβαίνοντος:** The participle συμβαίνοντος (pres.
  act. ptc. neut. gen. sg. of συμβαίνω) is synonymous with γινομένῃ

---

1. See Greg W. Forbes, *1 Peter*, EGGNT (Nashville: B&H Academic, 2014), 154.

in the previous phrase and is a genitive absolute with the noun ξένου functioning as the genitive subject of the construction. Because a genitive absolute is a type of adverbial participle, the context here calls for a conditional usage.

- **ἀλλὰ καθὸ κοινωνεῖτε τοῖς τοῦ Χριστοῦ παθήμασιν χαίρετε:** The genitive τοῦ Χριστοῦ, linked to the head noun τοῖς παθήμασιν (dative of direct object with the verb κοινωνέω), is a subjective genitive ("the sufferings of Christ" = "Christ suffers"). Again, note the sandwich construction: τοῖς <u>τοῦ Χριστοῦ</u> παθήμασιν.

- **ἵνα καὶ ἐν τῇ ἀποκαλύψει τῆς δόξης αὐτοῦ χαρῆτε ἀγαλλιώμε-νοι:** The genitive τῆς δόξης is an objective genitive ("the revelation of glory" = "[someone] reveals glory") and refers to the second coming of Christ at the final day. The adverbial participle ἀγαλ-λιώμενοι (pres. mid. ptc. masc. nom. pl. of ἀγαλλιάω) conveys the manner in which the main verb (χαρῆτε) is accomplished. Because the meanings of both verbs are virtually synonymous, the participle serves to intensify χαρῆτε: "rejoice with great joy" (CSB), "overjoyed" (NIV), "wonderful joy" (NLT), "be glad and shout for joy" (NRSVue).

FOR THE JOURNEY

Peter uses the metaphor of a "fiery trial" (ESV, NKJV) or "fiery ordeal" (CSB, NASB1995, NIV, NRSVue) to describe the situation that his readers are experiencing (see 1 Pet. 1:6–7). This metaphor of being tested by fire should be interpreted in light of the OT. In Ps. 66:10, we read, "For you, O God, have tested us; you have tried us as silver is tried" (ESV). Zechariah also applies this metaphor to the remnant left in the land: "I will put this third into the fire, and refine them as one refines silver, and test them as gold is tested" (13:9 ESV). Finally, Malachi speaks of the Lord coming to his "temple" and being "like a refiner's fire" who "will sit as a refiner and purifier of silver, and . . . purify the sons of Levi"; he will "refine them like gold and silver, and they will bring offerings in righteousness to the LORD" (3:1–3 ESV). Thus "their sufferings are not a sign of God's absence but his purifying presence."[2]

2. Thomas R. Schreiner, *1 & 2 Peter and Jude*, CSC (Nashville: Holman Reference, 2020), 252.

ANSWER KEY

1. *Parse:* (1) ξενίζεσθε (ξενίζω, pres. pass. impv. 2nd pl.), (2) κοινωνεῖτε (κοινωνέω, pres. act. ind. 2nd pl.), (3) χαίρετε (χαίρω, pres. act. ind. 2nd pl.), (4) χαρῆτε (χαίρω, aor. pass. subj. 2nd pl.).

2. *Identify:* (1) ἀγαπητοί (masc. voc. pl.), (2) τῇ πυρώσει (fem. dat. sg.), (3) ὑμῖν (dat. pl.), (4) πειρασμόν (masc. acc. sg.), (5) ξένου (neut. gen. sg.), (6) τοῖς παθήμασιν (neut. dat. pl.), (7) τοῦ Χριστοῦ (masc. gen. sg.), (8) τῇ ἀποκαλύψει (fem. dat. sg.), (9) τῆς δόξης (fem. gen. sg.), (10) αὐτοῦ (masc. gen. sg.).

3. *Translate:* "Beloved, do not be surprised at the fiery trial among you when it comes to test you, as if something strange were happening to you. But insofar as you share in the sufferings of Christ, rejoice, so that you may also rejoice as you exult at the revelation of his glory."

DAY 72: 1 PETER 4:14–15

STEP ONE: **Read** aloud the text at least five times.

εἰ ὀνειδίζεσθε ἐν ὀνόματι Χριστοῦ, μακάριοι, ὅτι τὸ τῆς δόξης καὶ τὸ τοῦ θεοῦ πνεῦμα ἐφ᾽ ὑμᾶς ἀναπαύεται. μὴ γάρ τις ὑμῶν πασχέτω ὡς φονεὺς ἢ κλέπτης ἢ κακοποιὸς ἢ ὡς ἀλλοτριεπίσκοπος.

STEP TWO: **Parse** the following verbs.

	Lexical Form	Tense	Voice	Mood	Pers.	Num.	Translation
(1) ὀνειδίζεσθε							
(2) ἀναπαύεται							
(3) πασχέτω							

STEP THREE: **Identify** the gender, case, and number of the following words.

	Gender	Case	Num.		Gender	Case	Num.
(1) ὀνόματι				(7) ὑμᾶς			
(2) Χριστοῦ				(8) τις			
(3) μακάριοι				(9) ὑμῶν			
(4) τὸ πνεῦμα				(10) φονεύς			
(5) τῆς δόξης				(11) κλέπτης			
(6) τοῦ θεοῦ				(12) κακοποιός			

STEP FOUR: **Translate** the text into understandable English.

VOCABULARY

ὀνειδίζω, I revile, reproach
ἀναπαύω, I rest upon
πάσχω, I suffer
φονεύς, ὁ, murderer

κλέπτης, ὁ, thief
κακοποιός, ὁ, evildoer
ἀλλοτριεπίσκοπος, ὁ, meddler

STEP FIVE: **Notice** significant exegetical and syntactical insights.

- εἰ ὀνειδίζεσθε ἐν ὀνόματι Χριστοῦ, μακάριοι: This is a first-class conditional clause introduced with εἰ. The dative construction ἐν ὀνόματι Χριστοῦ is probably causal (*"because of* the name of Christ," NIV). The term μακάριοι is a predicative adjective with an implied copulative verb (ἐστέ, "*You are* blessed").

- ὅτι τὸ τῆς δόξης καὶ τὸ τοῦ θεοῦ πνεῦμα ἐφ' ὑμᾶς ἀναπαύεται: This part of the verse echoes Isa. 11:2 LXX (καὶ ἀναπαύσεται ἐπ' αὐτὸν πνεῦμα τοῦ θεοῦ). The repetition of the article τό is unexpected and has caused much discussion. With just one article at the beginning of the phrase, it would read "the Spirit of glory and God." But with the reposition of the article, it is best to take the second phrase as epexegetical: "the Spirit of glory, that is, Spirit of God."

- μὴ γάρ τις ὑμῶν πασχέτω ὡς: The indefinite pronoun τις functions as the subject of the third-person imperative πασχέτω ("let no *one* suffer" or "he must not suffer").

FOR THE JOURNEY

Peter continues informing his readers that not only are believers commanded to rejoice in the midst of suffering, but they also are blessed by God when they are insulted. Based on the term used (ὀνειδίζεσθε), the type of persecution that the readers were facing appears to be primarily verbal abuse rather than physical harm. Even so, they are encouraged that such insults actually result in blessings. In particular, Peter states, they are blessed because God's Spirit rests on them. The very Spirit bestowed on Jesus is also given to God's people. So "Peter consoles his readers that because the same Spirit of glory and of God rests upon them, their current suffering is as Christ's was, a prelude to the glory to follow."[3]

3. Karen H. Jobes, *1 Peter*, BECNT (Grand Rapids: Baker Academic, 2005), 288.

ANSWER KEY

1. *Parse:* (1) ὀνειδίζεσθε (ὀνειδίζω, pres. pass. ind. 2nd pl.), (2) ἀναπαύεται (ἀναπαύω, pres. mid. ind. 3rd sg.), (3) πασχέτω (πάσχω, pres. act. impv. 3rd sg.).

2. *Identify:* (1) ὀνόματι (neut. dat. sg.), (2) Χριστοῦ (masc. gen. sg.), (3) μακάριοι (masc. nom. pl.), (4) τὸ πνεῦμα (neut. nom. sg.), (5) τῆς δόξης (fem. gen. sg.), (6) τοῦ θεοῦ (masc. gen. sg.), (7) ὑμᾶς (acc. pl.), (8) τις (masc. nom. sg.), (9) ὑμῶν (gen. pl.), (10) φονεύς (masc. nom. sg.), (11) κλέπτης (masc. nom. sg.), (12) κακοποιός (masc. nom. sg.).

3. *Translate:* "If you are reviled for the name of Christ, [you are] blessed, because the Spirit of glory and of God rests upon you. For let not anyone of you suffer as a murderer or a thief or an evildoer or a meddler."

DAY 73: 1 PETER 4:16

STEP ONE: **Read** aloud the text at least five times.

εἰ δὲ ὡς Χριστιανός, μὴ αἰσχυνέσθω, δοξαζέτω δὲ τὸν θεὸν ἐν τῷ ὀνόματι⁴ τούτῳ.

STEP TWO: **Parse** the following verbs.

	Lexical Form	Tense	Voice	Mood	Pers.	Num.	Translation
(1) αἰσχυνέσθω							
(2) δοξαζέτω							

STEP THREE: **Identify** the gender, case, and number of the following words.

	Gender	Case	Num.		Gender	Case	Num.
(1) Χριστιανός				(3) τῷ ὀνόματι			
(2) τὸν θεόν				(4) τούτῳ			

STEP FOUR: **Translate** the text into understandable English.

> VOCABULARY
>
> Χριστιανός, ὁ, Christian
> αἰσχύνω, I am ashamed

---

4. In preferring ὀνόματι over μέρει here, I depart from the reading found in NA²⁸ and UBS⁵ and follow most English Bible translations (e.g., NIV, NRSVue, CSB, ESV, NASB1995, NLT).

STEP FIVE: Notice significant exegetical and syntactical insights.

- εἰ δὲ ὡς Χριστιανός: Again, a first-class conditional clause is used here. The implied verb (τις πάσχει) comes from verse 15 ("if [anyone suffers] as a Christian"). The term Χριστιανός is a cognate of the noun Χριστός and is found only three times in the NT (Acts 11:26; 26:28).

- μὴ αἰσχυνέσθω: "This verb connotes not simply subjective shame, but anticipates the potential of a concrete denial of one's faith."[5] The middle voice is common with verbs of emotion.

- δοξαζέτω δὲ τὸν θεὸν ἐν τῷ ὀνόματι τούτῳ: The "name" referred to here is not the name of Χριστός but the name Χριστιανός. The Christian is to glorify God ἐν τῷ ὀνόματι τούτῳ ("in this name"). This construction is probably best understood as a dative of sphere.

FOR THE JOURNEY

In verse 13 believers were encouraged to rejoice in the midst of suffering. Jesus exhorts his disciples that when they are reviled and persecuted for being his followers, they should "rejoice and be glad, for your reward is great in heaven, for so they persecuted the prophets who were before you" (Matt. 5:12 ESV). Luke records that the apostles "left the presence of the council, rejoicing that they were counted worthy to suffer dishonor for the name" (Acts 5:41 ESV). Earlier Peter stated, "In this you rejoice, though now for a little while, if necessary, you have been grieved by various trials" (1 Pet. 1:6 ESV). Paul rejoiced while he was in prison as he wrote to the believers in Philippi. The way in which believers respond to suffering indicates whether we truly belong to God and trust in his promises. In other words, the belief that God will right all wrongs and deliver his people is what fuels our joy now. In verse 16, followers of Jesus are exhorted to glorify God as they bear the name "Christian," a term probably coined by outsiders as derogatory (Acts 11:26; 26:28). The name itself simply means "follower of Christ" (just as "Herodians" identifies those loyal to Herod and his family). Being ashamed of being a Christian leads to denying Christ or abandoning the

5. Mark Dubis, *1 Peter*, BHGNT (Waco: Baylor University Press, 2010), 152–53.

faith. Thus, believers "glorify God in the name 'Christian' by enduring such suffering with joy (v. 13), pleased that they are privileged to suffer because of their allegiance to Jesus Christ."[6]

ANSWER KEY

1. *Parse:* (1) αἰσχυνέσθω (αἰσχύνω, pres. mid. impv. 3rd sg.), (2) δοξαζέτω (δοξάζω, pres. act. impv. 3rd sg.).

2. *Identify:* (1) Χριστιανός (masc. nom. sg.), (2) τὸν θεόν (masc. acc. sg.), (3) τῷ ὀνόματι (neut. dat. sg.), (4) τούτῳ (neut. dat. sg.).

3. *Translate:* "But if [anyone suffers] as a Christian, let him not be ashamed, but let him glorify God in this name."

6. Schreiner, *1 & 2 Peter and Jude*, 261.

DAY 74: 1 PETER 4:17–18

STEP ONE: **Read** aloud the text at least five times.

ὅτι [ὁ] καιρὸς τοῦ ἄρξασθαι τὸ κρίμα ἀπὸ τοῦ οἴκου τοῦ θεοῦ· εἰ
δὲ πρῶτον ἀφ' ἡμῶν, τί τὸ τέλος τῶν ἀπειθούντων τῷ τοῦ θεοῦ
εὐαγγελίῳ; καὶ εἰ ὁ δίκαιος μόλις σῴζεται, ὁ ἀσεβὴς καὶ ἁμαρτωλὸς
ποῦ φανεῖται;

STEP TWO: **Parse** the following verbs.

	Lexical Form	Tense	Voice	Mood	Pers.	Num.	Translation
(1) σῴζεται							
(2) φανεῖται							

STEP THREE: **Identify** the gender, case, and number of the following words.

	Gender	Case	Num.		Gender	Case	Num.
(1) ὁ καιρός				(6) τὸ τέλος			
(2) τὸ κρίμα				(7) τῷ εὐαγγελίῳ			
(3) τοῦ οἴκου				(8) ὁ δίκαιος			
(4) τοῦ θεοῦ				(9) ὁ ἀσεβής			
(5) ἡμῶν				(10) ἁμαρτωλός			

STEP FOUR: **Translate** the text into understandable English.

VOCABULARY

κρίμα, τό, judgment
τέλος, τό, end, goal
ἀπειθέω, I disobey
μόλις, with difficulty

ἀσεβής, ungodly, impious
ἁμαρτωλός, τό, sinner
ποῦ, where?
φαίνω, I appear, shine

STEP FIVE: **Notice** significant exegetical and syntactical insights.

- ὅτι [ὁ] καιρὸς τοῦ ἄρξασθαι τὸ κρίμα ἀπὸ τοῦ οἴκου τοῦ θεοῦ: The articular infinitive τοῦ ἄρξασθαι (aor. mid. inf. of ἄρχομαι) is epexegetical to καιρός ("It is time *to begin*"). The accusative τὸ κρίμα functions as the subject of the infinitive.

- εἰ δὲ πρῶτον ἀφ' ἡμῶν, τί τὸ τέλος τῶν ἀπειθούντων τῷ τοῦ θεοῦ εὐαγγελίῳ: The articular participle τῶν ἀπειθούντων (pres. act. ptc. masc. gen. pl. of ἀπειθέω) functions substantively ("those who disobey"). The verb ἀπειθέω takes its direct object in the dative case (τῷ εὐαγγελίῳ). The genitive in the phrase τῷ τοῦ θεοῦ εὐαγγελίῳ ("the gospel of God") is best interpreted as an objective genitive ("the gospel *about* God").

- καὶ εἰ ὁ δίκαιος μόλις σῴζεται, ὁ ἀσεβὴς καὶ ἁμαρτωλὸς ποῦ φανεῖται; This phrase is almost a verbatim citation of Prov. 11:31 LXX. The verb σῴζεται is a gnomic present that expresses a general truth. The phrase ὁ ἀσεβὴς καὶ ἁμαρτωλός represents an example of the Granville Sharp Rule: two substantives with one article and connected by καί refer to the same person. Consequently, it could be rendered as a hendiadys ("ungodly sinner").

FOR THE JOURNEY

The judgment in the house of God refers to the persecution and insults that Christians were facing. In the OT, the house of God was the temple, the dwelling place of God. In the NT, believers are God's spiritual house/temple. For believers, the judgment is the "fiery trial" (v. 12) they were experiencing, which had refining purposes. This judgment involved not their destruction but their purification and refinement. Such tribulations constituted the beginning of God's eschatological judgment. Peter then uses an argument from lesser to greater. If the righteous go through fires of purification, what will become of the unrighteous? In other words, although believers go through persecution now (which is difficult), think about how much more unbearable it will be to experience God's full judgment.

ANSWER KEY

1. *Parse:* (1) σῴζεται (σῴζω, pres. pass. ind. 3rd sg.), (2) φανεῖται (φαίνω, fut. mid. ind. 3rd sg.).

2. *Identify:* (1) ὁ καιρός (masc. nom. sg.), (2) τὸ κρίμα (neut. acc. sg.), (3) τοῦ οἴκου (masc. gen. sg.), (4) τοῦ θεοῦ (masc. gen. sg.), (5) ἡμῶν (gen. pl.), (6) τὸ τέλος (neut. nom. sg.), (7) εὐαγγελίῳ (neut. dat. sg.), (8) ὁ δίκαιος (masc. nom. sg.), (9) ὁ ἀσεβής (masc. nom. sg.), (10) ἁμαρτωλός (masc. nom. sg.).

3. *Translate:* "Because [it is] the time for judgment to begin with the household of God, and if [it begins] with us first, what [will be] the end of those who disobey the gospel of God? And if the righteous [person] is saved with difficulty, where will the ungodly and sinner appear?"

DAY 75: 1 PETER 4:19

STEP ONE: **Read** aloud the text at least five times.

ὥστε καὶ οἱ πάσχοντες κατὰ τὸ θέλημα τοῦ θεοῦ πιστῷ κτίστῃ παρατιθέσθωσαν τὰς ψυχὰς αὐτῶν ἐν ἀγαθοποιΐᾳ.

STEP TWO: **Parse** the following verb.

	Lexical Form	Tense	Voice	Mood	Pers.	Num.	Translation
παρατιθέσθωσαν							

STEP THREE: **Identify** the gender, case, and number of the following words.

	Gender	Case	Num.		Gender	Case	Num.
(1) τὸ θέλημα				(4) τὰς ψυχάς			
(2) τοῦ θεοῦ				(5) αὐτῶν			
(3) κτίστῃ				(6) ἀγαθοποιΐᾳ			

STEP FOUR: **Translate** the text into understandable English.

VOCABULARY

πάσχω, I suffer
κτίστης, ὁ, the Creator
παρατίθημι, I entrust, give over
ἀγαθοποιΐα, ἡ, doing good

STEP FIVE: **Notice** significant exegetical and syntactical insights.

* **ὥστε καὶ οἱ πάσχοντες κατὰ τὸ θέλημα τοῦ θεοῦ:** The inferential conjunction ὥστε concludes verses 12–18. The articular participle οἱ πάσχοντες (pres. act. ptc. masc. nom. pl. of πάσχω) functions substantively ("those who suffer") as the subject of the imperative (παρατιθέσθωσαν). The genitive in the phrase τὸ θέλημα τοῦ

228

θεοῦ ("the will of God") is best interpreted as a subjective genitive ("God wills [something]").

- **πιστῷ κτίστῃ παρατιθέσθωσαν τὰς ψυχὰς αὐτῶν ἐν ἀγαθοποιΐᾳ:** The verb παρατίθημι takes its direct object in the dative case (πιστῷ κτίστῃ). The phrase ἐν ἀγαθοποιΐᾳ is either a dative of time ("*while* doing good") or means ("*by* doing good").

FOR THE JOURNEY

This section concludes with a summary statement: those who are suffering should entrust themselves to God. The meaning of "entrust" (παρατίθημι) was first modeled by Jesus, who did not threaten when he endured suffering "but entrusted himself to the One who judges justly" (1 Pet. 2:23 CSB). He later entrusted his spirit to God as he died on the cross (Luke 23:46). Paul and Barnabas entrusted their converts to God (Acts 14:23; 20:32). Paul entrusts the gospel to Timothy, who is to entrust the gospel message to faithful men who will likewise teach others (1 Tim. 1:18; 2 Tim. 2:2). In the same way, as believers we are to entrust our lives to our "faithful Creator," a reference that implies God's sovereignty over the world since he is its Creator. As Creator, God is "faithful to his promises and faithful to his people, never abandoning them in their time of need."[7] So, even when we suffer, it is "according to God's will," which "means that we can trust that God has a purpose in our suffering, that our suffering has meaning even if wicked people (rather than God) are the ones directly causing it."[8] Finally, we demonstrate that we trust in our faithful Creator by continuing to do good, even in the midst of suffering or insults.

ANSWER KEY

1. *Parse:* παρατιθέσθωσαν (παρατίθημι, pres. mid. impv. 3rd pl.).
2. *Identify:* (1) τὸ θέλημα (neut. acc. sg.), (2) τοῦ θεοῦ (masc. gen. sg.), (3) κτίστῃ (masc. dat. sg.), (4) τὰς ψυχάς (fem. acc. pl.), (5) αὐτῶν (masc. gen. pl.), (6) ἀγαθοποιΐᾳ (fem. dat. sg.).
3. *Translate:* "So then, let those who suffer according to the will of God entrust their souls to a faithful Creator in doing good."

7. Schreiner, *1 & 2 Peter and Jude*, 265.
8. Craig S. Keener, *1 Peter: A Commentary* (Grand Rapids: Baker Academic, 2021), 350.

ROUTE 16

Jude 17–25

STEP ONE: **Read** aloud the text at least five times.

Ὑμεῖς δέ, ἀγαπητοί, μνήσθητε τῶν ῥημάτων τῶν προειρημένων ὑπὸ τῶν ἀποστόλων τοῦ κυρίου ἡμῶν Ἰησοῦ Χριστοῦ ὅτι ἔλεγον ὑμῖν [ὅτι] Ἐπ' ἐσχάτου [τοῦ] χρόνου ἔσονται ἐμπαῖκται κατὰ τὰς ἑαυτῶν ἐπιθυμίας πορευόμενοι τῶν ἀσεβειῶν.

STEP TWO: **Parse** the following verbs.

	Lexical Form	Tense	Voice	Mood	Pers.	Num.	Translation
(1) μνήσθητε							
(2) ἔλεγον							
(3) ἔσονται							

STEP THREE: **Identify** the gender, case, and number of the following words.

	Gender	Case	Num.		Gender	Case	Num.
(1) ὑμεῖς				(7) ὑμῖν			
(2) ἀγαπητοί				(8) τοῦ χρόνου			
(3) τῶν ῥημάτων				(9) ἐμπαῖκται			
(4) τῶν ἀποστόλων				(10) τὰς ἐπιθυμίας			
(5) τοῦ κυρίου				(11) ἑαυτῶν			
(6) ἡμῶν				(12) τῶν ἀσεβειῶν			

STEP FOUR: **Translate** the text into understandable English.

VOCABULARY

μιμνῄσκω, I remember
προλέγω, I foretell
ἐμπαίκτης, ὁ, mocker
ἐπιθυμία, ἡ, desire, lust
ἀσέβεια, ἡ, ungodliness, impiety

STEP FIVE: **Notice** significant exegetical and syntactical insights.

- **μνήσθητε τῶν ῥημάτων τῶν προειρημένων:** The aorist imperative μνήσθητε is used to command a specific occurrence (which is common for the aorist and, like many verbs of remembering, takes its direct object in the genitive case [τῶν ῥημάτων]). The participle προειρημένων (perf. pass. ptc. neut. gen. pl. of προεῖπον) functions attributively, modifying τῶν ῥημάτων ("the *previously spoken* words").

- **ὅτι ἔλεγον ὑμῖν:** The imperfect verb ἔλεγον conveys "that the readers had already been told (προειρημένων) what he is about to say *on more than one occasion*."[1]

- **ἐπ᾽ ἐσχάτου χρόνου ἔσονται ἐμπαῖκται:** The preposition ἐπί is extremely versatile, and here it is used as "a marker of temporal associations" ("*in* the end time," BDAG 367). The noun ἐμπαῖκται functions as the nominative subject of ἔσονται ("mockers will be . . .").

- **κατὰ τὰς ἑαυτῶν ἐπιθυμίας πορευόμενοι τῶν ἀσεβειῶν:** The participle πορευόμενοι (pres. mid. ptc. nom. masc. pl. of πορεύομαι) functions attributively ("mockers *who go after* ungodly lusts"). The genitive phrase in the construction ἐπιθυμίας . . . τῶν ἀσεβειῶν is an attributive genitive ("lusts of ungodliness" = "ungodly lusts").

---

1. Peter H. Davids, *The Letters of 2 Peter and Jude*, BHGNT (Waco: Baylor University Press, 2011), 29.

FOR THE JOURNEY

Are we living in the "end times"? The NT unequivocally affirms that we have been in the end times since the first coming of Jesus—especially in his death, resurrection, ascension, and the subsequent coming of the Holy Spirit. Indeed, several different phrases are used that all refer to the same period: "in the last days" (Acts 2:17; 2 Tim. 3:1; Heb. 1:2; James 5:3; 2 Pet. 3:3), "the last day" (John 6:39–40, 44, 54; 11:24; 12:48), "the last hour" (1 John 2:18), "the last time" (1 Pet. 1:5), and "the later/latter times" (1 Tim. 4:1 NIV/KJV). The first coming of Jesus constitutes the initial fulfillment of God's promises to his people, which will only be finally realized when he comes again. The concept of the last days is rooted in OT expectations of a time when God would manifestly intervene to accomplish his purposes for the world and his people (cf. Isa. 2:2; Dan. 11:40–12:13). The NT writers firmly believed that the arrival, death, and resurrection of Jesus the Messiah inaugurated an eschatological shift indicating that the last days have now commenced and will be brought to the proper conclusion at the return of Christ.

ANSWER KEY

1. *Parse:* (1) μνήσθητε (μιμνήσκω, aor. pass. impv. 2nd pl.), (2) ἔλεγον (λέγω, impf. act. ind. 3rd pl.), (3) ἔσονται (εἰμί, fut. mid. ind. 3rd pl.).

2. *Identify:* (1) ὑμεῖς (nom. pl.), (2) ἀγαπητοί (masc. voc. pl.), (3) τῶν ῥημάτων (neut. gen. pl.), (4) τῶν ἀποστόλων (masc. gen. pl.), (5) τοῦ κυρίου (masc. gen. sg.), (6) ἡμῶν (gen. pl.), (7) ὑμῖν (dat. pl.), (8) τοῦ χρόνου (masc. gen. sg.), (9) ἐμπαῖκται (masc. nom. pl.), (10) τὰς ἐπιθυμίας (fem. acc. pl.), (11) ἑαυτῶν (masc. gen. pl.), (12) τῶν ἀσεβειῶν (fem. gen. pl.).

3. *Translate:* "But you, beloved, remember the words foretold by the apostles of our Lord Jesus Christ that they were saying to you that in the end time there will be mockers who go after their own ungodly lusts."

DAY 77: JUDE 19

STEP ONE: **Read** aloud the text at least five times.

Οὗτοί εἰσιν οἱ ἀποδιορίζοντες, ψυχικοί, πνεῦμα μὴ ἔχοντες.

STEP TWO: **Parse** the following verb.

	Lexical Form	Tense	Voice	Mood	Pers.	Num.	Translation
εἰσιν							

STEP THREE: **Identify** the gender, case, and number of the following words.

	Gender	Case	Num.		Gender	Case	Num.
(1) οὗτοί				(3) πνεῦμα			
(2) ψυχικοί							

STEP FOUR: **Translate** the text into understandable English.

_____

_____

VOCABULARY

ἀποδιορίζω, I divide, separate

ψυχικός, unspiritual, worldly

STEP FIVE: **Notice** significant exegetical and syntactical insights.

- **Οὗτοί εἰσιν οἱ ἀποδιορίζοντες:** The articular participle οἱ ἀποδιορίζοντες (pres. act. ptc. masc. nom. pl. of ἀποδιορίζω) functions substantively ("the ones who cause division") and is a predicate nominative.

- **ψυχικοί, πνεῦμα μὴ ἔχοντες:** The noun ψυχικοί is literally translated "natural" or "worldly" and refers to "the life of the natural world and whatever belongs to it, in contrast to the realm of experience whose central characteristic is πνεῦμα, *natural, unspiritual, worldly*" (BDAG 1100). This nominative form is in apposition to οἱ ἀποδιορίζοντες. The anarthrous participle ἔχοντες (pres. act. ptc. masc. nom. pl. of ἔχω) functions substantively ("[those] not having") and is in apposition to ψυχικοί.

FOR THE JOURNEY

Jude offers three descriptions of the false teachers. These opponents are divisive, worldly, and unspiritual. First, he calls them divisive, those who cause divisions. These are people who cause strife and partisanship that results in separation or division. John experienced a similar situation and speaks of those who "went out from us, but they were not of us" (1 John 2:19 KJV). Paul refers to those who formed cliques within the church (1 Cor. 1:11–12) and later writes "I hear that there are divisions among you" (1 Cor. 11:18 ESV). James mentions jealousy and selfish ambition in the church (James 3:14–16). Second, Jude says that they are natural or worldly. That is, they follow their natural, fleshly instincts instead of being led by the Spirit. Perhaps Jude is countering the claims of his opponents who claim to have the Spirit and can thus live as they please. The term ψυχικός is linked with "demonic" in James 3:15. Third, they are unspiritual ("not having the Spirit," CSB). Despite what they might claim, they are not led by the Spirit, since they do not possess the Spirit of God. They are led by purely natural, earthly impulses. Their lives reflect the one who leads them, as does ours.

ANSWER KEY

1. *Parse:* εἰσιν (εἰμί, pres. act. ind. 3rd pl.).
2. *Identify:* (1) οὗτοί (masc. nom. pl.), (2) ψυχικοί (masc. nom. pl.), (3) πνεῦμα (neut. acc. sg.).
3. *Translate:* "These are the ones who cause divisions, worldly people, not having the Spirit."

DAY 78: JUDE 20–21

STEP ONE: **Read** aloud the text at least five times.

ὑμεῖς δέ, ἀγαπητοί, ἐποικοδομοῦντες ἑαυτοὺς τῇ ἁγιωτάτῃ ὑμῶν πίστει, ἐν πνεύματι ἁγίῳ προσευχόμενοι, ἑαυτοὺς ἐν ἀγάπῃ θεοῦ τηρήσατε προσδεχόμενοι τὸ ἔλεος τοῦ κυρίου ἡμῶν Ἰησοῦ Χριστοῦ εἰς ζωὴν αἰώνιον.

STEP TWO: **Parse** the following verb.

	Lexical Form	Tense	Voice	Mood	Pers.	Num.	Translation
τηρήσατε							

STEP THREE: **Identify** the gender, case, and number of the following words.

	Gender	Case	Num.		Gender	Case	Num.
(1) ὑμεῖς				(8) ἀγάπη			
(2) ἀγαπητοί				(9) θεοῦ			
(3) ἑαυτούς				(10) τὸ ἔλεος			
(4) τῇ πίστει				(11) τοῦ κυρίου			
(5) ὑμῶν				(12) ἡμῶν			
(6) πνεύματι				(13) ζωήν			
(7) ἑαυτούς				(14) αἰώνιον			

STEP FOUR: **Translate** the text into understandable English.

VOCABULARY

ἐποικοδομέω, I build up, edify
προσδέχομαι, I wait for
ἔλεος, τό, mercy, compassion

STEP FIVE: **Notice** significant exegetical and syntactical insights.

- **ἐποικοδομοῦντες ἑαυτοὺς τῇ ἁγιωτάτῃ ὑμῶν πίστει:** The adverbial participle ἐποικοδομοῦντες (pres. act. ptc. masc. nom. pl. of ἐποικοδομέω) communicates means ("*by* building"). The adjective ἁγιωτάτῃ is the superlative form of ἅγιος ("most holy"). Superlative adjectives often have an elative sense ("very") in the Koine period, which seems to be the sense here since Jude is not comparing faith traditions according to their varying levels of holiness.

- **ἐν πνεύματι ἁγίῳ προσευχόμενοι:** The adverbial participle προσευχόμενοι (pres. mid. ptc. masc. nom. pl. of προσεύχομαι) communicates means ("*by* praying"). In other words, it is *by* building themselves up and *by* praying that the Christians will obey the command to keep themselves in the love of God. Specifically, Christians are expected to pray ἐν πνεύματι ἁγίῳ, which communicates agency ("*in/by* the Holy Spirit").

- **ἑαυτοὺς ἐν ἀγάπῃ θεοῦ τηρήσατε:** The noun θεοῦ is likely a subjective genitive (i.e., "the love of God" = the love that God has for his people). Robertson notes that in verse 1, the recipients of Jude's Letter are described as "kept by Jesus Christ" (Ἰησοῦ Χριστῷ τετηρημένοις), but here they are commanded to keep "themselves" (ἑαυτούς). He notes that, as in Phil. 2:12, "Human responsibility and divine sovereignty are presented side by side."[2]

- **προσδεχόμενοι τὸ ἔλεος τοῦ κυρίου ἡμῶν Ἰησοῦ Χριστοῦ εἰς ζωὴν αἰώνιον:** The adverbial participle προσδεχόμενοι (pres. mid. ptc. masc. nom. pl. of προσδέχομαι) functions temporally ("*as* you wait"). The preposition εἰς communicates result. The appearance of God's mercy at Christ's return results in eternal life.

2. A. T. Robertson, *Word Pictures* (Grand Rapids: Baker, 1960), 6:194–95.

FOR THE JOURNEY

These two verses have one imperative in the Greek: "Keep yourselves in the love of God" (v. 20). But how do we obey this command? Precisely how do we keep ourselves in a place where we experience God's love for us? The three participles communicate the means by which we accomplish this task. First, we do it *by building ourselves up in our most holy faith*. But as Davids notes, "the building is collective. It is not that the individual follower of Jesus is to build himself or herself up, but that the follower(s) of Jesus (individually or together) is (are) to build the community of Jesus up."[3] Second, we keep ourselves in God's love *by praying in the Holy Spirit*. Our prayers should be guided by God's Spirit and should therefore be consistent with God's will and God's word. Finally, we do it *by waiting expectantly for the mercy of our Lord*. Such waiting involves our eschatological hope, which is linked to Christ's return. Paul states that we are currently "waiting for our blessed hope, the appearing of the glory of our great God and Savior Jesus Christ" (Titus 2:13 ESV).

ANSWER KEY

1. *Parse:* τηρήσατε (τηρέω, aor. act. impv. 2nd pl.).

2. *Identify:* (1) ὑμεῖς (nom. pl.), (2) ἀγαπητοί (masc. voc. pl.), (3) ἑαυτούς (masc. acc. pl.), (4) τῇ πίστει (fem. dat. sg.), (5) ὑμῶν (gen. pl.), (6) πνεύματι (neut. dat. sg.), (7) ἑαυτούς (masc. acc. pl.), (8) ἀγάπῃ (fem. dat. sg.), (9) θεοῦ (masc. gen. sg.), (10) τὸ ἔλεος (neut. acc. sg.), (11) τοῦ κυρίου (masc. gen. sg.), (12) ἡμῶν (gen. pl.), (13) ζωήν (fem. acc. sg.), (14) αἰώνιον (fem. acc. sg.).

3. *Translate:* "But you, beloved, building up yourselves in your most holy faith, praying in the Holy Spirit, keep yourself in the love of God, waiting expectantly for the mercy of our Lord Jesus Christ for eternal life."

3. Davids, *Letters of 2 Peter and Jude*, 94.

DAY 79: JUDE 22–23

STEP ONE: **Read** aloud the text at least five times.

καὶ οὓς μὲν ἐλεᾶτε διακρινομένους, οὓς δὲ σῴζετε ἐκ πυρὸς ἁρπάζοντες, οὓς δὲ ἐλεᾶτε ἐν φόβῳ μισοῦντες καὶ τὸν ἀπὸ τῆς σαρκὸς
ἐσπιλωμένον χιτῶνα.

STEP TWO: **Parse** the following verbs.

	Lexical Form	Tense	Voice	Mood	Pers.	Num.	Translation
(1) ἐλεᾶτε							
(2) σῴζετε							

STEP THREE: **Identify** the gender, case, and number of the following words.

	Gender	Case	Num.		Gender	Case	Num.
(1) οὕς				(4) τὸν χιτῶνα			
(2) πυρός				(5) τῆς σαρκός			
(3) φόβῳ							

STEP FOUR: **Translate** the text into understandable English.

_____

_____

VOCABULARY

ἐλεάω, I have mercy on
διακρίνω, I doubt, waver
ἁρπάζω, I snatch, take away
φόβος, ὁ, fear
μισέω, I hate, detest
σπιλόω, I stain, defile
χιτών, ὁ, shirt, clothes

STEP FIVE: **Notice** significant exegetical and syntactical insights.

- **καὶ οὓς μὲν ἐλεᾶτε διακρινομένους:** The participle διακρινομένους (pres. mid. ptc. masc. acc. pl. of διακρίνω) functions attributively, modifying the relative pronoun οὕς ("those *who are doubting*"). The particle μέν introduces an idea that is contrasted with two other ideas, both introduced by δέ in verse 23, an example of a μέν ... δέ construction ("on the one hand ... on the other hand ...").

- **οὓς δὲ σῴζετε ἐκ πυρὸς ἁρπάζοντες:** The adverbial participle ἁρπάζοντες (pres. act. ptc. masc. nom. pl. of ἁρπάζω) communicates means ("*by* snatching").

- **οὓς δὲ ἐλεᾶτε ἐν φόβῳ:** The prepositional phrase ἐν φόβῳ ("with fear") communicates the manner in which believers are to show mercy. That is, as they help rescue sinners, they are to do so with a godly trepidation, reflecting on the personal danger to their spiritual lives as they come into close contact with deceitful wickedness.

- **μισοῦντες καὶ τὸν ἀπὸ τῆς σαρκὸς ἐσπιλωμένον χιτῶνα:** The adverbial participle μισοῦντες (pres. act. ptc. masc. nom. pl. of μισέω) conveys the manner in which mercy is to be shown, with a loving compassion that includes a holy hatred of sin. The participle ἐσπιλωμένον (perf. pass. ptc. masc. acc. sg. of σπιλόω) functions attributively, modifying χιτῶνα ("the clothing *stained*"). In fact, the noun τὸν ... χιτῶνα is modified by the entire phrase (ἀπὸ τῆς σαρκὸς ἐσπιλωμένον) that is sandwiched between the article and the noun.

FOR THE JOURNEY

Jude informs his readers that they are to do three things in relation to those who are in danger of leaving the true path. First, they should "have mercy on those who doubt" (v. 22). Jude has already wished for mercy for his readers (v. 2), and it is what they hope to receive from Christ (v. 21). Thus it is fitting that those who receive mercy extend it to others. Second, they are to "save others by snatching them from the fire" (v. 23 NIV). "In Jude's picture the flames of judgment already lap around their feet; one must snatch them away before they are fully in flame and lost forever."⁴ They are proleptically pictured as in the fires of Gehenna (see Amos 4:11; Zech. 3:2; Matt. 5:22; 18:8). Third, they are to "have mercy on others with fear" (v. 23). Mercy is emphasized a second time, but it must be offered in a reverent manner, hating "the clothing stained by the flesh." As we show mercy to others who are near hellfire, we must be careful not to endanger ourselves and fall into the same sin.

ANSWER KEY

1. *Parse:* (1) ἐλεᾶτε (ἐλεάω, pres. act. impv. 2nd pl.), (2) σῴζετε (σῴζω, pres. act. impv. 2nd pl.).

2. *Identify:* (1) οὕς (masc. acc. pl.), (2) πυρός (neut. gen. sg.), (3) φόβῳ (masc. dat. sg.), (4) τὸν χιτῶνα (masc. acc. sg.), (5) τῆς σαρκός (fem. gen. sg.).

3. *Translate:* "And have mercy on those who doubt. And save others by snatching [them] from the fire, and have mercy on others with fear, even hating the clothing stained by the flesh."

4. Davids, *Letters of 2 Peter and Jude*, 102.

DAY 80: JUDE 24–25

STEP ONE: **Read** aloud the text at least five times.

Τῷ δὲ δυναμένῳ φυλάξαι ὑμᾶς ἀπταίστους καὶ στῆσαι κατενώπιον τῆς δόξης αὐτοῦ ἀμώμους ἐν ἀγαλλιάσει, μόνῳ θεῷ σωτῆρι ἡμῶν διὰ Ἰησοῦ Χριστοῦ τοῦ κυρίου ἡμῶν δόξα μεγαλωσύνη κράτος καὶ ἐξουσία πρὸ παντὸς τοῦ αἰῶνος καὶ νῦν καὶ εἰς πάντας τοὺς αἰῶνας, ἀμήν.

STEP TWO: **Parse** any verbs.
There are no verbs.

STEP THREE: **Identify** the gender, case, and number of the following words.

	Gender	Case	Num.		Gender	Case	Num.
(1) ἀπταίστους				(8) μεγαλωσύνη			
(2) τῆς δόξης				(9) κράτος			
(3) ἀμώμους				(10) ἐξουσία			
(4) ἀγαλλιάσει				(11) παντός			
(5) σωτῆρι				(12) τοῦ αἰῶνος			
(6) τοῦ κυρίου				(13) πάντας			
(7) δόξα				(14) τούς αἰῶνας			

STEP FOUR: **Translate** the text into understandable English.

VOCABULARY

φυλάσσω, I guard, protect
ἄπταιστος, without stumbling
κατενώπιον, before (place)
ἄμωμος, blameless
ἀγαλλίασις, ἡ, gladness, joy

σωτήρ, ὁ, savior, deliverer
μεγαλωσύνη, ἡ, majesty
κράτος, τό, power
πρό, before (time)

STEP FIVE: **Notice** significant exegetical and syntactical insights.

- **Τῷ δὲ δυναμένῳ φυλάξαι ὑμᾶς ἀπταίστους:** The participle τῷ ... δυναμένῳ (pres. mid. ptc. masc. dat. sg. of δύναμαι) functions substantively ("to the one who is able"). The verb φυλάξαι (aor. act. inf. of φυλάσσω) is a complementary infinitive, taking a double accusative: ὑμᾶς (the direct object) and ἀπταίστους (the predicate object or complement).

- **καὶ στῆσαι κατενώπιον τῆς δόξης αὐτοῦ ἀμώμους ἐν ἀγαλλιάσει:** The verb στῆσαι (aor. act. inf. of ἵστημι) is the second complementary infinitive in verse 24, both linked to the substantival participle δυναμένῳ. The adjective ἀμώμους is the object-complement in another double accusative construction (but this time with ὑμᾶς implied). The prepositional phrase ἐν ἀγαλλιάσει ("with joy") communicates the manner in which God's people stand before him (i.e., joyfully).

- **μόνῳ θεῷ σωτῆρι ἡμῶν διὰ Ἰησοῦ Χριστοῦ τοῦ κυρίου ἡμῶν:** The dative nouns μόνῳ θεῷ ("the only God") and σωτῆρι ("Savior") are in apposition to δυναμένῳ. The genitive noun τοῦ κυρίου is in apposition to Ἰησοῦ Χριστοῦ.

- **δόξα μεγαλωσύνη κράτος καὶ ἐξουσία πρὸ παντὸς τοῦ αἰῶνος καὶ νῦν καὶ εἰς πάντας τοὺς αἰῶνας, ἀμήν:** There is an ellipsis of the verb εἴη ("may it be," pres. act. opt. 3rd sg. of εἰμί) or some similar verb.

FOR THE JOURNEY

Jude appropriately ends his short letter with a doxology (a praise to God). He describes God as the one who is able "to keep/guard" his people and "to present us blameless." Earlier in his letter, Jude stated that believers are "kept" (τετηρημένοις) by Jesus Christ (v. 1). Jesus prays that his disciples are "kept" (τήρησον) in God's name and that he might "keep" (τηρήσης) them from the evil one (John 17:11, 15). Paul states that God will establish and "guard" his people "against the evil one" (2 Thess. 3:3). And Peter reminds his readers that by God's power they are "being guarded [φρουρουμένους] through faith" (1 Pet. 1:5).

But God not only guards and protects his people; he also will "present" them as blameless. The verb translated "present" means "to cause to stand," a verb that contrasts with falling or stumbling mentioned in verse 24. Davids remarks, "If one does not fall in the world, then one stands before God, and both standing and being without fault are products of God's actions" (*Letters of 2 Peter and Jude*, 110).

ANSWER KEY

1. *Parse:* No verbs to parse.
2. *Identify:* (1) ἀπταίστους (masc. acc. pl.), (2) τῆς δόξης (fem. gen. sg.), (3) ἀμώμους (masc. acc. pl.), (4) ἀγαλλιάσει (fem. dat. sg.), (5) σωτῆρι (masc. dat. sg.), (6) τοῦ κυρίου (masc. gen. sg.), (7) δόξα (fem. nom. sg.), (8) μεγαλωσύνη (fem. nom. sg.), (9) κράτος (neut. nom. sg.), (10) ἐξουσία (fem. nom. sg.), (11) παντός (masc. gen. sg.), (12) τοῦ αἰῶνος (masc. gen. sg.), (13) πάντας (masc. acc. pl.), (14) τούς αἰῶνας (masc. acc. pl.).
3. *Translate:* "To him who is able to keep you from stumbling and to make you stand blameless before his glory with gladness, to the only God our Savior through Jesus Christ our Lord [be] glory, majesty, power, and authority before every age and both now and into the ages, amen."

ROUTE 17

Hebrews 3:1–6

STEP ONE: **Read** aloud the text at least five times.

Ὅθεν, ἀδελφοὶ ἅγιοι, κλήσεως ἐπουρανίου μέτοχοι, κατανοήσατε τὸν ἀπόστολον καὶ ἀρχιερέα τῆς ὁμολογίας ἡμῶν Ἰησοῦν, πιστὸν ὄντα τῷ ποιήσαντι αὐτὸν ὡς καὶ Μωϋσῆς ἐν [ὅλῳ] τῷ οἴκῳ αὐτοῦ.

STEP TWO: **Parse** the following verb.

	Lexical Form	Tense	Voice	Mood	Pers.	Num.	Translation
κατανοήσατε							

STEP THREE: **Identify** the gender, case, and number of the following words.

	Gender	Case	Num.		Gender	Case	Num.
(1) ἀδελφοί				(7) τῆς ὁμολογίας			
(2) κλήσεως				(8) ἡμῶν			
(3) ἐπουρανίου				(9) Ἰησοῦν			
(4) μέτοχοι				(10) πιστόν			
(5) τὸν ἀπόστολον				(11) τῷ οἴκῳ			
(6) ἀρχιερέα				(12) αὐτοῦ			

STEP FOUR: Translate the text into understandable English.

VOCABULARY

ὅθεν, therefore
κλῆσις, ἡ, calling
ἐπουράνιος, heavenly
μέτοχος, ὁ, partaker
κατανοέω, I consider
ὁμολογία, ἡ, confession

STEP FIVE: Notice significant exegetical and syntactical insights.

- Ὅθεν, ἀδελφοὶ ἅγιοι, κλήσεως ἐπουρανίου μέτοχοι: The noun κλήσεως is genitive because of its syntactical relationship with μέτοχοι, which takes a genitive (BDAG 643). The noun μέτοχοι is vocative because it is in apposition to ἀδελφοὶ ἅγιοι.

- κατανοήσατε τὸν ἀπόστολον καὶ ἀρχιερέα τῆς ὁμολογίας ἡμῶν Ἰησοῦν: The object of the verb κατανοήσατε ("consider") is Ἰησοῦν. The phrase τὸν ἀπόστολον καὶ ἀρχιερέα is in apposition to Ἰησοῦν. The Granville Sharp rule applies to τὸν ἀπόστολον καὶ ἀρχιερέα (two substantives governed by one article connected by καί refer to one entity), which signifies that Jesus is both the apostle and high priest.

- πιστὸν ὄντα τῷ ποιήσαντι αὐτὸν ὡς καὶ Μωϋσῆς ἐν [ὅλῳ] τῷ οἴκῳ αὐτοῦ: The participle ὄντα (pres. act. ptc. masc. acc. sg. of εἰμί) functions attributively, modifying Ἰησοῦν ("Jesus, who was faithful"). The participle τῷ ποιήσαντι (aor. act. ptc. masc. dat. sg. of ποιέω) functions substantively, referring to God.

FOR THE JOURNEY

The author of Hebrews establishes that Jesus is superior to what the old covenant had to offer. Therefore, it would be foolish to return to the old system and forsake the one who is greater than the prophets, angels, Joshua, Aaron, and, yes, even Moses. The readers are exhorted to "consider" Jesus, who is "the apostle and high priest" of God. These two designations of Jesus are unique to the author of Hebrews. Jesus is first the apostle of our confession because he was sent by God to accomplish the mission of establishing the new covenant. He was sent to secure salvation by being obedient to the Father, accomplishing all that he was sent to do. Just as the Lord sent Moses to deliver his people from slavery in Egypt, so too Jesus is God's final and definitive ambassador to deliver his people from their bondage to sin. As a high priest, Jesus became fully human in order to offer himself as the perfect substitute, enabling us to have access to God. "For by a single offering he has perfected for all time those who are being sanctified" (Heb. 10:14 ESV). Moses was a faithful servant of God, but Jesus is greater—by far!

ANSWER KEY

1. *Parse:* κατανοήσατε (κατανοέω, aor. act. impv. 2nd pl.).
2. *Identify:* (1) ἀδελφοί (masc. voc. pl.), (2) κλήσεως (fem. gen. sg.), (3) ἐπουρανίου (fem. gen. sg.), (4) μέτοχοι (masc. voc. pl.), (5) τὸν ἀπόστολον (masc.
   acc. sg.), (6) ἀρχιερέα (masc. acc. sg.), (7) τῆς ὁμολογίας (fem. gen. sg.),
   (8) ἡμῶν (gen. pl.), (9) Ἰησοῦν (masc. acc. sg.), (10) πιστόν (masc. acc. sg.),
   (11) τῷ οἴκῳ (masc. dat. sg.), (12) αὐτοῦ (masc. gen. sg.).
3. *Translate:* "Therefore, holy brothers, partakers of the heavenly calling, consider
   Jesus, the apostle and high priest of our confession, who was faithful to him
   who appointed him just as Moses also [was] in all his house."

DAY 82: HEBREWS 3:3

STEP ONE: **Read** aloud the text at least five times.

πλείονος γὰρ οὗτος δόξης παρὰ Μωϋσῆν ἠξίωται, καθ' ὅσον πλείονα
τιμὴν ἔχει τοῦ οἴκου ὁ κατασκευάσας αὐτόν·

STEP TWO: **Parse** the following verbs.

	Lexical Form	Tense	Voice	Mood	Pers.	Num.	Translation
(1) ἠξίωται							
(2) ἔχει							

STEP THREE: **Identify** the gender, case, and number of the following words.

	Gender	Case	Num.		Gender	Case	Num.
(1) πλείονος				(5) πλείονα			
(2) οὗτος				(6) τιμήν			
(3) δόξης				(7) τοῦ οἴκου			
(4) ὅσον				(8) αὐτόν			

STEP FOUR: **Translate** the text into understandable English.

VOCABULARY

ἀξιόω, I consider/count worthy
τιμή, ἡ, honor
κατασκευάζω, I build, prepare

STEP FIVE: **Notice** significant exegetical and syntactical insights.

* **πλείονος γὰρ οὗτος δόξης παρὰ Μωϋσῆν ἠξίωται:** The comparative adjective πλείονος is fronted for emphasis. The near demonstrative pronoun οὗτος refers back to Ἰησοῦν (v. 1). The preposition παρά followed by the accusative Μωϋσῆν communicates comparison.

- καθ' ὅσον πλείονα τιμὴν ἔχει τοῦ οἴκου ὁ κατασκευάσας αὐτόν: The noun τοῦ οἴκου is a comparative genitive (*"than* the house"). The participle ὁ κατασκευάσας functions substantively ("the builder"), with Jesus as its referent, and is the subject of the verb ἔχει.

FOR THE JOURNEY

When a child's team wins a baseball game, that is a worthy accomplishment. But if your favorite team wins the World Series, that is a far greater achievement. Both are good, but one is better. Moses deserves a place of honor for being one of God's chief servants. But Jesus should be considered worthy of far more honor than Moses. The analogy used is one of a house and of an architect/builder of a house. When someone sees a finely constructed house, they don't compliment the house itself; instead, they congratulate the builder of the house. In the same way, Moses (compared to the house) deserves some honor as God's servant. But Jesus is the one who built the house (probably a reference to God's people). As the builder, he is to receive honor and glory. As Ellingworth explains, "Praise of Jesus does not entail blame of Moses. . . . Jesus' faithfulness is more highly honoured than that of Moses, not because Moses' faithfulness was in any way defective, but because that of Jesus was displayed in a higher office."[1] As the great apostle and high priest, Jesus is deserving of our praise.

ANSWER KEY

1. *Parse:* (1) ἠξίωται (ἀξιόω, perf. pass. ind. 3rd sg.), (2) ἔχει (ἔχω, pres. act. ind. 3rd sg.).

2. *Identify:* (1) πλείονος (fem. gen. sg.), (2) οὗτος (masc. nom. sg.), (3) δόξης (fem. gen. sg.), (4) ὅσον (neut. acc. sg.), (5) πλείονα (fem. acc. sg.), (6) τιμήν (fem. acc. sg.), (7) τοῦ οἴκου (masc. gen. sg.), (8) αὐτόν (masc. acc. sg.).

3. *Translate:* "For this one has been considered worthy of more glory than Moses, as much more honor as the builder than the house itself."

1. Paul Ellingworth, *The Epistle to the Hebrews*, NIGTC (Grand Rapids: Eerdmans, 1993), 203.

DAY 83: HEBREWS 3:4

STEP ONE: **Read** aloud the text at least five times.

πᾶς γὰρ οἶκος κατασκευάζεται ὑπό τινος, ὁ δὲ πάντα κατασκευάσας θεός.

STEP TWO: **Parse** the following verb.

	Lexical Form	Tense	Voice	Mood	Pers.	Num.	Translation
κατασκευάζεται							

STEP THREE: **Identify** the gender, case, and number of the following words.

	Gender	Case	Num.		Gender	Case	Num.
(1) πᾶς				(4) πάντα			
(2) οἶκος				(5) θεός			
(3) τινος							

STEP FOUR: **Translate** the text into understandable English.

<hr />

<hr />

> VOCABULARY
>
> κατασκευάζω, I build, prepare

STEP FIVE: **Notice** significant exegetical and syntactical insights.

- **πᾶς γὰρ οἶκος κατασκευάζεται ὑπό τινος**: The present-tense κατασκευάζω is gnomic, which conveys a general, timeless truth and is often used for proverbial statements or general maxims (see Wallace, *GGBB* 523–25).

- **ὁ δὲ πάντα κατασκευάσας θεός**: The participle ὁ κατασκευάσας (aor. act. ptc. masc. nom. sg. of κατασκευάζω) functions substantively ("the one who builds"). The noun θεός functions as the

predicate nominative with an implied copulative verb (e.g., ἐστιν).[2]
When verses 3 and 4 are considered together, the implication is
that Jesus is God: Jesus is worthy of more glory than Moses since
he is the builder of the house; God is the builder of all things;
therefore, Jesus is God.

FOR THE JOURNEY

The author of Hebrews implicitly claims that Jesus is the Creator of all
things. But can such a statement be validated by other NT passages?
In Colossians, Paul states, "For by him [i.e., Jesus] all things were created, in heaven and on earth, visible and invisible, whether thrones or
dominions or rulers or authorities—all things were created through him
and for him" (Col. 1:16 ESV). John informs us that Jesus was there in
the beginning with God and that "All things were made through him, and
without him was not any thing made that was made" (John 1:3 ESV).
As the "Alpha and Omega," he not only has no beginning and no end,
but he was there in the beginning, forming and fashioning the universe.
He is also called "the first and the last" (Rev. 1:17; 2:8; 22:13), "the
beginning and the end" (21:6; 22:13). Bauckham argues that these titles
in Revelation do not "designate him a second god . . . but includes him
in the eternal being of the one God of Israel who is the only source and
goal of all things."[3] As the master builder, Jesus is the master of all that
he built—and he built all things.

ANSWER KEY

1. *Parse:* κατασκευάζεται (κατασκευάζω, pres. pass. ind. 3rd sg.).
2. *Identify:* (1) πᾶς (masc. nom. sg.), (2) οἶκος (masc. nom. sg.), (3) τινος (masc. gen. sg.), (4) πάντα (neut. acc. pl.), (5) θεός (masc. nom. sg.).
3. *Translate:* "For every house is built by someone, and the one who built all things is God."

---

2. Wallace (*GGBB* 43) notes that when there is doubt, the articular substantive will be the subject.

3. Richard Bauckham, *Theology of the Book of Revelation* (Cambridge: Cambridge University Press, 1993), 58.

DAY 84: HEBREWS 3:5

STEP ONE: **Read** aloud the text at least five times.

καὶ Μωϋσῆς μὲν πιστὸς ἐν ὅλῳ τῷ οἴκῳ αὐτοῦ ὡς θεράπων εἰς μαρτύριον τῶν λαληθησομένων,

STEP TWO: **Parse** any verbs.
There are no verbs.

STEP THREE: **Identify** the gender, case, and number of the following words.

	Gender	Case	Num.		Gender	Case	Num.
(1) πιστός				(4) θεράπων			
(2) τῷ οἴκῳ				(5) μαρτύριον			
(3) αὐτοῦ							

STEP FOUR: **Translate** the text into understandable English.

VOCABULARY

θεράπων, ὁ, servant, steward
μαρτύριον, τό, testimony

STEP FIVE: **Notice** significant exegetical and syntactical insights.

- **καὶ Μωϋσῆς μὲν πιστὸς ἐν ὅλῳ τῷ οἴκῳ αὐτοῦ:** The adjective πιστός is the predicate nominative of an implied copulative verb (e.g., ἦν).

- **ὡς θεράπων εἰς μαρτύριον τῶν λαληθησομένων:** The term θεράπων can be glossed as "servant" (most English versions), "attendant" (YLT), or "steward." The prepositional phrase εἰς μαρτύριον communicates purpose. The participle τῶν λαληθησομένων (fut. pass. ptc. masc. gen. pl. of λαλέω) functions substantively ("of what things would be said"). The future form of a participle only occurs 12 times in the NT, with this being the only future passive form.

FOR THE JOURNEY

Although almost all English versions translate the noun θεράπων as "servant," such a gloss might not convey the significance of this term. This is not merely a low position of someone who serves others but, especially in a religious/cultic context, it is an honorific designation of one who holds the elevated status. In the OT, the term is used in relation to the status of Moses: "Israel saw the great power that the LORD used against the Egyptians, so the people feared the LORD, and they believed in the LORD and in his *servant* Moses" (Exod. 14:31 ESV). Again we read: "O Lord GOD, you have only begun to show your *servant* your greatness and your mighty hand. For what god is there in heaven or on earth who can do such works and mighty acts as yours?" (Deut. 3:24 ESV). Finally, and this is the text cited by the author of Hebrews, Num. 12:6–8 mentions how God communicates with lesser prophets through visions or dreams, but "not so with my servant Moses. He is faithful in all my house" (v. 7), and so God speaks with him directly and plainly (literally, "mouth to mouth"). In these texts the powerful works of God are displayed, with Moses serving as God's agent and spokesman. Hebrews tells us that Moses functioned as a witness of what God would communicate later to his people. Thus, Moses had an important prophetic role, but his testimony pointed toward something greater. Moses bore witness to Jesus as John the Baptist did, and John said that Jesus was greater than John the Baptist, who described himself as unworthy even to untie Jesus's sandals (Mark 1:7). Moses was a faithful servant, but he wrote about one who was greater. That one has now come.

ANSWER KEY

1. *Parse:* No verbs to parse.
2. *Identify:* (1) πιστός (masc. nom. sg.), (2) τῷ οἴκῳ (masc. dat. sg.), (3) αὐτοῦ (masc. gen. sg.), (4) θεράπων (masc. nom. sg.), (5) μαρτύριον (neut. acc. sg.).
3. *Translate:* ". . . and Moses was faithful in all his house as a servant for a testimony of what would be said."

DAY 85: HEBREWS 3:6

STEP ONE: **Read** aloud the text at least five times.

Χριστὸς δὲ ὡς υἱὸς ἐπὶ τὸν οἶκον αὐτοῦ· οὗ οἶκός ἐσμεν ἡμεῖς,
ἐάν[περ] τὴν παρρησίαν καὶ τὸ καύχημα τῆς ἐλπίδος κατάσχωμεν.

STEP TWO: **Parse** the following verbs.

	Lexical Form	Tense	Voice	Mood	Pers.	Num.	Translation
(1) ἐσμεν							
(2) κατάσχωμεν							

STEP THREE: **Identify** the gender, case, and number of the following words.

	Gender	Case	Num.		Gender	Case	Num.
(1) Χριστός				(6) οἶκος			
(2) υἱός				(7) ἡμεῖς			
(3) τὸν οἶκον				(8) τὴν παρρησίαν			
(4) αὐτοῦ				(9) τὸ καύχημα			
(5) οὗ				(10) τῆς ἐλπίδος			

STEP FOUR: **Translate** the text into understandable English

---

VOCABULARY

ἐάνπερ, if
παρρησία, ἡ, boldness, confidence
καύχημα, τό, boast
κατέχω, I hold fast/firm

253

JOURNEY 3 · DIFFICULT

STEP FIVE: **Notice** significant exegetical and syntactical insights.

- **Χριστὸς δὲ ὡς υἱὸς ἐπὶ τὸν οἶκον αὐτοῦ:** The fronted position of Χριστός conveys emphasis. Moses was a servant *in* (ἐν) God's house, but Christ is Son *over* (ἐπί) God's house. Although a servant receives some benefits from the owner of the house, the son is the heir (see Heb. 1:2). The adjective πιστός is implied from verse 5.

- **οὗ οἶκός ἐσμεν ἡμεῖς:** The antecedent of the genitive relative pronoun οὗ is God.

- **ἐάν[περ] τὴν παρρησίαν καὶ τὸ καύχημα τῆς ἐλπίδος κατάσχωμεν:** This is a third-class conditional statement (ἐάν + subj. = uncertain but likely fulfillment).

FOR THE JOURNEY

This section ends with a conditional statement: we are God's house *if* we continue to hold firm to our hope. The theme of hope is frequently mentioned in this epistle: (1) "so that by two unchangeable things, in which it is impossible for God to lie, we who have fled for refuge might have strong encouragement to hold fast to the *hope* set before us" (6:18 ESV), (2) "(for the law made nothing perfect); but on the other hand, a better *hope* is introduced, through which we draw near to God" (7:19 ESV), (3) "Let us hold fast the confession of our *hope* without wavering, for he who promised is faithful" (10:23 ESV), (4) "Now faith is the assurance of things *hoped* for, the conviction of things not seen" (11:1). Since Jesus has given us the better and final word, we should continue to hold fast to our hope. Why go back to Moses and the OT sacrificial system when Moses himself prophesied regarding a greater prophet? Schreiner summarizes the message of this verse: "Believers in Jesus Christ must hold onto their faith until the end. It would be lamentable to revert to the revelation given through Moses, for Moses was a faithful servant of the Lord, but Jesus is God's faithful Son. . . . Moses himself looked forward to a further word from God, to the fulfillment of what was proclaimed, and Jesus constitutes that fulfillment."[4] May we, through the power of God, hold firm until the end.

4. Thomas R. Schreiner, *Commentary on Hebrews*, BTCP (Nashville: Holman Reference, 2015), 119–20.

ANSWER KEY

1. *Parse:* (1) ἐσμεν (εἰμί, pres. act. ind. 1st pl.), (2) κατάσχωμεν (κατέχω, aor. act. subj. 1st pl.).

2. *Identify:* (1) Χριστός (masc. nom. sg.), (2) υἱός (masc. nom. sg.), (3) τὸν οἶκον (masc. acc. sg.), (4) αὐτοῦ (masc. gen. sg.), (5) οὖ (masc. gen. sg.), (6) οἶκος (masc. nom. sg.), (7) ἡμεῖς (nom. pl.), (8) τὴν παρρησίαν (fem. acc. sg.), (9) τὸ καύχημα (neut. acc. sg.), (10) τῆς ἐλπίδος (fem. gen. sg.).

3. *Translate:* "But Christ [is/was faithful] as a son over his house; whose house we are if we hold firm our confidence and boasting of our hope."

ROUTE 18

Hebrews 13:20–25

STEP ONE: **Read** aloud the text at least five times.

Ὁ δὲ θεὸς τῆς εἰρήνης, ὁ ἀναγαγὼν ἐκ νεκρῶν τὸν ποιμένα τῶν προβάτων τὸν μέγαν ἐν αἵματι διαθήκης αἰωνίου, τὸν κύριον ἡμῶν Ἰησοῦν,

STEP TWO: **Parse** any verbs.
There are no verbs.

STEP THREE: **Identify** the gender, case, and number of the following words.

	Gender	Case	Num.		Gender	Case	Num.
(1) ὁ θεός				(7) αἵματι			
(2) τῆς εἰρήνης				(8) διαθήκης			
(3) νεκρῶν				(9) αἰωνίου			
(4) τὸν ποιμένα				(10) τὸν κύριον			
(5) τῶν προβάτων				(11) ἡμῶν			
(6) τὸν μέγαν				(12) Ἰησοῦν			

256

STEP FOUR: **Translate** the text into understandable English.

VOCABULARY

ἀνάγω, I bring/lead up

ποιμήν, ὁ, shepherd

πρόβατον, τό, sheep

διαθήκη, ἡ, covenant

STEP FIVE: **Notice** significant exegetical and syntactical insights.

- Ὁ δὲ θεὸς τῆς εἰρήνης: Verses 20–21 begin the final benediction. There is an implied optative form of εἰμί (i.e., εἴη). The noun τῆς εἰρήνης is genitive of source (God is the source who grants peace).

- ὁ ἀναγαγὼν ἐκ νεκρῶν τὸν ποιμένα τῶν προβάτων τὸν μέγαν ἐν αἵματι διαθήκης αἰωνίου: The participle ὁ ἀναγαγών (pres. act. ptc. masc. nom. sg. of ἀνάγω) functions substantively and is in apposition to ὁ θεός (or possibly Ἰησοῦν if Jesus is taken as the direct object of the participle). The prepositional phrase ἐν αἵματι διαθήκης αἰωνίου most likely communicates means (*"by* the blood of the eternal covenant"*).

- τὸν κύριον ἡμῶν Ἰησοῦν: The accusative τὸν κύριον is in apposition to τὸν ποιμένα, and Ἰησοῦν is in apposition to τὸν κύριον (or vice versa).

FOR THE JOURNEY

In this benediction, the author mentions God's raising Jesus from the dead. The resurrection of Jesus appears in several places throughout the book of Hebrews. In chapter 5, we read, "In the days of his flesh, Jesus offered up prayers and supplications, with loud cries and tears, to him who *was able to save him from death,* and he was heard because of his reverence" (5:7 ESV, with added emphasis). Death did not have the final word over Jesus. Chapter 6 says that Jesus entered the heavenly temple as our forerunner and is a high priest "according to the order of Melchizedek" (6:19–20 CSB). In chapter 7, we are reminded that Jesus "continues a priest forever" because of his resurrection (7:3). Unlike mortal priests who die, Jesus is the priest who "lives" (7:8) because he has "an indestructible life" (7:16). The priests after the Aaronic order (Levites) "were prevented by death from continuing in office, but [Jesus] holds his priesthood permanently, because he continues forever" (7:23–24). Thus, "he always lives to make intercession for [believers]" (7:25). In fact, he is the reigning Sovereign and seated at God's right hand (1:3, 13; 8:1; 10:12; 12:2). The resurrection of Jesus is the foundation of the Christian faith and Christian hope.

ANSWER KEY

1. *Parse:* No verbs to parse.
2. *Identify:* (1) ὁ θεός (masc. nom. sg.), (2) τῆς εἰρήνης (fem. gen. sg.), (3) νεκρῶν (masc. gen. pl.), (4) τὸν ποιμένα (masc. acc. sg.), (5) τῶν προβάτων (neut. gen. pl.), (6) τὸν μέγαν (masc. acc. sg.), (7) αἵματι (neut. dat. sg.), (8) διαθήκης (fem. gen. sg.), (9) αἰωνίου (fem. gen. sg.), (10) τὸν κύριον (masc. acc. sg.), (11) ἡμῶν (gen. pl.), (12) Ἰησοῦν (masc. acc. sg.).
3. *Translate:* "Now the God of all peace, the one who brought up from the dead the great Shepherd of the sheep by the blood of his eternal covenant, our Lord Jesus, . . ."

DAY 87: HEBREWS 13:21

STEP ONE: **Read** aloud the text at least five times.

… καταρτίσαι ὑμᾶς ἐν παντὶ ἀγαθῷ εἰς τὸ ποιῆσαι τὸ θέλημα αὐτοῦ, ποιῶν ἐν ἡμῖν τὸ εὐάρεστον ἐνώπιον αὐτοῦ διὰ Ἰησοῦ Χριστοῦ, ᾧ ἡ δόξα εἰς τοὺς αἰῶνας [τῶν αἰώνων], ἀμήν.

STEP TWO: **Parse** the following verb.

	Lexical Form	Tense	Voice	Mood	Pers.	Num.	Translation
καταρτίσαι							

STEP THREE: **Identify** the gender, case, and number of the following words.

	Gender	Case	Num.		Gender	Case	Num.
(1) ὑμᾶς				(7) τὸ εὐάρεστον			
(2) παντί				(8) Ἰησοῦ Χριστοῦ			
(3) ἀγαθῷ				(9) ᾧ			
(4) τὸ θέλημα				(10) ἡ δόξα			
(5) αὐτοῦ				(11) τοὺς αἰῶνας			
(6) ἡμῖν				(12) τῶν αἰώνων			

STEP FOUR: **Translate** the text into understandable English.

VOCABULARY

καταρτίζω, I equip, restore
εὐάρεστος, pleasing, acceptable

STEP FIVE: **Notice** significant exegetical and syntactical insights.

- καταρτίσαι ὑμᾶς ἐν παντὶ ἀγαθῷ εἰς τὸ ποιῆσαι τὸ θέλημα αὐτοῦ: The verb καταρτίσαι is in the optative mood, a somewhat rare mood that indicates volition or a wish. It occurs only 68 times in the NT (and in Hebrews only here). The adjective ἀγαθῷ is used substantively ("good thing"). The infinitival phrase εἰς τὸ ποιῆσαι (aor. act. inf. of ποιέω) communicates purpose ("that you might do").

- ποιῶν ἐν ἡμῖν τὸ εὐάρεστον ἐνώπιον αὐτοῦ διὰ Ἰησοῦ Χριστοῦ: The participle ποιῶν (pres. act. ptc. masc. nom. sg. of ποιέω) functions instrumentally (*"by* doing"). The adjective τὸ εὐάρεστον is used substantively ("what is pleasing").

- ᾧ ἡ δόξα εἰς τοὺς αἰῶνας [τῶν αἰώνων], ἀμήν: The antecedent for the relative pronoun ᾧ is most likely "the God of peace" (v. 20; cf. 13:15), but proximity supports Jesus Christ as the antecedent.

FOR THE JOURNEY

In this final verse of the benediction, the author reminds us that God has equipped us for good things so that we might do his will by working in us what is pleasing to him. Indeed, *pleasing service* is a key feature of OT worship that is carried into the NT. In Heb. 12:28, the author states, "So since we are receiving an unshakable kingdom, let us give thanks, and through this let us offer worship *pleasing* [εὐαρέστως] to God in devotion and awe" (NET). We are exhorted to worship or serve God in a way that is pleasing or acceptable to him. In 13:15–16, he adds, "Through him then let us continually offer up a sacrifice of praise to God, that is, the fruit of lips that acknowledge his name. Do not neglect to do good and to share what you have, for such sacrifices are pleasing [εὐαρεστεῖται] to God" (ESV). We know that Enoch lived a life that was pleasing to God (11:5) and that "without faith it is impossible to please" God (11:6 ESV). In our own strength, our righteousness is as filthy rags. But when we receive the life-giving power of God, he works in us "both to will and to work for his good pleasure" (Phil. 2:13 ESV).

ANSWER KEY

1. *Parse:* καταρτίσαι (καταρτίζω, aor. act. opt. 3rd sg.).

2. *Identify:* (1) ὑμᾶς (acc. pl.), (2) παντί (neut. dat. sg.), (3) ἀγαθῷ (neut. dat. sg.), (4) τὸ θέλημα (neut. acc. sg.), (5) αὐτοῦ (masc. gen. sg.), (6) ἡμῖν (dat. pl.), (7) τὸ εὐάρεστον (neut. acc. sg.), (8) Ἰησοῦ Χριστοῦ (masc. gen. sg.), (9) ᾧ (masc. dat. sg.), (10) ἡ δόξα (fem. nom. sg.), (11) τοὺς αἰῶνας (masc. acc. pl.), (12) τῶν αἰώνων (masc. gen. pl.).

3. *Translate:* ". . . may he equip you with every good thing to do his will, working in us what [is] pleasing before him through Jesus Christ, to whom [be] the glory into the ages of ages, amen."

DAY 88: HEBREWS 13:22

STEP ONE: **Read** aloud the text at least five times.

Παρακαλῶ δὲ ὑμᾶς, ἀδελφοί, ἀνέχεσθε τοῦ λόγου τῆς παρακλήσεως,
καὶ γὰρ διὰ βραχέων ἐπέστειλα ὑμῖν.

STEP TWO: **Parse** the following verbs.

	Lexical Form	Tense	Voice	Mood	Pers.	Num.	Translation
(1) παρακαλῶ							
(2) ἀνέχεσθε							
(3) ἐπέστειλα							

STEP THREE: **Identify** the gender, case, and number of the following words.

	Gender	Case	Num.		Gender	Case	Num.
(1) ὑμᾶς				(4) τῆς παρακλήσεως			
(2) ἀδελφοί				(5) βραχέων			
(3) τοῦ λόγου				(6) ὑμῖν			

STEP FOUR: **Translate** the text into understandable English.

VOCABULARY
ἀνέχω, I endure, bear with
παράκλησις, ἡ, exhortation
βραχύς, small, short
ἐπιστέλλω, I write (a letter)

STEP FIVE: **Notice** significant exegetical and syntactical insights.

- **Παρακαλῶ δὲ ὑμᾶς, ἀδελφοί:** Typically, παρακαλῶ is complemented by an infinitive, but occasionally an imperative is found, as it is here (see also 1 Cor. 16:15; 1 Pet. 5:1).

- **ἀνέχεσθε τοῦ λόγου τῆς παρακλήσεως:** The verb ἀνέχω takes a genitive direct object (i.e., τοῦ λόγου). The noun τῆς παρακλήσεως functions as a descriptive genitive (a word characterized by exhortation).

- **καὶ γὰρ διὰ βραχέων ἐπέστειλα ὑμῖν:** The prepositional phrase διὰ βραχέων functions adverbially ("briefly"; cf. δι᾽ ὀλίγων in 1 Pet. 5:12). The verb ἐπέστειλα is an epistolary aorist. Also, because lambda (λ) is a liquid consonant, the sigma (σ) is rejected, causing compensatory lengthening of the vowel (ε → ει).

FOR THE JOURNEY

The author describes his sermon-letter as a "word of exhortation." This same phrase is used in Acts 13:15 for a synagogue sermon given by Paul. William Lane explains, "This expression appears to have been an idiomatic designation for the homily or edifying discourse that followed the public reading from the designated portions of Scripture in the Hellenistic synagogue." In Hebrews, this "exhortation consisted of strong encouragement and stern warning."[1] In fact, the Letter to the Hebrews is peppered with five such warning passages:

- Warning 1: Don't ignore the revelation of God's Son (2:1–4): "Therefore we must pay much closer attention to what we have heard, lest we drift away from it" (2:1).

- Warning 2: Don't harden your heart (3:7–19): "Therefore, as the Holy Spirit says, 'Today, if you hear his voice, do not harden your hearts as in the rebellion, on the day of testing in the wilderness'" (3:7–8).

- Warning 3: Don't be spiritually immature (5:12–6:8): "For though by this time you ought to be teachers, you need someone to teach

---

1. William L. Lane, *Hebrews 9–13*, WBC 47B (Dallas: Word, 1991), 568.

you again the basic principles of the oracles of God. You need milk, not solid food" (5:12).

- Warning 4: Don't forsake Christ (10:26–31): "For if we go on sinning deliberately after receiving the knowledge of the truth, there no longer remains a sacrifice for sins, but a fearful expectation of judgment, and a fury of fire that will consume the adversaries" (10:26–27).
- Warning 5: Don't refuse God's grace (12:18–29): "See that you do not refuse him who is speaking. For if they did not escape when they refused him who warned them on earth, much less will we escape if we reject him who warns from heaven" (12:25).

ANSWER KEY

1. *Parse:* (1) παρακαλῶ (παρακαλέω, pres. act. ind. 1st sg.), (2) ἀνέχεσθε (ἀνέχω, pres. mid. impv. 2nd pl.), (3) ἐπέστειλα (ἐπιστέλλω, aor. act. ind. 1st sg.).

2. *Identify:* (1) ὑμᾶς (acc. pl.), (2) ἀδελφοί (masc. voc. pl.), (3) τοῦ λόγου (masc. gen. sg.), (4) τῆς παρακλήσεως (fem. gen. sg.), (5) βραχέων (masc./neut. gen. pl.), (6) ὑμῖν (dat. pl.).

3. *Translate:* "I exhort you, brothers, bear with this word of exhortation, for also I have written to you briefly."

DAY 89: HEBREWS 13:23

STEP ONE: **Read** aloud the text at least five times.

Γινώσκετε τὸν ἀδελφὸν ἡμῶν Τιμόθεον ἀπολελυμένον, μεθ' οὗ ἐὰν τάχιον ἔρχηται ὄψομαι ὑμᾶς.

STEP TWO: **Parse** the following verbs.

	Lexical Form	Tense	Voice	Mood	Pers.	Num.	Translation
(1) γινώσκετε							
(2) ἔρχηται							
(3) ὄψομαι							

STEP THREE: **Identify** the gender, case, and number of the following words.

	Gender	Case	Num.		Gender	Case	Num.
(1) τὸν ἀδελφόν				(4) οὗ			
(2) ἡμῶν				(5) ὑμᾶς			
(3) Τιμόθεον							

STEP FOUR: **Translate** the text into understandable English.

> **VOCABULARY**
>
> τάχιον, sooner, quicker (comparative form of adv. ταχέως, "soon, quickly," from adj. ταχύς, "soon, quick")

STEP FIVE: **Notice** significant exegetical and syntactical insights.

- **Γινώσκετε τὸν ἀδελφὸν ἡμῶν Τιμόθεον ἀπολελυμένον:** The verb γινώσκετε can be either an indicative ("you know") or an imperative ("you should know," ESV, NET; "be aware," CSB; "I want you to know," NIV, NRSVue, NLT; "take notice," NASB1995; "know," NKJV). If the indicative is meant, then the author is reminding them of what they already know. If the imperative is meant, he is giving them new information. The hortatory context favors the imperative (which is reflected in most English versions). The name Τιμόθεον is in apposition to ἀδελφόν (or vice versa). The participle ἀπολελυμένον (perf. pass. ptc. masc. acc. sg. of ἀπολύω) functions as a predicate.

- μεθ' οὗ ἐὰν τάχιον ἔρχηται ὄψομαι ὑμᾶς: The antecedent of the relative pronoun οὗ is Τιμόθεον. The conditional marker ἐάν introduces a third-class conditional sentence (ἐάν + subj.).

FOR THE JOURNEY

Because Timothy is mentioned without further reference, he is probably the same Timothy who was mentored by the apostle Paul. What do we know about Timothy? He was one of Paul's closest and most trusted partners in the gospel. Timothy was circumcised in order to effectively minister among Jews (Acts 16:1–3). He joined Paul on his second missionary journey and became a nearly constant companion of the apostle. He and Silas were left behind in Berea after Paul was encouraged by the local believers to flee the city (Acts 17:14). Later, Timothy became Paul's emissary to Thessalonica to help strengthen their faith (1 Thess. 3:2–3). Paul sent Timothy, along with Erastus, to Macedonia while Paul himself remained in Asia (Acts 19:22). Timothy was also chosen by Paul to travel to Corinth so that he could remind them of Paul's ways in Christ (1 Cor. 4:17). During his first Roman imprisonment, Paul made plans to send Timothy to Philippi, although there is no clear indication in Scripture that he actually traveled there during that time (Phil. 2:19). Finally, Paul had Timothy remain in Ephesus to combat the false teaching that had infiltrated the church (1 Tim. 1:3). Timothy continued his missionary efforts and, following the example of his mentor Paul, spent time in prison. Yet in his kindness, God orchestrated Timothy's release (Heb. 13:23). As far as we know, Timothy was a faithful servant of the Lord Jesus until the end of his days. May God grant us strength to do the same.

ANSWER KEY

1. *Parse:* (1) γινώσκετε (γινώσκω, pres. act. ind./impv. 2nd pl.), (2) ἔρχηται
(ἔρχομαι, pres. mid. subj. 3rd sg.), (3) ὄψομαι (ὁράω, fut. mid. ind. 1st sg.).

2. *Identify:* (1) τὸν ἀδελφόν (masc. acc. sg.), (2) ἡμῶν (gen. pl.), (3) Τιμόθεον
(masc. acc. sg.), (4) οὗ (masc. gen. sg.), (5) ὑμᾶς (acc. pl.).

3. *Translate:* "Know that our brother Timothy has been released, with whom, if he
comes soon, I shall see you."

DAY 90: HEBREWS 13:24–25

STEP ONE: **Read** aloud the text at least five times.

Ἀσπάσασθε πάντας τοὺς ἡγουμένους ὑμῶν καὶ πάντας τοὺς ἁγίους.
ἀσπάζονται ὑμᾶς οἱ ἀπὸ τῆς Ἰταλίας. ἡ χάρις μετὰ πάντων ὑμῶν.

STEP TWO: **Parse** the following verbs.

	Lexical Form	Tense	Voice	Mood	Pers.	Num.	Translation
(1) ἀσπάσασθε							
(2) ἀσπάζονται							

STEP THREE: **Identify** the gender, case, and number of the following words.

	Gender	Case	Num.		Gender	Case	Num.
(1) πάντας				(5) τῆς Ἰταλίας			
(2) ὑμῶν				(6) ἡ χάρις			
(3) τοὺς ἁγίους				(7) πάντων			
(4) ὑμᾶς							

STEP FOUR: **Translate** the text into understandable English.

VOCABULARY

ἡγέομαι, I lead, guide
Ἰταλία, ἡ, Italy

STEP FIVE: **Notice** significant exegetical and syntactical insights.

- **Ἀσπάσασθε πάντας τοὺς ἡγουμένους ὑμῶν καὶ πάντας τοὺς ἁγίους:** Why is the verb ἀσπάσασθε in the aorist tense-form (perfective aspect)? The answer most likely lies in the procedural nature of the action. That is, the verb ἀσπάζομαι is a telic action that takes

268

only a few moments to complete and therefore naturally favors the aorist tense-form. Indeed, it would be difficult to envision the verb as a present imperative (imperfective aspect) conveying a progressive or ongoing action since the verb is completed in a few short moments. Consequently, the author really does not have much of a choice because in the imperative mood, ἀσπάζομαι occurs 27 times in the aorist tense-form and only once in the present tense-form.[2] The participle ἡγουμένους (pres. mid. ptc. masc. acc. pl. of ἡγέομαι) functions substantively ("those who lead" or "the leaders").

- **ἀσπάζονται ὑμᾶς οἱ ἀπὸ τῆς Ἰταλίας:** The article οἱ functions as a substantivizer, turning the prepositional phrase ἀπὸ τῆς Ἰταλίας into a virtual noun ("those from Italy"). This reference "could . . . refer to Italians not living in Italy who sent their greetings to a group who was in Italy . . . or . . . to Italians in Italy greeting a group not in Italy."[3] The first option is preferable.

- **ἡ χάρις μετὰ πάντων ὑμῶν:** This is a standard benediction. The exact wording is also found in Titus 3:15.

FOR THE JOURNEY

Being a Christian means being part of God's family. This also means that believers are family. Family members care for one another. Family members love one another. Consequently, family members also greet one another. The first group singled out for greeting is "all your leaders" (πάντας τοὺς ἡγουμένους ὑμῶν). Earlier the author exhorted the congregation, "Remember your leaders [τῶν ἡγουμένων ὑμῶν], those who spoke to you the word of God. Consider the outcome of their way of life, and imitate their faith" (13:7 ESV). Later, he added, "Obey your leaders [τοῖς ἡγουμένοις ὑμῶν] and submit to them, for they are keeping watch over your souls, as those who will have to give an account" (13:17 ESV). These leaders are implicitly commended for faithfully teaching God's word, being examples to others, and shepherding the souls of the congregation. The second group that the author

---

2. Interestingly, the one present tense-form is used distributively: ἀσπάζου τοὺς φίλους κατ᾽ ὄνομα (3 John 15).
3. Dana M. Harris, *Hebrews*, EGGNT (Nashville: B&H Academic, 2019), 429.

greets is "all the saints." Of course, "saints" (ἅγιοι) is simply another designation for Christians, as those who are set apart to God. Even those who are with the author send their greetings ("those from Italy greet you," 13:24). "The church of Jesus Christ is a family. Greetings and news about one another are significant, for every person matters; every person is important. Part of what it means to love one another is to greet one another warmly and in love."[4]

ANSWER KEY

1. *Parse:* (1) ἀσπάσασθε (ἀσπάζομαι, aor. mid. impv. 2nd pl.), (2) ἀσπάζονται (ἀσπάζομαι, pres. mid. ind. 3rd pl.).

2. *Identify:* (1) πάντας (masc. acc. pl.), (2) ὑμῶν (gen. pl.), (3) τοὺς ἁγίους (masc. acc. pl.), (4) ὑμᾶς (acc. pl.), (5) τῆς Ἰταλίας (fem. gen. sg.), (6) ἡ χάρις (fem. nom. sg.), (7) πάντων (masc. gen. pl.).

3. *Translate:* "Greet all your leaders and all the saints. Those from Italy greet you. Grace [be] with you all."

---

4. Thomas R. Schreiner, *Commentary on Hebrews*, BTCP (Nashville: Holman Reference, 2015), 432.

Appendix

SUPPLEMENTAL VOCABULARY

Words That Occur More Than
50 Times in the New Testament

Numbers in parentheses indicate how many times a form of the word occurs in the New Testament.

Ἀβραάμ, ὁ Abraham (73)
ἀγαθός good, useful (102)
ἀγαπάω I love (143)
ἀγάπη, ἡ love (116)
ἀγαπητός beloved, dear (61)
ἄγγελος, ὁ angel, messenger (175)
ἅγιος holy, saints (pl.) (233)
ἄγω I lead, bring (68)
ἀδελφός, ὁ brother, fellow believer (343)
αἷμα, -ατος, τό blood, death (97)
αἴρω I take (up/away), raise (101)
αἰτέω I ask (for), demand (70)
αἰών, -ῶνος, ὁ eternity, age, world (122)
αἰώνιος eternal (71)
ἀκολουθέω I follow, accompany (90)

ἀκούω I hear, listen, obey (428)
ἀλήθεια, ἡ truth, truthfulness (109)
ἀλλά but, yet, rather, nevertheless (638)
ἀλλήλων one another, each other (100)
ἄλλος other, another, different (155)
ἁμαρτία, ἡ sin, sinfulness (173)
ἀμήν amen, truly, so be it (129)
ἄν (conditional particle used with subj.) (166)
ἀναβαίνω I go up, ascend (82)
ἀνήρ, ἀνδρός, ὁ man, husband (216)
ἄνθρωπος, ὁ man, human being, husband (550)
ἀνίστημι I stand up, arise, raise, bring to life (108)
ἀνοίγω I open (77)
ἀπέρχομαι I go away, depart, pass by (117)
ἀπό (away) from, with, for (646)
ἀποθνῄσκω I die (111)

ἀποκρίνομαι I answer, reply (231)
ἀποκτείνω I kill, put to death (74)
ἀπόλλυμι I destroy, ruin, lose (90)
ἀπολύω I release, dismiss, divorce (66)
ἀποστέλλω I send (out/away) (132)
ἀπόστολος, ὁ apostle, messenger (80)
ἄρτος, ὁ bread, loaf, food (97)
ἀρχή, ἡ beginning, origin, ruler (55)
ἀρχιερεύς, -έως, ὁ high priest (122)
ἄρχω I rule; begin (mid.) (86)
ἀσπάζομαι I greet, welcome (60)
αὐτός, ή, ό he, she, it; self, same (5,597)
ἀφίημι I leave, forgive, divorce (143)

βάλλω I throw, cast, put (122)
βαπτίζω I immerse, dip, baptize (77)
βασιλεία, ἡ kingdom, reign, rule (162)
βασιλεύς, -έως, ὁ king (115)
βλέπω I see, look at, watch (132)

Γαλιλαία, ἡ Galilee (61)
γάρ for, because, so, then (1,041)
γεννάω I beget, give birth to (97)
γῆ, ἡ earth, land, ground (250)
γίνομαι I become, come, exist, am born (669)
γινώσκω I know, understand, perceive, acknowledge (222)
γλῶσσα, ἡ tongue, language (50)
γραμματεύς, -έως, ὁ scribe, scholar, expert in the law (63)
γραφή, ἡ writing, scripture (50)
γράφω I write, record (191)
γυνή, -αικός, ἡ woman, wife, bride (215)

δαιμόνιον, τό demon, evil spirit (63)
Δαυὶδ, ὁ David (59)
δέ but, and, rather, now (2,788)
δεῖ it is necessary, one must (101)

δεξιός right (hand/side) (54)
δέχομαι I take, receive, welcome (56)
διά though, during, with, at, by (gen.); because of (acc.) (667)
διδάσκαλος, ὁ teacher (59)
διδάσκω I teach (97)
δίδωμι I give, grant (415)
δίκαιος righteous, just, right (79)
δικαιοσύνη, ἡ righteousness, justice (92)
διό therefore, for this reason (53)
δοκέω I think, suppose, seem (62)
δόξα, ἡ glory, majesty, splendor (166)
δοξάζω I glorify, praise, honor (61)
δοῦλος, ὁ slave (124)
δύναμαι I can, am able (210)
δύναμις, -εως, ἡ power, ability, miracle (119)
δύο two (135)
δώδεκα twelve (75)

ἐάν if, when (333)
ἑαυτοῦ (of) himself, herself, itself (319)
ἐγείρω I raise up, restore, awaken (144)
ἐγώ, ἡμεῖς I; we (2,570)
ἔθνος, -ους, τό nation, gentiles, people (162)
εἰ if, since, whether (502)
εἰμί I am, exist (2,463)
εἰρήνη, ἡ peace (92)
εἰς into, in, to, for (1,768)
εἷς, μία, ἕν one, single (345)
εἰσέρχομαι I come in, go in, enter (194)
εἴτε if, whether (65)
ἐκ from, (out) of, away from (914)
ἕκαστος each, every (82)
ἐκβάλλω I cast out, drive out, lead out (81)
ἐκεῖ there, in that place (95)
ἐκεῖνος that (person) (240)

ἐκκλησία, ἡ congregation, assembly, church (114)

ἐλπίς, -ίδος, ἡ hope (53)

ἐμός my, mine (76)

ἐν in, on, at, to, by, among, with (2,752)

ἐντολή, ἡ commandment, command, law (67)

ἐνώπιον before, in the presence of (94)

ἐξέρχομαι I go out, come up (218)

ἐξουσία, ἡ authority, right, power (102)

ἔξω outside, outer, out (63)

ἐπαγγελία, ἡ promise, pledge (52)

ἐπερωτάω I ask (for) (56)

ἐπί on (gen.); on, at, in (dat.); on, to, for (acc.) (890)

ἑπτά seven (88)

ἔργον, τό work, deed, action (169)

ἔρχομαι I come, go (631)

ἐρωτάω I ask, request (63)

ἐσθίω I eat, consume (158)

ἔσχατος last, end (52)

ἕτερος other, another, different (98)

ἔτι still, yet (93)

εὐαγγελίζω I announce good news, proclaim, preach (54)

εὐαγγέλιον, τό good news, gospel (76)

εὐθύς immediately, at once (51)

εὑρίσκω I find, discover; obtain (mid) (176)

ἔχω I have, possess, hold (708)

ἕως until, while (146)

ζάω I live, recover (140)

ζητέω I seek, look for (117)

ζωή, ἡ life (135)

ἤ or, than (343)

ἤδη now, already (61)

ἡμέρα, ἡ day, time (389)

θάλασσα, ἡ sea, lake (91)

θάνατος, ὁ death (120)

θέλημα, -ατος, τό will, wish, desire (62)

θέλω I will, want, desire, wish (208)

θεός, ὁ God, god (1,317)

θεωρέω I look at, perceive, see (58)

θρόνος, ὁ throne (62)

ἴδιος one's own; home; individually (114)

ἰδού see! behold! look! (200)

ἱερόν, τό temple, sanctuary (70)

Ἱεροσόλυμα, ἡ/τά Jerusalem (62)

Ἱερουσαλήμ, ἡ Jerusalem (77)

Ἰησοῦς, ὁ Jesus, Joshua (918)

ἱμάτιον, τό garment, coat, robe (60)

ἵνα that, in order that, so that (663)

Ἰουδαῖος Jewish; a Jew (195)

Ἰσραήλ, ὁ Israel (68)

ἵστημι I stand, set (155)

Ἰωάννης, -ου, ὁ John (135)

κἀγώ and I, but I, I also (84)

κάθημαι I sit (down), stay, live (91)

καθώς as, just as, even as (182)

καί and, even, also, but (8,998)

καιρός, ὁ time, season, age (85)

κακός bad, evil (50)

καλέω I call, address, invite (148)

καλός good, beautiful, useful (100)

καρδία, ἡ heart, mind (156)

καρπός, ὁ fruit, crop, result (66)

κατά down, against (gen.); according to, along (acc.) (473)

καταβαίνω I go down, descend (81)

κεφαλή, ἡ head, authority, source (75)

κηρύσσω I proclaim, announce, preach (61)

κόσμος, ὁ world, earth, universe; adornment (186)

κράζω I cry out, call out (55)

κρίνω I judge, decide, condemn (114)

κύριος, ὁ lord, master, sir, Lord (716)

λαλέω I speak, say (296)

λαμβάνω I take, receive, seize (258)

λαός, ὁ people, crowd (142)

λέγω I say, speak, call (2,353)

λίθος, ὁ stone (59)

λόγος, ὁ word, Word, message, statement, account (330)

λοιπός remaining, rest, other (55)

μαθητής, ὁ disciple, follower (261)

μακάριος blessed, fortunate (50)

μᾶλλον more, rather (81)

μαρτυρέω I bear witness, testify, approve (76)

μέγας, μεγάλη, μέγα large, great, important (243)

μέλλω I am about to, am going to, intend (109)

μέν on the one hand, indeed (179)

μένω I remain, stay, abide, live (118)

μέσος middle (58)

μετά with, among, against (gen.); after (acc.) (469)

μή not (with non-ind. verbs and questions expecting a negative answer) (1,042)

μηδέ and not, but not, nor (56)

μηδείς, μηδεμία, μηδέν no; no one (90)

μήτηρ, -τρός, ἡ mother (83)

μόνος only, alone, deserted (114)

Μωϋσῆς, -έως, ὁ Moses (80)

νεκρός dead, useless (128)

νόμος, ὁ law, rule, principle (194)

νῦν now, the present (147)

νύξ, νυκτός, ἡ night (61)

ὁ, ἡ, τό the (19,864)

ὁδός, -οῦ, ἡ road, way, journey (101)

οἶδα I know, am acquainted with, understand (318)

οἰκία, ἡ house(hold), home, family (93)

οἶκος, ὁ house(hold), home, family, temple (114)

ὅλος whole, all, entire (109)

ὄνομα, -ατος, τό name, title, reputation (228)

ὅπου where, since (82)

ὅπως in order that, that, how (53)

ὁράω I see, perceive (452)

ὄρος, -ους, τό mountain, hill (63)

ὅς, ἥ, ὅ who, which, what, that (1,407)

ὅσος as much as, as many as, as great as (110)

ὅστις, ἥτις, ὅ τι who, whoever (144)

ὅταν whenever, when (123)

ὅτε when, while (103)

ὅτι that, because, for (1,296)

οὐ not (with ind. verbs and questions expecting a positive answer) (1,621)

οὐδέ and not, neither, nor (143)

οὐδείς, οὐδεμία, οὐδέν no one, nothing, no (234)

οὖν so, then, therefore, consequently (498)

οὐρανός, ὁ heaven, sky (273)

οὔτε neither, nor, and not (87)

οὗτος, αὕτη, τοῦτο this; he, she, it (1,384)

οὕτως in this manner, thus, so (208)

οὐχί not, no (used with questions expecting a positive answer) (54)

ὀφθαλμός, ὁ eye, sight (100)

ὄχλος, ὁ crowd, multitude (175)

παιδίον, τό child, infant (53)

πάλιν again, furthermore (141)

παρά from (gen.); with, beside (dat.); at, on (acc.) (194)

παραβολή, ἡ parable, comparison, symbol (50)

παραδίδωμι I hand over, betray, entrust (119)

παρακαλέω I exhort, comfort, urge (109)

πᾶς, πᾶσα, πᾶν every, all; everyone, everything (1,243)

πατήρ, πατρός, ὁ father, Father, ancestor, forefather (413)

Παῦλος, ὁ Paul (158)

πείθω I persuade, convince (52)

πέμπω I send, appoint (79)

περί about, concerning (gen.); around, near (acc.) (333)

περιπατέω I walk, live, conduct myself (95)

Πέτρος, ὁ Peter (156)

Πιλᾶτος, ὁ Pilate (55)

πίνω I drink (73)

πίπτω I fall (down), perish (90)

πιστεύω I believe (in), have faith (in), trust, entrust (241)

πίστις, -εως, ἡ faith, belief, trust, faithfulness, doctrine (243)

πιστός faithful, reliable, believing, trusting (67)

πληρόω I (ful)fill, complete (86)

πλοῖον, τό boat, ship (67)

πνεῦμα, -ατος, τό spirit, Spirit, wind, breath (379)

ποιέω I do, practice, make (568)

πόλις, -εως, ἡ city, town (162)

πολύς, πολλή, πολύ much, many, large, great (416)

πονηρός evil, bad, wicked, sick (78)

πορεύομαι I go, travel (153)

πούς, ποδός, ὁ foot (93)

πρεσβύτερος older; elder, presbyter (66)

πρός for (gen.); at (dat.); to, for, against, with, at, by (acc.) (700)

προσέρχομαι I come/go to, approach (86)

προσεύχομαι I pray (85)

προσκυνέω I worship (60)

πρόσωπον, τό face, appearance, person (76)

προφήτης, -ος, ὁ prophet (144)

πρῶτος first, earlier, foremost (155)

πῦρ, -ός, τό fire (71)

πῶς how? in what way? (103)

ῥῆμα, -ατος, τό word, saying, object (68)

σάββατον, τό Sabbath, week (68)

σάρξ, σαρκός, ἡ flesh, body, sinful nature (147)

σημεῖον, τό sign, miracle, wonder (77)

Σίμων, -ωνος, ὁ Simon (75)

σοφία, ἡ wisdom, insight (51)

σπείρω I sow (52)

στόμα, -ατος, τό mouth, speech (78)

σύ, ὑμεῖς you (sg.); you (pl.) (2,900)

σύν (together) with, accompany, besides (128)

συνάγω I gather, bring together (59)

συναγωγή, ἡ synagogue, assembly (56)

σώζω I save, preserve, heal, deliver (106)

σῶμα, -ατος, τό body, corpse (142)

τέ and, so (215)

τέκνον, τό child, son, descendent (98)

τηρέω I keep, guard, obey (70)

τίθημι I put, place, appoint (100)

τις, τι someone, anyone, certain one, something (533)

τίς, τί who? which? what? why? (554)

τοιοῦτος, -αύτη, -οῦτον of such a kind, such (57)

τόπος, ὁ place, location (94)

τότε then (160)

τρεῖς, τρία three (68)

τρίτος third (56)

τυφλός blind (50)

ὕδωρ, -ατος, τό water (76)

υἱός, ὁ son, Son, descendent, child (377)

ὑπάγω I go away, depart (79)

ὑπάρχω I am, exist, am present (60)

ὑπέρ for, on behalf of, about (gen.); above, beyond (acc.) (150)

ὑπό by (gen.); under, below (acc.) (220)

Φαρισαῖος, ὁ Pharisee (98)

φέρω I bear, carry, endure (66)

φημί I say, affirm (66)

φοβέω I fear, am afraid, reverence (95)

φωνή, ἡ voice, sound, call (139)

φῶς, φωτός, τό light (73)

χαίρω I rejoice, am glad; greetings (74)

χαρά, ἡ joy (59)

χάρις, -ιτος, ἡ grace, favor, thanks (155)

χείρ, χειρός, ἡ hand, power (177)

Χριστός, ὁ Messiah, Christ, Anointed One (529)

χρόνος, ὁ time (54)

ψυχή, ἡ soul, life, living being (103)

ὧδε here, in this place (61)

ὥρα, ἡ hour, moment, time (106)

ὡς as, like, that, about (504)

ὥστε so that, in order that (83)

AUTHOR INDEX

SCRIPTURE INDEX